Key Concepts in
Race and Ethnicity

Recent volumes include:

Key Concepts in Migration
David Bartram, Maritsa Poros and
Pierre Monforte

Key Concepts in Sociology
Peter Bramham

**Key Concepts in Childhood
Studies 2e**
Allison James and
Adrian James

Key Concepts in Youth Studies
Mark Cieslik and Donald Simpson

Key Concepts in Family Studies
Jane Ribbens McCarthy and Rosalind
Edwards

Key Concepts in Drugs and Society
Ross Coomber, Karen McElrath, Fiona
Measham and Karenza Moore

Key Concepts in Classical Social Theory
Alex Law

Key Concepts in Social Work Practice
Aidan Worsley, Tim Mann, Angela
Olsen and Elizabeth Mason

The SAGE Key Concepts series provides students with accessible and authoritative knowledge of the essential topics in a variety of disciplines. Cross-referenced throughout, the format encourages critical evaluation through understanding. Written by experienced and respected academics, the books are indispensable study aids and guides to comprehension.

THIRD EDITION

Key Concepts in
Race and Ethnicity

NASAR MEER

Los Angeles | London | New Delhi
Singapore | Washington DC

Los Angeles | London | New Delhi
Singapore | Washington DC

SAGE Publications Ltd
1 Oliver's Yard
55 City Road
London EC1Y 1SP

SAGE Publications Inc.
2455 Teller Road
Thousand Oaks, California 91320

SAGE Publications India Pvt Ltd
B 1/I 1 Mohan Cooperative Industrial Area
Mathura Road
New Delhi 110 044

SAGE Publications Asia-Pacific Pte Ltd
3 Church Street
#10-04 Samsung Hub
Singapore 049483

Editor: Chris Rojek
Editorial assistant: Gemma Shields
Production editor: Katherine Haw
Copyeditor: Neil Dowden
Marketing manager: Michael Ainsley
Cover design: Wendy Scott
Typeset by: C&M Digitals (P) Ltd, Chennai, India
Printed in India at Replika Press Pvt Ltd

© Nasar Meer 2014

First published 2014

Apart from any fair dealing for the purposes of research or private study, or criticism or review, as permitted under the Copyright, Designs and Patents Act, 1988, this publication may be reproduced, stored or transmitted in any form, or by any means, only with the prior permission in writing of the publishers, or in the case of reprographic reproduction, in accordance with the terms of licences issued by the Copyright Licensing Agency. Enquiries concerning reproduction outside those terms should be sent to the publishers.

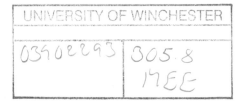

UNIVERSITY OF WINCHESTER

03902293   305.8
          MEE

Library of Congress Control Number: 2013955942

British Library Cataloguing in Publication data

A catalogue record for this book is available from the British Library

ISBN 978-0-85702-867-9
ISBN 978-0-85702-868-6 (pbk)

At SAGE we take sustainability seriously. Most of our products are printed in the UK using FSC papers and boards. When we print overseas we ensure sustainable papers are used as measured by the Egmont grading system. We undertake an annual audit to monitor our sustainability.

To all my family, and most recently Rashida Clarke Meer (b. 2011) who arrived early to meet Khizer Mohammed Meer (1927–2012)

contents

About the Author   xi
Acknowledgements   xii

Introduction   1
Why a New Book on Race and Ethnicity?   1
Carving Nature at its Joints   2
Identity and Dispersion   3
Reflexivity   5
How to Use This Book   6

Antisemitism   8
The Object–Subject Distinction   8
From Bigotry to Racism   9
Hierarchies and the New Antisemitism   10

Blackness   13
An Etymology of Blackness   14
Blackness as Double Consciousness   15
Blackness as a Political Identity   16
The Black Atlantic   17

Citizenship   19
The Challenge of Citizenship   19
What the Greeks and Romans Did For Us   20
Marshall and Beyond: Equality and Culture   22
National and Post-National Citizenship   23
Citizenship and New Social Movements   24

Diaspora   27
Co-ordinates of Diaspora   28
Diasporas and Groups   29
Diasporic Space   30

Equalities and Inequalities   31
Foot Races and Starting Lines   32
Groups and Experiences   33
Recognition and Redistribution   35

Ethnicity   37
Subjectivities and Primordialisms   38
Ethnic Boundaries and Ethnic Assertiveness   38

New and Old Ethnicities 40
Boundaries and Drawbacks 41

Euro-Islam **43**
Euro-Islam as a Multidirectional Process 43
Euro-Islam as Muslim Adaptation 45
Re-locating the Muslim Subject 46

Health and Well-being **47**
Ethnicity and Health 47
Disease and Categories 48
Ethnic Variations 50

Hybridity **52**
Hybridity as Translation 52
Hybridity as Identity 53

Integration **55**
Two Uses 55
Diversity and Integration 56
Integration as a Vortex Issue 57

Interculturalism **59**
Communication Beyond Co-existence? 60
Free from Cultural Groups 61
A Stronger Sense of the Whole 62
Illiberalism and Culture 63

Intersectionality **64**
Structural or Political Intersectionality? 65
Intra-Categorical, *Anti*-Categorical and *Inter*-Categorical 66
Unitary, Multiple and Intersectional 67

Islamophobia **69**
Challenges and Responses 70
Intersectional Islamophobia: Gender and Civilisation 72

Migration **75**
Recent Trends in Migration 76
Three Ages of *Mass* Migration 76
Theorising Migration 78

Mixedness **80**
Mixedness as Population Change 80
Mixedness as Racial Formation 81

key concepts in
race and ethnicity

Multiculturalism 83
A Philosophical Rationale 83
Political Provenance(s) 84
Intellectual Calibrations 85
Known Knowns, Known Unknowns 88
The Backlash and Beyond 89

Nationalism 92
Nationalism and the State 92
What is a Nation? 93
Imagined Communities 94
Ethnies amd Pre-modernity 95
The Bad and the Banal 96

Orientalism 98
Muslim *Society* 98
A Style of Thought 99
Neo-Orientalism? 101

Political Participation 103
The Function of Political Rights 104
Political Participation as the Franchise 106
Securing Representation 107

Post-colonialism 109
Post or Present? 110
Politics, Culture or Both? 111
Addressing or Ignoring the Post-Colonial? 112

Race 113
History and Categorisation 114
A Biological Category 115
Post-Race or the Paradox of Race? 116

Race Relations 119
Origins 120
British Race Relations 121
Six Orders of Race Relations 121
Status and Party 123

Racialisation 125
Intellectual Provenances 125
Historical Racialisation 126
Contemporary Racialisation 127

Positive Racialisation and Model Minorities   127
Institutional Racisms   128

Recognition   **130**
The Range of Recognition   131
Phenomenology and Ethics   131
Critical Theory and Race   132
Multicultural Turns   133
Democratic Participation   134
The Emergence of *Mis*recognition   134

Secularism   **136**
Contemporary Meanings   137
Secularisation   137
Secularism and State   138
Secularism and Autonomy   139
Secularism and Citizenship   141
Post-Secularism   142

Super-diversity   **144**
A Concept for Our Time?   145
What is New That is 'Super'?   146

Transnationalism   **147**
The Conditions of Transnationalism   148
Social Morphology and Consciousness   148
Cultural Reproduction and Capital   149
Political Engagement and Space   150

Whiteness   **152**
White or Western?   153
Racial Supremacy and Privilege   154
Class and Negotiating Identity   155

Index   **159**

key concepts in
race and ethnicity

x

about the author

Dr Nasar Meer is Reader in Comparative Social Policy and Citizenship, and Chancellor's Fellow in the Faculty of Humanities and Social Sciences at the University of Strathclyde. He has been a Minda de Gunzberg Fellow at Harvard University, a Resident Fellow with the Institute for Advanced Studies in the Humanities (IASH) at the University of Edinburgh, and a member of the British Council's Outreach Programme. He is currently a Routledge 'Super Author' and has previously studied at the Universities of Essex, Edinburgh and Bristol, and held a Visiting Fellowship with the W.E.B. Du Bois Institute for African and African-American Research, Harvard University, and the Department of Political Science and Government at Aarhus University. Nasar was previously a Reader, Co-Director of the Centre for Civil Society and Citizenship (CCSC), and senior lecturer at Northumbria University, a lecturer at the University of Southampton, and a researcher at the Centre for the Study of Ethnicity and Citizenship (CSEC), Bristol University, where he is an Honorary Fellow. www.nasarmeer.com

acknowledgements

This book reflects an accumulated process of learning; something that arguably places me in a debt to both my teachers and students alike. Inevitably this debt takes a diffuse course and could not be traced to one or other class room, whether I was in the audience or at the podium. Nonetheless, and as I set out in more detail in the discussion of reflexivity, the book relies on continuous thinking made possible through collaboration and dialogue with friends and colleagues. Amongst those who I would especially like to name here include Tariq Modood, John Solomos, Anna Triandafyllidou, Per Mouritsen, Anoop Nayak, Varun Uberoi, Claire Alexander, Ray Taras, Jan Dobbernack, Brian Klug, Therese O'Toole, Tehseen Noorani, Derek McGhee, Pnina Werbner, Claire Blencowe, Bernard Harris, Carol Stephenson, Les Back and Ruth Lewis. Significant thanks are owed to Chris Rojek who commissioned the book some years ago when I was at Southampton University, and waited patiently with Gemma Shields and Katherine Haw at SAGE. The majority of the book was penned during my time at Northumbria University, and I will always be grateful to colleagues for creating and sustaining an intellectually rewarding space in the Department of Social Sciences and Languages. I am obliged to SAGE Publications for kind permission to reproduce a figure from Pieterse, J. N. (2001) 'Hybridity, so what? The anti-hybridity backlash and the riddles of recognition', *Theory, Culture and Society*, 18 (2–3): 219–45. Finally, the book would never have been completed without the support and encouragement of Katherine Smith, and for which I am profoundly fortunate.

key concepts in race and ethnicity

WHY A NEW BOOK ON RACE AND ETHNICITY?

The study of race and ethnicity is a dynamic field. For some readers this will be self-evidently the case. Why? Because human populations and the social relations they constitute are constantly developing, and so our conceptual language needs to meet the challenge of valid description. But the task for social scientists is much greater than may at first appear. In order for our analyses to be meaningful they also have to be reflexive. In our case this means that we need to think critically about the intellectual *frames* through which we have come to understand what we name as racial and ethnic differences amongst and across populations. Meeting this challenge is important. Not doing so invites the risk that we can ignore how – through our concepts – we sometimes help constitute those social relations we wish to study.

As a teacher and researcher in race and ethnicity studies, it has become clear to me that while the status of some concepts has been so significant that they have helped structure the field (e.g. blackness, ethnicity, integration, race, race relations), and while others are much more novel (e.g. hybridity, intersectionality, mixedness, transnationalism, whiteness), the status of established and novel concepts does not necessarily reflect an incremental development in our learning. To put it another way, more recent concepts do not necessarily describe more recent phenomena. So while there are several introductory books on race and ethnicity, one of the strengths of this collection is that it is able to illustrate how it may equally be the case that our conceptualisation of 'new' phenomena is only now able to register something that may have long been in evidence. This is not to say other things remain the same (on the contrary) but instead that few other introductory collections seek to offer the analytical range of this book – not merely in describing but also critiquing with real world examples.

What the book tries to do therefore is move a little beyond the conventional inventory of core categories by additionally surveying and interrogating those concepts which for too long have been left out of our repertoires (e.g. equalities and inequalities, health and well-being, political participation, post-colonialism). The collection is more than a historical corrective, however. Several of us working in this field have noted that the place of religion as minority identity, one that is shaped by processes of racialisation, must also be brought under scrutiny. This realisation is reflected in this book (e.g. antisemitism, Euro-Islam, Islamophobia). Other concepts have been knocking at the door but often refused entry as they complicate existing configurations. These are included too (e.g. interculturalism, recognition, secularism, transnationalism).

1

Some concepts were initially placed together to avoid artificial breaks, but in fact it was decided that it would be more useful to split them into several concepts. For example, mixedness is discussed separately from hybridity (as an example of racial formation), while post-colonialism is considered separately from Orientalism (even though there is a profound relationship between the two). In organising it this way I have thought long and hard about the approach, testing it with my students and established scholars in the field. The consensus was that the discussion would be of greater benefit if it were able to offer a fuller and more focused account. I agree with this view and have tried to offer distinct concepts throughout but have refrained from making artificial breaks. The underlying intellectual question this invites, however, is what constitutes a concept in the fields of race and ethnicity?

CARVING NATURE AT ITS JOINTS

It is sometimes said that concepts in the Platonic sense should 'carve at the joints' (Phaedrus 265d–266a, in Plato, 1989). By this it is meant that the given properties that make up any concept should not be arbitrary or selected at random, but should instead reflect the organisation of repeated phenomena. The task of any researcher is to separate the segments at the appropriate points, just like a butcher carving up an animal at the 'joints' instead of randomly across the social field (or indeed carcass). This assessment begins to set a 'concept' apart from merely a 'term'.

This does mean that a term is without any analytical depth. On the contrary, as Cantwell-Smith elaborates (1996: 16), a term too can come to be 'a significant index of how we think. Also, more actively, it is a significant factor in determining how we think.' The point is that while a term and a concept can offer interpretative order to our understanding of the social world, a concept offers us something weightier, something thicker. Of course there is a much deeper theoretical argument that can help us to locate the place of a concept, one that is related to ways in which we can conceptualise language and text, in a manner that has profound implications for social scientific inquiry. This cannot properly be summarised here but, briefly, we might point to a tradition of scholarship that is influenced by the later work of the analytical philosopher Ludwig Wittgenstein (1953), and especially the idea that we should understand language as a coherent (though diverse) set of games that are governed by common rules. The rules bear resemblance to one another and emphasise the ways in which human agents 'are intentionally speaking according to their mentality and consciousness' (Garling, 2013: 18). Here local context is important (e.g. in terms of the rules of the game) but in a way that is different from a second tradition, known as structuralism, which also views language as a system which can be studied according to the rules that are deemed to *structure* it. Owing much to the work on linguistics by Ferdinand Saussure (2006 [1916]), this tradition views 'words as not mere vocal labels or communicational adjuncts superimposed upon an already given order of things. They are collective products of social interaction, essential instruments through which human beings constitute and articulate their world' (Harris, 1988: ix).

For people influenced by the first tradition, the focus tends to be on the 'players'. For those influenced by the second tradition, the prevailing focus is on the 'rules'. The challenge for a social scientific concept is that it has to be alive to both of these concerns. John Brewer (1982: 392) once described the task as follows:

> What makes a concept sociologically significant is that the classification of empirical reality it institutes is one which succeeds in capturing without distortion ... Unfortunately this offers a range of possibilities. The word 'concept' ... is a blank cheque: its potential value depends on its use.

This excellent observation is useful in a number of respects. First, it reminds us that even a theoretical concept, one which claims utility in helping to explain the social world, must bear some relationship to empirical phenomena. This need not lead eventually to positivism; for it may lead us to consider a variety of 'data' including biography. As such each of the concepts in this book does just that. From antisemitism to whiteness there is either reference to historical record or live data against which the discussion of the concept can take shape. Second, Brewer points to the chameleonic quality of concepts where similar (perhaps the same) concepts may be adopted variously in the service of different arguments (Smith, 2010). This is not to say that knowledge is relativistic, but that it is socially constructed and so there can be a politics to its appropriation. The debates over concepts of new antisemitism, Euro-Islam and interculturalism show different forms this politics can take. This assessment perhaps raises another question concerning the nature of the relationship between subjectivity and research. For while this book does not set out to discuss concepts with anything like a narrative inquiry approach that would have very little distance between the subject and the inquiry, neither has it adopted a very positivistic approach that decouples social contingency from political issues. This is an important point that has a number of implications discussed below.

IDENTITY AND DISPERSION

Before we can turn to the issue of reflexivity and the role it assumes in this book, we need first to understand something of how the concept of identity is being understood here. For instead of restricting this to a single entry, identity is dispersed across all the concepts in this book.

Zygmunt Bauman (1995: 22) has argued that identities necessarily have 'the ontological status of a project and a *postulate*'. He continues: 'To say "postulated identity" is to say one word too many, as there is not nor can there be any other identity but a postulated one' (ibid.). This is not the same as saying that identities are a fiction. What it means, and as will be explored at length in the discussion of nationalism, is that all identities are imagined and often amount to an unfinished conversation, as the discussion of recognition theorises and the concept of blackness and Muslim subjectivity illustrates. Either way, identity is not something that can reasonably be contained within a short discussion. To some extent this is remarkable when we recall that identity is a concept that has been *imported* into the social sciences.

If we step back from its social scientific usage, we can note Hawthorne's (2004: 99) description that identity, in its simplest sense, reflects the relationship 'that each thing has to itself and to nothing else'. This he traces to traditions of thinking about identity in mathematical forms, something that Calhoun (1994) broadens out when he situates the provenance of identity within 'a technical origin in philosophy, beginning from the ancient Greeks, as well as in mathematics and biology. Aristotle pursued identity in terms of the relationship between "essence" and "appearance", or between the true nature of phenomena and epiphenomenal variations' (quoted in Sicakkan and Lithman, 2005: 3). What is interesting is that even following its migration into the social sciences, identity has not until relatively recently enjoyed the centrality it does today. This has changed partly because of a wider set of methodological developments in the social sciences, including the cultural turn and elevation of the *subject*. As Hall (1992: 275–6) has written, this reflected

> the growing complexity of the modern world and the awareness that this inner core of the subject was not autonomous and self-sufficient, but was formed in relation to 'significant others', who mediated the subject values, meanings and symbols – the culture – of the world he/she inhabited. ... Identity in this socio-logical conception, bridges the gap between the 'inside' and the 'outside' – between the personal and the public worlds. The fact that we project 'ourselves' into these cultural identities, at the same time internalizing their meanings and values, making them 'part of us', helps to align our subjective feelings with the objectives places we occupy in the social and cultural world.

The cultivation of a critical and visible study of race and ethnicity has been central to developing this understanding, something that has not been universally welcomed. Consistent with his critique of diaspora discussed later, Rogers Brubaker (Brubaker and Cooper, 2000: 1) deems the social sciences in thrall to identity, something that he concludes has regressive outcomes:

> the social sciences and humanities have surrendered to the word 'identity'; that this has both intellectual and political costs ... and tends to mean too much (when understood in a strong sense), too little (when understood in a weak), or nothing at all (because of its sheer ambiguity).

Part of Brubaker's complaint is that identity has become a ubiquitous explanation rather than something in need of explaining. In other words, social sciences conflate categories of *practice* with categories of *analysis* (or indeed explanans with explanandum). Key here is how the study of race and ethnicity often emphasises the importance of group identities. A thoughtful example is Guttman's (2003: 2) observation that 'group identities help individuals have a more secure sense of self and social belonging', not least the ways in which it allows 'disadvantaged minorities to counteract inherited negative stereotypes, defend more positive self-images, and develop respect for members of their groups'. This is partly the role we can observe ethnicity as playing in terms of self-definition. This does not mean that ethnic and racial groups have singular identities; the discussion of hybridity shows why this is increasingly rarely the case. The objective instead is to register, as Young (1995: 187) describes, the ways in which 'as products of social relations, groups are fluid; they come into being and fade away'. In this respect we often find that 'group identity may become salient only under specific circumstances' since 'most people in modern societies have multiple group identifications, moreover, and therefore groups themselves are not discrete unities' (ibid.).

One route or means of overcoming this tension is to differentiate between conceptualising people's identities and processes of identification. This appears to allow social scientists to understand how social and political processes help forge identities, individual and group. To Sicakkan and Lithman (2005: 2) 'the term "identification" enables one to conceptualise identity both in terms of individuals' own chosen choices of identity references and of other persons' identity attributions. That is, individuals can both identify with and be identified as "something".' The important point here, as we learn when we explore the concepts of race and ethnicity, is that processes of identification are rarely straightforward issues of choice for they often comprise a response (often a challenge) to prior processes of categorisation. There is a political implication to this, which is explored through the works of Modood in the discussion of multiculturalism, but which also has implications for how we go about inquiry, and it is to this that we now turn.

REFLEXIVITY

In an interesting discussion of religion, Garling (2013: 18) has recently reminded readers that 'the formation of a category or concept itself should be the focus of empirical research, rather than just criticising its (mis)use within power relations'. For our purposes, a way of reading this is to state that the formulation of concepts presented here has not pursued a conscious line of normative coupling or detachment. Given the kinds of issues and the examples that the topic is enmeshed in, however, a certain degree of sympathy is clearly apparent throughout the book. For instance, it draws attention to a political problem, namely the frequent disadvantage of racial and ethnic minorities, and it does not pretend that we should be happy about this. So by identifying a 'problem', a normative perspective is already in operation. Not approaching this topic entirely neutrally, however, is the standard of all work on race and ethnicity. By that it is meant that while researchers undertake work with rigour and deploy standards of self-criticism and external criticism, it is clear that terms like racialisation contain both a 'positive' and a 'negative'.

Yet it is unusual to hear that a researcher 'likes' racialisation. Hence, while the concepts here are a-symmetrical it makes sense to say that racial inequality is a bad thing and we should do something about it. This is consistent with Taylor's (1989) description of the research field as more like a slope on which political concepts take the researcher in, rather than a level playing field. It means then that on the one hand our identity makes the difference as to what we may be more likely to empathise with, while on the other hand the whole field is structured around identifying problems and pointing towards remedies. A book like this therefore necessarily reflects an accumulated expertise, which in turn means returning to and revising some previously published arguments. Inevitably this takes a diffuse course as it is impossible to trace all of one's thoughts to one or other output. There are nonetheless a few exceptions, so I would like to gratefully acknowledge that the discussions of interculturalism and multiculturalism partly reproduce my work with Tariq Modood, recognition with Wendy Martineau and Simon Thompson, new social movements with Narzanin Massoumi, and health and well-being with Katherine Smith. I therefore thank them, and also Routledge, Sage and Oxford University Press, for drawing on these here.

HOW TO USE THIS BOOK

Each concept is introduced with a short summary, and then an accessible interpretation of it is presented to the reader. This includes emboldened cross-references to other concepts elsewhere in the book. At the end of each concept there is a references section which provides material both on the sources and for wider reading. This is important as the reader will soon discover that concepts in the study of race and ethnicity are interrelated and do not stand alone. Equally, key concepts in this field are necessarily interdisciplinary and so any introduction to them must take in different branches of the social sciences (e.g. sociology, politics and anthropology) as well as some humanities (e.g. history, English literature and religious studies). As such the book is designed for both students and researchers on the basis that an intelligent and research-informed discussion of key concepts in race and ethnicity should be accessible to all who are interested.

REFERENCES

Bauman, Z. (1995) *Life in Fragments: Essays in Postmodern Morality*. Oxford: Blackwell.
Brewer, J. (1982) 'Racial politics and nationalism: the case of South Africa', *Sociology*, 16: 390–405.
Brubaker, R. and Cooper, F. (2000) 'Beyond identity', *Theory and Society*, 29 (1), 1–47.
Calhoun, C. (1994) *Social Theory and the Politics of Identity*. Oxford: Blackwell.
Cantwell-Smith, W. (1996) *The Meaning and End of Religion*. Minneapolis: Fortress Press.
Garling, S. (2013) 'Approaching religion through linguistics: methodological thoughts on a linguistic analysis of religion in political communication', *Approaching Religion*, 3 (1), 16–24.
Guttman, A. (2003) *Identity and Democracy*. Princeton: Princeton University Press.
Hall. S. (1992) 'The question of cultural identity', in S. Hall, D. Held and T. McGrew (eds) *Modernity and its Futures*. Cambridge: Polity Press.
Harris, R. (1988) *Language, Saussure and Wittgenstein*. London: Routledge.
Hawthorne. J. (2004) 'Identity', in M. J. Loux and D. W. Zimmerman (eds) *The Oxford Handbook of Metaphysics*. Oxford: Oxford University Press.

Plato (1989) *Phaedrus, in: Plato: Complete Works*, ed. J. M. Cooper, trans. A. Nehamas and P. Woodruff. London: Hackett Publishing.

Saussure, F. (2006 [1916]) *Course in General Linguistics*. London: Open Court.

Sicakkan, G. H. and Lithman, Y. (2005) 'Politics of identity. Modes of belonging and citizenship: an overview of conceptual and theoretical challenges', in G. H. Sicakkan and Y. Lithman (eds) *Changing the Basis of Citizenship in the Modern State*. Lampeter: The Edwin Mellen Press.

Smith, K. E. (2010) 'Research, policy and funding – academic treadmills and the squeeze on intellectual spaces', *British Journal of Sociology*, 61 (1): 176–95.

Taylor, C. (1989) *Sources of the Self*. Cambridge: Cambridge University Press.

Wittgenstein, L. (1953) *Philosophical Investigations*. Oxford: Blackwell.

Young, I. M. (1995) 'Polity and group difference: a critique of the ideal of the universal citizenship', in R. Beiner (ed.) *Theorising Citizenship*. Albany: State University of New York Press.

> Antisemitism describes the suspicion, dislike or hatred of Jewish individuals or groups. This can be attitudinal or structural, and proceeds from a real or assumed 'Jewishness'. It therefore reflects a racial and not just theological character (as in anti-Judaism), and can take a number of forms spanning behaviours, discourse and state policies.

The term *antisemitism* (also spelled *anti-Semitism*) can be traced to a publication penned in 1873 by a German polemicist named Wilhelm Marr. This was entitled *The Victory of the Jewish Spirit over the Germanic Spirit*, and in it Marr used the word 'Semitismus' interchangeably with 'Judentum' to describe what he understood as the relationship between 'Jewry' (Jewish people) and 'Jewishness' (the content and culture of Jewish people). Marr was motivated by the view that Jews in Europe posed a subversive threat to national cultures, a reading that arguably drew upon a much deeper historical current that came to assume a particular role in twentieth-century European nation-states, and which sanctioned intellectual and political support for enormous violence and discrimination towards Jewish minorities. These included pogroms and forced expulsions from Eastern Europe, restrictions on participation in public life in Western Europe, a widespread public discourse characterising Jews as a pernicious and deleterious presence, and of course the planned genocide of Jews and others in the Holocaust (known in Hebrew as the *Shoa*).

THE OBJECT–SUBJECT DISTINCTION

In contemporary discussion the prevailing convention is not to use a hyphen in antisemitism as no phenomenon such as *Semitism* has ever existed. This is so even though there is a racial-linguistic genealogy of *Semites* that some trace to Noah's son *Shem* in the Old Testament, and of course this includes other ethno-religious groups too (see Firestone, 2010). So while hostility towards Jews is a great deal older than the nineteenth-century term antisemitism, the work of Brian Klug (2004) has been helpful in unpicking what is valuable about the term at a deeper level and in a more generalised sense. Specifically, Klug maintains that the logic of antisemitism is 'a priori' in so far as antisemites do not generalise from specific instances but are disposed to see Jews in a certain negative light. That is to say that our working definition of antisemitism as *suspicion, dislike or hatred of Jews* should be understood as *suspicion, dislike or hatred of Jews* 'as Jews', 'in which Jews are perceived as something other than what they are. Or, more accurately, hostility towards Jews as *not* Jews' (Klug, 2003: 123). He elaborates:

For the 'Jew' toward whom the antisemite feels hostile is not a *real* Jew at all. ... Antisemitism is best defined not by an attitude to Jews but by a definition of the 'Jew'. ... Wilhelm Marr, who founded the Antisemitism Liga in Germany in 1879, described Jews as ... 'a flexible, tenacious, intelligent, foreign tribe that knows how to bring abstract reality into play in many different ways. Not individual Jews, but the Jewish spirit and Jewish consciousness have conquered the world.' ... In short, anti-Semitism is the process of turning Jews into 'Jews'.

So the emphasis is not on religion or religious doctrine per se – on *Judaism* – but on an imagined and generalised 'collective Jew'. While this allows us to differentiate antisemitism from what Iganski and Kosmin (2003) term 'Judeophobia', which focuses more on the object of Judaism than the subject of Jews as people, it should not confer the impression the anti-Jewish sentiment commences with antisemitism. For as Jacobson (2009: 305) reminds us, 'the history of racial Jewishness is not merely the history of antisemitism; it encompasses the ways in which both Jews and non-Jews have construed Jewishness ... over time.' Indeed, on surveying the nineteenth century, the philosopher Hannah Arendt (1968: xiv) once quipped that 'whereas anti-Jewish sentiments were widespread among the educated classes of Europe throughout the nineteenth century, antisemitism as an ideology remained, with very few exceptions, the prerogative of crackpots in general and the lunatic fringe in particular'.

FROM BIGOTRY TO RACISM

What is interesting therefore is the role of racial mechanics, especially **racialisation**, in how 'the move from *Judenhass* (Jew hatred) to antisemitism marks a crucial turning point of the late 19th century ... as a shift in alterity from religion to race' (Bunzl, 2005: 537). Yet this question remains understudied, and in their wide-ranging reader on theories of race and racism, Back and Solomos (2000: 257) remark that 'one of the regrettable features of much contemporary theorising about race and racism has been the tendency to leave the question of anti-Semitism to one side, treating it as almost a separate issue'. This is unfortunate, because as Mosse (2009: 260) describes: 'The mystery of race transformed the Jew into an evil principle. This was nothing new for the Jews; after all, anti-Christ had been a familiar figure during the Middle Ages.' A good example of how we might begin to address what has been overlooked is by revisiting the experiences of Jewish minorities in Elizabethan England, who were yet to be formally readmitted following their expulsion in 1290 by a decree of King Edward I. As such there was no 'official' Jewish presence in Britain until 1656 during the Interregnum of Oliver Cromwell (though some people practised Judaism secretly). Nonetheless, the most celebrated Elizabethan playwright, William Shakespeare, in his play *The Merchant of Venice*, imbues his Jewish character, Shylock, with many of the prevailing negative characterisations of Jews: deceiving, money grabbing, constantly plotting, etc. This is because the character of Shylock was at least partly sustained by a mythology and 'threat of Jews circumcising Englishmen, taking Christian servants, and racially contaminating the English nation' (Shapiro, 2000: 128). In the terms of Pnina Werbner, this would be analogous to the 'malevolent witch' who 'crystallises fears of a hidden, disguised, malevolent stranger, of a general breakdown of trust, of a nation divided against itself' (Werbner, 2005: 6). The point is that, for Shakespeare no less than his audiences, these ideas of 'the Jew' had achieved traction as corporeal shorthand for non-Christian difference, and in so doing problematise the familiar Atlantic-centred narrative of **race**. As Thomas (2010: 1738–9) summarises:

> Most scholars still conceive of race as a post-Enlightenment ideology built upon the Atlantic slave trade, hinged upon observable phonotypical human differentiation .... Yet, discourses of modern racism not only antedate the social taxonomies arising out of nineteenth-century scientific thought, but it was Christianity which provided the vocabularies of difference for the Western world ...

The overlap of race and religion is therefore evident prior to the formation of modernity – an overlap that subsequently proliferated through an 'emphasis on epistemology and the knowing subject' (Amin, 2010: 8). This conceptual intermingling is supported by Thomas's (2010) challenging critique of the omission of historical Jewish–Christian relations from understandings of race and racism, and so is consistent with the view that Jews have been important subjects in the emergence of race. However, it is a provenance which is frequently ignored in theories of racism as modern and premised upon biology as *the* principle marker of difference (over and above religion).

HIERARCHIES AND THE NEW ANTISEMITISM

A further obstacle to an alignment in our understanding of antisemitism and other forms of racism are the contentions over what Pnina Werbner (2013) describes as globally transmitted violent encounters, which can transform racist imaginaries (about the essential and unchanging nature of protagonists) amongst Jews as well as beyond them. She examines the particular conundrums associated with the state of Israel, anti-Zionism, and its equation with a 'new antisemitism'. The conceptual implications of this equation are forensically explored by Klug (2013), who focuses on the analytical utility of designating hostility to Israel and Zionism as a new form of antisemitism. His assessment is that antisemitism *can* take this form. But, he maintains, in the literature that detects a new antisemitism something greater is proposed:

> At its strongest, there is the qualitative claim that anti-Zionism and hostility to Israel are, *per se*, antisemitic. At other times, the claim is quantitative: it

amounts to saying that, predominantly and for the most part, these attitudes are antisemitic, and therefore, in any given case, the burden of proof is on those who deny the allegation of anti-Semitism. (Klug, 2013: 479)

This, he argues, is an over-simplification which does more to obscure our understanding of the topic than to illuminate it. The issue is also taken up by Tony Kushner who challenges the terms of our framing and reading of contemporary controversies surrounding the new antisemitism, reminding us that 'the Jewish experience has not always been about persecution' (Kushner, 2013: 448). The issue, however, is understandably complex and inevitably takes in a number of scales, and so is reminiscent of how Webber (1997: 268) once observed that:

> European Jews thus live with the awareness that many Israelis see them as part of a people inhabiting an incurably antisemitic environment, and some may well accept this to be true. It is quite a different picture from one promoted for example by the European Union. But what, indeed, is more typical for Jews as a model of contemporary Europe: Maastricht or Auschwitz? In practice, many minority groups, Jews included, hold more than one model in their heads at any one time; some models out of date, some deriving from the inside, and some presented to them from the outside.

So alongside the 'new antisemitism' thesis rests another reading of an environment that may decrease antisemitism. That is to say that while it is sociologically documented that Jews have historically been accused of interfering with the alleged purity of nation-states (Arendt, 1968: 11–53), from the vantage point of a supranational Europe, Jewish minorities are 'one of us'. This means they have moved on from being the perpetual 'historical outsiders'. As Bunzl (2005: 502) elaborates:

> consider Europe's realities against the backdrop of anti-Semitism's political project. That project sought to secure the purity of the ethnic nation-state, a venture that has become obsolete in the supranational context of the European Union. There, Jews no longer figure as the principal Other but as the veritable embodiment of the post national order.

Analytically, this problematises the bifurcation proposed by some authors that the study of antisemitism is incommensurable with the study of other forms of **racialisation** such as **Islamophobia**. Amongst others, Rensmann and Schoeps (2011: 52) have argued: 'antisemitism has motivated mass movements, declared Jews as "enemies of mankind", and, in its past and present forms, attributes to Jews global conspiracies, hidden power, control over the media and politics, the subterranean global destruction of societies … none of which we tend to find even in the most radical forms of public anti-Muslim resentments.'

A cursory, let alone detailed, reading of history is replete with evidence of the ways in which Jewish experience(s) have given rise to new vocabularies of persecution. Racial logics, however, do not respect Rensmann and Schoeps' hierarchies. One need not look far for evidence of this. The widely received conspiracy theory, initially proposed by the polemicist Bat Ye'or (2001, 2005), reflected in the notion of 'Eurabia' – foretelling the planned numerical and cultural domination of Europe by Muslims and Islam – has achieved significant traction and features prominently in the accounts of various best-selling authors. In this regard, contemporary antisemitism may also be studied in parallel with other forms of racial discrimination, in a manner that is reminiscent of Taguieff's (2004: 127, n. 8) observation that 'in the late nineteenth century some of the so-called anti-Semitic literature was, in varying proportions, both anti-Jewish and anti-Islamic'.

REFERENCES

Agamben, G. (1999) *Remnants of Auschwitz: The Witness and the Archive*. New York: Zone Books.

Amin, A. (2010) 'Remainders of race', *Theory, Culture and Society*, 27 (1): 1–23.

Arendt, H. (1968) *Antisemitism*. New York: Harcourt Brace Jovanovich.

Back, L. and Solomos, J. (2000) (eds) *Theories of Race and Racism*. New York: Routledge.

Bunzl, M. (2005) 'Between anti-Semitism and Islamophobia: some thoughts on the new Europe', *American Ethnologist*, 32 (4): 499–508.

Firestone, R. (2010) 'Islamophobia & antisemitism: history and possibility', *Arches Quarterly*, 4 (7): 42–53.

Iganski, P. and Kosmin, B. (2003) 'Globalized Judeophobia and its ramifications for British society', in P. Iganski and B. Kosmin (eds) *A New Antisemitism? Debating Judeophobia in 21st-Century Britain*. London: Institute for Jewish Policy Research.

Jacobson, M. F. (2009) 'Looking Jewish, seeing Jews', in L. Back and J. Solomos (eds) *Theories of Race and Racism*. New York: Routledge.

Klug, B. (2003) 'The collective Jew: Israel and the new antisemitism', *Patterns of Prejudice*, 37 (2): 1–19.

Klug, B. (2004) 'The myth of the new anti-Semitism', *The Nation*, 15 January, p. 7.

Klug, B. (2013) 'Interrogating "new antiSemitism"', *Ethnic and Racial Studies*, 36 (3), 468–82.

Kushner, A. (2013) 'Anti-Semitism in Britain: continuity and the absence of a resurgence?', *Ethnic and Racial Studies*, 36 (3): 434–49

Lerner, S. (2000) 'Wilhelm S and Shylock', in C. M. S. Alexander and S. Wells (eds) *Shakespeare and Race*. Cambridge: Cambridge University Press.

Mosse, G. L. (2009) 'The Jews: myth and counter-myth', in L. Back and J. Solomos (eds) *Theories of Race and Racism: A Reader*. London: Routledge.

Omi, M. and Winnant, H. (1994) *Racial Formation in the United States*. New York: Routledge.

Peace, T. (2009) 'Un antisemitisme nouveau? The debate about a "new anti-Semitism" in France', *Patterns of Prejudice*, 43 (2): 103–21.

Rensmann, L. and Schoeps, J. H. (2011) *Antisemitism and Counter-Cosmopolitanism in the European Union*. Leiden: Brill.

Shapiro, J. (1996) *Shakespeare and the Jews*. New York: Columbia University Press.

Shapiro, J. (2000) *Oberammergau: The Troubling Story of the World's Most Famous Passion Play*. New York: Pantheon Books.

Taguieff, P.-A. (2004) *Rising from the Muck: The New Anti-Semitism in Europe*. Chicago: Ivan R. Dee.

Thomas, J. M. (2010) 'The racial formation of medieval Jews: a challenge to the field', *Ethnic & Racial Studies*, 33 (10): 1737–55.

Webber, J. (1997) 'Jews and Judaism in contemporary Europe', *Ethnic & Racial Studies*, 20 (2): 257–79.

Werbner, P. (2005) 'Islamophobia: incitement to religious hatred – legislating for a new fear?', *Anthropology Today*, 21 (1): 5–9.

Werbner, P. (2013) 'Folk devils and racist imaginaries in a global prism: Islamophobia and anti-Semitism in the twenty-first century', *Ethnic and Racial Studies*, 36 (3): 450–67.

Ye'or, B. (2001) *Islam and Dhimmitude: Where Civilizations Collide*. Madison, NJ: Dickinson University Press.

Ye'or, B. (2005) *Eurabia: The Euro Arab Axis*. Madison, NJ: Dickinson University Press.

Blackness

> *Blackness is a relational term to whiteness that has historically been imbued with negative connotations (which conversely endowed whiteness with positive qualities). One consequence is that social differences according to registers of colour have been framed by this language even while they have taken distinct forms in the organisation of social relations. As such, blackness cannot be discussed separately from a fuller elaboration of these dynamics offered in the concept of **race**. The important point to understand is that blackness has been, is and will continue to be a significant vehicle for mobilisation and advancement amongst black communities, to critique and challenge prevailing **inequalities**. This has often taken the form of **political participation** and struggle, but there is also a cultural and aesthetic dimension to this.*

In a recent film that marks a retrospective of his life and work, the pioneering scholar of cultural studies Stuart Hall (2012) says that 'black identity is an ongoing and unfinished conversation'. By 'conversation' Hall means that identities are necessarily forged in dialogue with others, precisely as discussed in **recognition**. Where blackness is concerned, these dialogues have been occurring over a long duration. Hence the title of Gilroy's (1993a) important work *The Black Atlantic* charts an ongoing cultural dialogue between West Africa, North America and Europe (which together constitutes one meaning of contemporary blackness). For Gilroy (1993a, 1993b) the outcome is something that is expressed in literary, aesthetic and other cultural forms. What this and related work also seek to show, however, is that blackness as a subject position, as a site and resource for identity construction, is not easily charted because it has been, and continues to be, patterned by a number of competing standpoints.

AN ETYMOLOGY OF BLACKNESS

As the discussion of **race** illustrates, there is a long-standing debate about the relationship between terms that mark out difference, and how those terms are imbued with social and political significance. Blackness is a pre-eminent example of this. It is hard to do justice to the multilayered fashion in which the word 'blackness' is stitched into the English language but, *minimally*, we can say that it serves a relational function to contrast with **whiteness**. Jordan (2009: 38) puts this succinctly when he notes that 'long before they found that some men were black, Englishmen found in the idea of blackness a way of expressing some of their most ingrained values'. He continues:

> No other colour *except white* conveyed so much emotional impact. As described in the *Oxford English Dictionary*, the meaning of *black* before the sixteenth century included 'Deeply stained with dirt; soiled, dirty, foul … Having dark or deadly purposes, malignant; pertaining to or involving death. Deadly; baneful, disastrous, sinister …' Black was an emotionally partisan colour, the handmaid and symbol of baseness and evil, a sign of danger and repulsion … Embedded in Blackness was its direct opposite – whiteness. No other colours so clearly implies opposition … no others were so frequently used to denote polarization. (Ibid.)

Jordan is effective in showing how an emotive language of blackness creates the means through which a subsequent social category might be constructed. As with the biblical stories explored in our discussion of **race**, the language of blackness sets the tone for how societies have understood it as social phenomena. A poignant illustration of what is meant by this can be found in W. E. B. Du Bois's collection of essays *The Souls of Black Folk* (1903). For Du Bois how Blackness came to represent a lower status in an alleged hierarchy of humanity has had profound implications not only for how black and white people feel and relate to each other, but also how they feel and relate to themselves. He elaborates what he means in an essay on the political development of America, where he argues that the fate of American consciousness is dependent upon an unfolding dialogue or interaction between black and white subjectivities, as two separate but entwined forms of consciousness. These *dialectics* will, for Du Bois, determine the course of American history as a whole.

Another excavation of blackness can been found in the writings of the Martique and French scholar Frantz Fanon (1965 [1959], 1968 [1961], 1970 [1952]). For Fanon blackness and whiteness are not only things in the body, but also internalised in the psyche. For Fanon, signs of blackness are inhabited as deeply psychological processes, as captured in the title of his critically acclaimed volume *Black Skin, White Masks*. Here we learn how 'The Antilles Negro who wants to be white will be the whiter as he gains greater mastery of the tool that language is' (1970 [1952]: 29). In one example, Fanon tells of how, when watching *Tarzan* as a child, he would also self-identify with the white figure. Fanon's poignant critique of Western modernity (see especially Fanon, 1968 [1961]) reminds us of the traumatic and scarring effect that race encounters have. 'All this whiteness that burns me', he wrote (1970[1952]: 81).

BLACKNESS AS DOUBLE CONSCIOUSNESS

Fanon's thinking about blackness was arguably informed by an observation Du Bois had made many years earlier. Du Bois argued that the prevailing understanding of how blackness has come to be understood creates what he called 'double consciousness'. He outlines this in the following passage, which is worth quoting at length because it is possibly one of the most important passages in the critical scholarship of race that has ever been penned:

> the Negro is ... born with a veil, and gifted with a second-sight in this American world, – a world which yields to him no true self consciousness, but only lets him see himself through the revelation of the other world. It is a peculiar sensation, this double-consciousness, this sense of always looking at one's self through the eyes of others, of measuring one's soul by the tape of a world that looks on in amused contempt and pity. One ever feels his twoness, – an American, a Negro; two souls, two thoughts, two unreconciled strivings; two warring ideals in one dark body, whose dogged strength alone keeps it from being torn asunder. The history of the American Negro is the history of this strife, – this longing to attain self-conscious manhood, to merge his double self into a better and truer self. In this merging he wishes neither of the older selves to be lost. He would not Africanize America, for America has too much to teach the world and Africa. He would not bleach his Negro soul in a flood of white Americanism, for he knows that Negro blood has a message for the world. He simply wishes to make it possible to be both a Negro and an American, without being cursed and spat upon by his fellows, without having the doors of Opportunity closed roughly in his face. (Du Bois, 1999 [1903]: 10–11)

On the surface, this passage has as its fundamental theme a duality in black American life. Fuelled largely – but not exclusively – by colour racism, this duality is a kind of paradox which stems from being intimately part of a society while excluded from its public culture, or, as Du Bois characteristically puts it, 'being an outcast and stranger in mine own house' (ibid.). Yet further scrutiny reveals four different issues, loosely grouped into two sets, which encompass much more than an outcome of colour racism. Moreover, there are a range of issues signalled in his description of double consciousness, and this range attempts to mediate between agency and structure, individual and society, and ultimately between whiteness and blackness.

In the opening half of the passage, Du Bois outlines his reading of the *self*, specifically the significance of the internalisation by blacks of the contempt white America has for them, and the creation of an additional perspective in the form of a 'gifted second sight' to which experiencing this gives rise. In the second half of the passage he identifies how societal incongruencies emerge from conceiving of blacks as having fewer civic rights but no less the duties or responsibilities of an American citizenship, and diverging sets of unreconciled ideals or 'strivings' held by black Americans which are objected to by white society, specifically emerging from an 'enduring hyphenation' signalled in his notion of 'two-ness'. In sum, these four interacting constructs give rise to a condition of double consciousness as Du Bois understood it.

BLACKNESS AS A POLITICAL IDENTITY

The discussion thus far perhaps gives the impression that blackness is a passive identity. This would be a profound error, not least because blackness finds a qualitatively novel expression in Black Power movements, originally pioneered in the USA from the early 1960s onwards, which sought to challenge the prevailing system of ingrained domination that deeply impinged on African American life. As Marable (1984: 110) describes, Black Power did not comprise a 'coherent ideology, and never developed into a unitary program which was commonly supported by a majority of its proponents'. Instead, Black Power informed a disparate range of possibilities: e.g. as 'black capitalism' where corporate sponsorship and private enterprise were deemed a means of tackling African American exclusion; 'black nationalism' where a cultural agenda, sometimes related to 'Afrocentrism', promoted the discovery and imagination of aesthetic and wider cultural content that was suppressed and denied during slavery and its aftermath; or 'black revolution' where engaging in the prevailing system was considered ineffective because it was so inherently implicated in the oppression of blacks. As Shukra (1998: 28–9) describes, this articulation of Black Power gave rise to social movement organisations like the Black Panther Party, who developed a holistic ten-point programme spanning health and social care and political enfranchisement:

> The Panthers viewed racism as integral to the capitalist social formation and therefore considered that society would need to be restructured in order to eliminate racism. Black people were seen as the key agent in that process of change. … This approach was the most threatening form of black power for the American establishment. Consequently the Black Panthers became the targets of FBI Counter Intelligence programs and violent repression until the organization was destroyed.

While the story of the Black Panthers is a specific account about an American organisation, it is underwritten by a rationale that the terms of protest against discrimination both should refuse and accept the group identities upon which discrimination is based. In the case of political blackness this relied on how a 'search for a black consciousness called for the acquisition of a black identity through the recognition of a distinct culture through black solidarity, pride and history' (Shukra, 1998: 39). Sometimes then, as discussed in the concept of **equality**, demands for inclusion necessarily invoke and repudiate the differences that have been denied inclusion in the first place. As Gilroy (1987: 23) once argued, in the discussion of 'class relations inside the black communities', observers often overlook this and the significance of 'the effects of popular and institutional racisms in drawing together various black groups with different histories is unexplored'. Often, he continues, 'the idea that these relationships might create a new definition of black out of various different experiences of racial subordination is not entertained.'

Gilroy's objection stems from an observation he made in earlier collaborative work with the Race and Politics Group at the Centre for Contemporary Cultural Studies (CCCS), especially in *The Empire Strikes Back: Race and Racism in 70s Britain* (1982). The concern here, repeated in Gilroy's comment above, was that the idea of **race** should not only be viewed as something that is used to regulate and racialise ethnic minorities, but that 'the meaning of race as a social construction is contested and fought over' (Solomos and Back, 1996: 10). Blackness here could be spoken through collective identities of race, community and locality, in ways that may become powerful means to engender solidarity. This was particularly the case, according to the CCCS (1982: 277), where the 'politics of race' had been successful in forging communities of resistance in the absence of white working-class solidarity. Hence they complained:

> [T]he British left has been reluctant to approach the Pandora's box of racial politics. They have remained largely unaffected by over sixty years of black critical dialogue … The simplistic reduction of race to class, which has guided their practice has been thrown into confusion by intense and visible *black* struggles …

The key shift here involves an objection to viewing 'black' communities as passive objects of study in favour of viewing them as active partners in the creation of black political subjectivities. According to Solomos (1993: 30), 'a multiplicity of political identities' could from here fall into 'an inclusive notion of black identity', while allowing 'heterogeneity of national and cultural origins within this constituency'. These could then resist racialisation processes through co-ordinated action – not least through anti-racist struggles. So in the past a notion of a 'black' identity was taken to incorporate minorities of both south Asian and African Caribbean origin in Britain, specifically in contesting racism as something based upon colour prejudice. Thus a dominant strand of anti-racism once sought to organise minority ethnic populations through a politicised – but racialised – colour-based **ethnicity**.

THE BLACK ATLANTIC

One of the paradoxes of using **race** to underwrite black mobilizations for inclusion, as Gilman (2009: 295) observes, is that 'in reversing the idea of "race", we have not eliminated its negative implications'. Gilman puts his finger on something that a later Gilroy has struggled with, and which has led him to another idea of blackness. Broadly, it is a position which encourages a recognition of **hybridity**, and a reflexive understanding between origin and destination, between what Gilroy (1993a) has called 'roots' and 'routes', arguing not only that there is space for both, but that both be positively cultivated in an effort to develop a new synthesis or hyphenation. While Gilroy gives it a novel form, intriguingly it is a task that Du Bois started to pursue in his misleadingly entitled essay *The Conservation of Races*:

> Here, then, is the dilemma, and it is a puzzling one, I admit. No Negro who has given earnest thought to the situation of his people in America has failed, at some time in life, to find themselves at these crossroads; has failed to ask at some time: What, after all, am I? Am I an American or am I a Negro? Can I be both? ... We are Americans, not only by our birth and citizenship, but by our diverging political ideals ... (Du Bois, 1995 [1897]: 24)

Gilroy wants to answer the conundrum that Du Bois identifies by moving the idea of blackness outside of national registers. He thus turns to 'debates about African art history and the debates about African art history', from where he takes the title of his book *The Black Atlantic* (1993a). In this he relocates blackness to 'the recognizably African cultures in the Western hemisphere and the West African cultures from which they partially stem'. He elaborates:

> I borrowed [the term *Black Atlantic*] it because I wanted to supplement the Diaspora idea with a concept that emphasized the in-between and the intercultural ... Investigating the black Atlantic diaspora means that you have to reckon with the creolization process as a founding moment, a point in time when new relations, cultures and conflicts were brought into being. (Gilroy, 1993b: 208)

What Gilroy is thus challenging readers with is a conception of contemporary blackness that is not rooted in a singular nation or culture. On the contrary, he has in mind an idea of blackness that *travels* and so is shaped by multiple sites of geography and so cannot be anchored in a single point of origin. The important implication for understanding blackness in this fashion is that it requires a reconceptualisation not only of black identities, but also of European and, more broadly, Western imaginaries too.

REFERENCES

Centre for Contemporary Cultural Studies (CCCS) (1982) *The Empire Strikes Back*. London: Hutchinson.

Du Bois, W. E. B. (1939) *Black Folk Then and Now*. New York: Holt.

Du Bois, W. E. B. (1971) 'Does the Negro Need Separate Schools?', in J. Lester (ed.) *The Seventh Son: The Thought and Writings of Web Du Bois*. New York: Random House.

Du Bois, W. E. B. (1995 [1897]) *The Conservation of Race*. Reproduced in D. Lewis (ed.) *W.E.B. Du Bois: A Reader*. New York: Henry Holt.

Du Bois, W. E. B. (1999 [1903]) *The Souls of Black Folk*, Centenary Edition, ed. H. L. Gates Jr and H. Oliver. London: Norton Critical Edition.

Fanon, F. (1965 [1959]) *A Dying Colonialism*. New York: Grove Press.

Fanon, F. (1968 [1961]) *The Wretched of the Earth*. New York: Grove Weidenfeld.

Fanon, F. (1970 [1952]) *Black Skin, White Masks: The Experiences of a Black Man in a White World*. London: Paladin.

Gilman, S. (2009) 'Are Jews white?', in L. Back and J. Solomos (eds) *Theories of Race and Racism: A Reader*. London: Routledge.

Gilroy, P. (1982) 'Steppin' out of Babylon – race, class and autonomy', in CCCS (ed.) *The Empire Strikes Back*. London: Hutchinson.

Gilroy, P. (1987) *Their Ain't No Black in the Union Jack ... the Cultural Politics of Race and Nation*. London: Hutchinson.

Gilroy, P. (1993a) *The Black Atlantic: Modernity and Double Consciousness*. London: Verso.

Gilroy, P. (1993b) *Small Acts: Thoughts on the Politics of Black Cultures*. London: Serpent's Tail.

Hall, S. (2012) Interviewed by Sut Jhally, available on-line at: http://vimeo.com/53879491 [accessed 26 September, 2013].

Jordan, W. D. (2009) 'First impressions', in L. Back and J. Solomos (eds) *Theories of Race and Racism: A Reader*. London: Routledge.

Marable, M. (1984) *Race Reform and Rebellion*. London: Macmillan Press.

Shukra, K. (1998) *The Changing Pattern of Black Politics in Britain*. London: Pluto.

Solomos, J. (1993) *Race and Racism in Britain*. Basingstoke: Macmillan Press.

Solomos, J. and Back, L. (1996) *Racism and Society*. Basingstoke: Palgrave Macmillan.

Citizenship

Citizenship is a multi-faceted and historically rich concept that describes a category of membership which seeks to reconcile rights with responsibilities. It is sometimes configured closely to a national culture and identity, and in contemporary usage it has grown to be explicitly coupled to ideas of national unity as well as debates over post-national membership and social movements more broadly.

There is a very deep and expansive literature on the idea and practice of citizenship, and this reflects an incredible variety in its philosophical, legal, social and political framings. For our purposes a good place to enter a conceptualisation of citizenship would be to note how it is a sign of the times that it appears clichéd to state that ethnic and racial minorities have increasingly 'challenged' the rights and status conferred upon them by various programmes of democratic citizenship.

THE CHALLENGE OF CITIZENSHIP

Amy Gutmann (1994: 3) declared two decades ago that 'it is hard to find a democratic or democratising society these days that is not the site of some significant controversy over whether and how its institutions should better recognize the identities of cultural and disadvantaged minorities'. Such contestations might surround the separation of public and private spheres (Parekh, 2000), or the way in which a country's self-image is configured (Uberoi and Modood, 2012), or emerge in what can either be conceived as mundane or politicised calls for dietary or uniform changes in places of school and work (Meer, 2010). What these all share in common is the view that conceptions of citizenship cannot ignore the internal plurality of societies that play host to 'difference'.

So, while citizenship takes a legal form, it also operates socially through the reciprocal balance of rights and responsibilities that confer upon its bearers a civic status, one that affords those bearers equal opportunity, dignity and confidence. One view, building on this foundation is that citizenship represents a field in which 'political and social rights, and cultural obligations [can be] contested by collective action' (Statham, 1999: 599), often with the aim of overcoming narrow ethno-cultural components that make formal citizenship *exclusive in practice* in the ways elaborated below. Collective action is not here limited to 'direct action' as much as the continual negotiations under the terms of a meta-membership which, in Tilly's terms (1997: 600), designates 'a set of mutually enforceable claims relating categories of persons to agents of governments'.

To appreciate what is meant by this we need to register how the very idea of citizenship has contained, since it earliest formulations, a dialectical tension between notions of inclusion and exclusion, for the citizenship of certain types of people implies the non-citizenship of others. This is to say that citizenship is a relational idea that is identified in as much by what it is not as by that which it is. Simultaneously, just as this tension is evident *within* citizen-and-non-citizen distinctions, so it is *across* citizen distinctions. This requires some elaboration, for what is being argued is that ideas and practices of citizenship need not be fixed in one mould or another. Quite the contrary – through forms of contestation, programmes of citizenship can change and develop.

WHAT THE GREEKS AND ROMANS DID FOR US

In the Western tradition, citizenship was born of an Athenian city-state participatory model in which political engagement (in a male-only public sphere) was the highest form of activity (Aristotle, 1986: 61–2). In this formulation it was anticipated that a group who united to make laws for the common good, and who would freely consent to be bound by these laws, could create order from chaos in behaving rationally as citizens. These qualities are proclaimed in Pericles' apocryphal funeral oration commemorating Athenian soldiers lost to Sparta during the Peloponnesian Wars. It is an account that famously illustrates how by 'establishing a rule of law within and without' (Castles and Davidson, 2000: 29), the Athenians were able to conceive of themselves *as a citizenry*, in distinction to their barbarous neighbours. In Athens, Pericles insisted, 'the freedom we enjoy in our government extends also to our ordinary life' so that 'far from exercising a jealous surveillance over each other, we do not feel called upon to be angry with our neighbour for doing what he likes ... We throw open our city to the world, and never by alien acts exclude foreigners from any opportunity of learning or observing ....' (Thucydides, 1964: 116–17).

It is worth remembering how this very self-consciously noble and ancient of formulations, in which it was proclaimed that 'no-one, so long as he has it to be of service to the state, is kept in political obscurity' (ibid.), restricted participation in excluding women, those without property, slaves, newcomers to Athens and so forth. Recalling this helps illustrate how, although the idea of citizenship can contain a powerful democratic and inclusive thrust, 'the speed of its progress towards ... inclusion will depend upon the openness of its rules of admission' (Castles and Davidson, 2000: 31). This is returned to below, and specifically how during the Enlightenment a justification of subject-hood developed notions of consent and contract, opening the way to liberalism's language of individual rights: a component in contemporary accounts of both citizenship *and* belonging presented in formulations of *jus soli* (territory of birth) and *jus sanguinis* (origin through lineage). These later formulations were themselves only made possible by the development of the idea of citizenship as a juridical concept of legal status (by another Western tradition, specifically the Roman need to incorporate very disparate groups within a single empire (Dynesson, 2001)). We see the imprints of these historical developments in the modern scholarship of liberal citizenship. Macedo (1990: 10), for example, maintains that:

> Liberal political institutions and public policies should be concerned to promote not simply freedom, order and prosperity, but the preconditions of active citizenship: the capacities and dispositions conducive to thoughtful participation in the activities of modern politics and civil society. A commitment to individual freedom as a paramount virtue is no warrant for neglecting the civic dimension of our lives.

This has all of the hallmarks of a Greek and Roman inheritance, and the discussion, while brief, implores us to consider, first, whether contemporary citizenship continues to reflect tensions arising from its exclusionary aspects, and how this may be particularly evidenced around sociological cleavages of gender, sexuality, class, race, ethnicity, religion and so forth. For example, Scott (1999: 4) argues:

> The relationship among equalities, social positions, and rights has varied over time. Since the democratic revolutions of the eighteenth century, equality in the West has most often referred to rights – rights that were deemed the universal possession of individuals regardless of their different social characteristics. In fact, the abstract notion of the individual was not as universally inclusionary as it sounded.

Second, it reminds us that an inclusive citizenship capable of challenging or overcoming these cleavages – through contestation – is a relatively recent development in accounts of citizenship and civic status.

MARSHALL AND BEYOND: EQUALITY AND CULTURE

In his landmark essay *Citizenship and Social Class* (1997 [1950]), T. H. Marshall displays the Greek and Roman inheritance in his view that the central feature of citizenship should be 'a status bestowed on all those who are full members of the community' (ibid.: 300). He deepened this formulation of citizenship to span both a right *and* a duty. This prospect of membership *through citizenship* undoubtedly heralded an increase in the rights enjoined by all. For example, Marshall identified a tripartite taxonomy of citizenship made up of the civil, the political and the social. While the *civil* element was composed of 'rights necessary for individual freedom – liberty of the person, freedom of speech … the right to own property and conclude valid contracts, and the right to justice' (ibid.: 294), the *political* referred to an extension of the franchise and the 'right to participate in the exercise of political power, as a member of a body invested with political authority or as an elector of the members of such a body' (ibid.). The third *social* element described a 'right to a modicum of economic welfare and security to the right to share in the full social heritage and to live the life of a civilised being according to the standards prevailing in the society' (ibid.).

To maintain this sort of citizenship 'contract', the state would guarantee such rights while the individual is duty bound to pay taxes and obey the law, and so forth. The tension, however, in Marshall's account arises from his focus on the majority (in his case the British white working class) in a way that prevented him from seeing cultural minority rights as a factor of full citizenship. That is to say that Marshall's approach is a classic, though nuanced, illustration of an account of citizenship that simultaneously upholds the promise of formal (and in many important respects substantive) equality while passing over the sources of inequality that require an account of differences.

It would be unreasonable to make this a specific charge against Marshall without appreciating the period in which he was writing. Indeed, it is arguable that Marshall proposed a progressive formulation of citizenship that advanced the philosophical conceptions of John Stuart Mill, the 'new Liberals' T. H. Green and L. T. Hobhouse, and economists such as Alfred Marshall and John Maynard Keynes. These figures cumulatively contributed to the idea that citizenship should constitute a positive freedom that would supplement the minimum of 'Life, Liberty, and Property' that had been advocated since at least the seventeenth century by classical liberals who

> [s]aw such rights as limited, for the most part opposing even the public provision of education, under the period of the welfare state the entitlement to membership and participation also came to embody rights to work, to health, and to security. As such, *a universal citizenship* expressed the new positive role of the state as the embodiment of social democracy. (Olssen, 2004: 180, emphasis added)

Nevertheless, and while his conception of citizenship was a relative advance that marked an important progress on earlier settlements, Marshall's conception of citizenship embodied a central feature of liberalism to be found in its 'universalism'. Criticisms of this tendency have been mounted from various quarters, not least in recent years from those engaged in the 'multicultural turn' (May et al., 2004: 1–19). Authors from this tradition have argued that one problem with the liberal conception of universal citizenship is that it is blind to the injustices that might arise from treating people marked by social, cultural and political differences in a uniform manner. As Squires (2002: 117) has argued, however, it is imperative to distinguish *this* complaint from a rejection of universal social and political inclusion per se, so that what is being advocated is 'a differentiated universalism as opposed to the false universalism of traditional citizenship theory' (ibid.).

NATIONAL AND POST-NATIONAL CITIZENSHIP

At the root of another complaint is that Marshallian-style traditional citizenship theory proceeds from a view of a national community, prevalent since the mid-seventeenth century in Europe at least, in which 'the individual enjoys the rights associated with citizenship because she or he belongs to a political community defined as a nation – the nation-state' (Martinello, 2002: 117). The critique of Marshall, and the question this raises, is not so much *who* makes up the nation part of this citizenship equation, as much as *whether* there is a tendency for some people to be left out of its construction. For example, according to Walzer (1997: 25) it is indeed the case that the 'nation' results from 'a single dominant group [that] organises the common life in a way that reflects its own authority and culture'. This is a source of concern amongst scholars who have argued that minorities will 'feel crucially left out [when] the majority understand the polity as an expression of their nation, or agreed purpose, whatever it may be' (Taylor, 2001: 123) (see the discussion of **nationalism**).

To be sure, much of what is encapsulated in the idea of **multiculturalism** raises this concern and critiques 'the myth of homogeneous and monocultural nation-states' when it advocates the right of minority 'cultural maintenance and community formation, linking these to social equality and protection from discrimination' (Castles, 2000: 5). Another persistent and related charge surrounds the extent to which the non-private 'civic' realm represents the particular communal interests and values of a dominant group, as if these were (or ought to be) equally held by all. Multicultural theorists unite in their conviction that a blanket reliance on difference-blind individual rights cannot sufficiently register the injustices of inevitable partialities that are contained in such things as public institutions, and which favour majority cultural norms. Hence Taylor (1994: 43–4) characterises the 'supposedly neutral set of difference-blind principles' that are sometimes said to underpin public institutions as reflecting 'one hegemonic culture ... a particularism masquerading as the universal'. These can include those principles that inform a society's laws, its values and dominant practices, and which are presented as the natural order of things when in fact they are an extension of the majority group's culture. This is an ever present tendency, according to Morris (1997: 194), because the Westphalian European nation-state has

> grown up around an 'ideal' of cultural homogeneity, established and reinforced through the state controlled acquisition of literate culture, alongside state control over entry and the acquisitions of citizenship: thus the nation represents territorialized cultural belonging, while the state formalises and controls legal membership.

As such, post-nationalism and post-war cosmopolitanism more broadly have put forward a challenge to citizenship (Meer and Modood, 2014). This is particularly true of those accounts which saw as the future of citizenship a retention and administration of citizenship rights in cross-national human rights covenants, which would be materially supported by international law (Soysal, 1994). Others, simultaneously, anticipated a diminution in the 'particularistic' content of political communities, such that the boundaries between nations, states, cultures or indeed societies might become empirically porous and even morally irrelevant (Archibugi et al., 2005). Each of these positions has had to grapple with something of a trend in the valorisation of national identities in nation-state citizenship across Western Europe, something that may be characterised as a re-nationalisation of various citizenship regimes (Tryandafyllidou et al., 2011).

CITIZENSHIP AND NEW SOCIAL MOVEMENTS

One of the parallel innovations in conceptualisations of citizenship centre on new social movements, which emerges from a twentieth-century politics of group-based movements (see Massoumi and Meer (2014) on which this section draws). Viewing these as historically new, some theorists explain the development of such movements as a result of changes in the form of modernisation, as a product of post-material values resulting from macro structural changes to a post-industrial society (Melucci, 1989, 1996). Touraine (1981) characterises new social movements as struggling for democracy and control rather than economic survival, aiming at expanding freedom rather than achieving it. As a result, the focus of much social movement activity is on expressing identity, a new 'moral concern' that seeks to gain recognition for new identities (Meluccci, 1996: 24). These movements challenged dominant narratives and cultural codes. More specifically, mobilisations seeking to rectify a lack of recognition of particular ethnic and racial identities were forging new meanings about the way in which 'difference' is dealt with (Melucci, 1996).

In his seminal work *Nomads of the Present*, Alberto Melucci (1989) claims that social movements 'operate as signs, in the sense that they translate their actions into symbolic challenges to the dominant codes' (1989: 12), emphasising the procedural aspects of social movements – the ways they produce meanings, communicate and make decisions. Theorising social movements in this way, Melucci claims that visibility is not the main strength of a social movement; movements are only visible at times of public conflict. It is what goes on behind the scenes of these movements which is more important 'in the everyday network of social relations, in the capacity and will to reappropriate space and time, and in the attempt to practise alternative life-styles' (1989: 71). These 'submerged networks', in their creation of new political cultures, hold the greatest potency for change (see Massoumi and Meer, 2014).

The emergence of new social movements marks an important shift in the theorisation of citizenship, towards a more positive understanding of movements not as a result of strain in society but as rational political actions by actors who did not have access to the main channels of the political system (McAdam: 1982: 23). New social movement theory (Touraine, 1981; Melucci, 1989, 1996) was the first concerted theoretical attempt to develop an analysis of the role of identity within social movements sparking a 'cultural turn' in the analysis of social movements. This provoked the more rationalist strand of social movement theory, such as resource mobilisation and political process theory, to develop an understanding of identity and culture. For resource mobilisation theorists, identity plays a role in social movements in providing solidary incentives, a collective sense of mutual solidarity that can motivate people to participate in collective action and overcome the 'free rider' problem.

While new social movement theory offers a 'bottom-up' understanding of politics – including the role of everyday subversive practices in collective action – it neglects politics in the wider sense, by relying on a false separation between culture as opposed to politics and political economy. Movements for recognition should not be simply conceptualised as aimed at cultural and expressive goals in contradistinction from movements aimed at political and economic change (Bernstein, 2008: 286; see also Bernstein, 2005). In their attempt to challenge the state-centredness of political process theories, new social movement theorists only attribute transformative value to the expressive dimensions of social movements. However, *if we adopt a pluralistic conception of oppression*, as operating through interlocking systems, movements formed on the basis of **race** and **ethnicity** are not simply engaging in cultural politics, but are actually engaged in political action where the goal is to challenge decision-making processes, division of labour and evaluation of worth in society (Young, 1990). This means that in order to understand why movements are seeking **recognition** of a devalued identity, we must understand that identities are linked to structure and interest (Bernstein, 2008: 286; Fraser, 1997), and so need to be understood within a wider register of citizenship.

REFERENCES

Archibugi, M. K., Held, D. and Zuran, M. (2005) *Global Governance and Public Accountability*. Hoboken: Wiley-Blackwell.

Aristotle (1986) *The Politics*. Harmondsworth: Penguin.

Bernstein, M. (2005) 'Identity politics', *Annual Review of Sociology*, 31: 47–74.

Bernstein, M. (2008) 'The analytic dimensions of identity: a political identity framework,' in J. Reger, D. Myers, and R. Einwohner (eds) *Identity Work in Social Movements*. Minneapolis: University of Minnesota Press.

Castles, S. (2000) *Ethnicity and Globalisation: From Migrant Worker to Transnational Citizen.* London: Sage.

Castles, S. and Davidson, A. (2000) *Citizenship and Migration.* Basingstoke: Palgrave.

Dynesson, T. L. (2001) *Civism: Cultivating Citizenship in European History.* New York: Peter Lang.

Fraser, N. (1991) 'Rethinking the public sphere: a contribution to the critique of actually existing democracy', in C. Calhoun (ed.) *Habermas and the Public Sphere.* Cambridge, MA: MIT Press.

Fraser, N. (1997) *Justice Interruptus: Critical Reflections on the 'Postsocialist' Condition.* London: Routledge.

Gutmann, A. (1994) 'Introduction', in A. Gutmann (ed.) *Multiculturalism: Examining the Politics of Recognition.* Princeton: Princeton University Press.

Macedo, S. (1990) *Liberal Virtues: Citizenship, Virtue and Community in Liberal Constitutionalism.* Oxford: Clarendon Press.

Marshall, T. H. (1997 [1950]) *Citizenship and Social Class and Other Essays.* Cambridge: Cambridge University Press.

Martinello, M. (2002) 'Citizenship', in T. D. Goldberg and J. Solomos (eds) *A Companion to Racial and Ethnic Studies.* London: Blackwell.

Massoumi, N. and Meer, N. (2014) 'Multiculturalism and Citizenship', in H-R Heijden (ed.) *Handbook of Political Citizenship and Social Movements.* Cheltenham: Edward Elgar Press.

May, S., Modood, T. and Squires, J. (2004) (eds) *Ethnicity, Nationalism, and Minority Rights.* Cambridge: Cambridge University Press.

McAdam, D. (1982) *Political Process and the Development of Black Insurgency 1930–1970.* Chicago: University of Chicago Press.

McAdam, D. (2002) 'Beyond structural analysis: toward a more dynamic understanding of social movements', in M. Diani and D. McAdam (eds) *Social Movements and Networks: Relational Approaches to Collective Action.* Oxford: Oxford University Press. pp.281–98.

Meer, N. (2010) *Citizenship, Identity and the Politics of Multiculturalism.* Basingstoke: Palgrave.

Meer, N. (2010) 'The incorporation of European Equality Directives into British anti-discrimination legislation', *Policy and Politics*, 38 (2): 197–215.

Meer, N. and Modood, T. (2014) 'Cosmopolitanism and integrationism: Is multiculturalism in Britain a zombie category?', *Identities: Global Studies in Culture and Power.* On-Line Early.

Melucci, A. (1989) *Nomads of the Present: Social Movements and Individual Needs in Contemporary Society.* London: Hutchinson.

Melucci, A. (1996) *Challenging Codes: Collective Action in the Information Age.* Cambridge: Cambridge University Press.

Morris, L. (1997) 'Globalization, migration and the nation-state: the path to a post-national Europe?', *British Journal of Sociology*, 48 (2): 192–209.

O'Leary, B. (2006) 'Liberalism, multiculturalism, Danish cartoons, Islamist fraud, and the rights of the ungodly', *International Migration*, 44 (5): 22–33.

Olssen, M. (2004) 'From Crick report to Parekh report: multiculturalism, cultural difference, and democracy – the re-visioning of citizenship education', *British Journal of Sociology of Education*, 25 (2): 179–91.

Parekh, B. (2000) *Rethinking Multiculturalism.* Basingstoke: Palgrave.

Parekh, B. (1994) 'Minority right, majority values' in D. Miliband (ed.) *Re-inventing the Left.* Cambridge: Polity Press.

Scott, J. (1999) 'The conundrum of equality', Paper Number 2, School of Social Sciences, Institute for Advanced Study, Princeton University.

Soysal, Y. (1994) *Limits of Citizenship.* Chicago: Chicago University Press.

Squires, J. (2002) 'Culture, equality and diversity', in P. Kelly (ed.) *Multiculturalism Reconsidered.* Oxford: Polity.

Statham, P. (1999) 'Political mobilisation by minorities in Britain: a negative feedback of "race relations"?', *Journal of Ethnic and Migration Studies*, 25 (4): 597–626.

Taylor, C. (1994) 'The politics of recognition', in A. Gutmann (ed.) *Multiculturalism and the Politics of Recognition*. Princeton: Princeton University Press.

Taylor, C. (2001) 'Multiculturalism and political identity', *Ethnicities*, 1: 122–8.

Thucydides (1964) *The Peloponnesian War*. Harmondsworth: Penguin.

Tilly, C. (1997) 'A primer on citizenship', *Theory and Society*, 26: 599–602.

Touraine A. (1981) *The Voice and the Eye: An Analysis of Social Movements*. Cambridge: Cambridge University Press.

Triandafyllidou, A., Modood, T. and Meer, N. (eds) (2011) *European Multiculturalism(s): Cultural, Religious and Ethnic Challenges*. Edinburgh: Edinburgh University Press.

Uberoi, V. and Modood, T. (2012) 'Inclusive Britishness – a multiculturalist advance', *Political Studies*, 61 (1): 23–41.

Walzer, M. (1997) *On Tolerance*. New Haven: Yale University Press.

Young, I. M. (1989) 'Polity and group difference: a critique of the ideal of universal citizenship', *Ethics*, 99: 250–74.

Young, I. M. (1990) *Justice and the Politics of Difference*. Princeton: Princeton University Press.

Diaspora

While the idea of a diaspora is in one respect ancient it has not remained static; on the contrary it has been modified and changed (sometimes profoundly) in its usage over time. Originally conceived to describe how – following forced expulsions – Jewish groups cultivated a sense of community and idea of home, in recent years it has come to rely less on a coherent idea of a centred homeland (from which a group is absent) and more a condition of identity that is re-imagined in ways that sustain a diasporic space.

The word 'diaspora' owes its provenance to the conjoined ancient Greek meanings of 'scattering' (*sperio*) and 'thoroughly' (*dio*) (Ember et al., 2004). But this gives us only one half of the circle, for the *concept* of diaspora tries to theorise how members of a non-territorial imagined community *self-identify*, namely through utilising social and cultural connections that can transcend time and distance. In this respect, argue Adamson and Demetriou (2007: 497), a diaspora

> can be identified as a social collectivity that exists across state borders and that has succeeded over time to 1) sustain a collective national, cultural or religious identity through a sense of internal cohesion and sustained ties with a real or imagined homeland and 2) display an ability to address the collective interests of members of the social collectivity through a developed internal organizational framework and transnational links.

As explored in the account of **transnationalism**, these concepts are intertwined but still distinct enough to be discussed separately. Diasporas were initially related to the Jewish story, where Roman expulsion from Jerusalem resulted in the creation, re-imagining and sustaining of communities in exile. Yet as Clifford (1994: 306) argues, 'we should be able to recognize the strong entailment of Jewish history on the language of diaspora without making that history a definitive model'. This is especially the case when we think of diasporas as 'non-normative starting points for a discourse that is travelling or hybridizing in new global conditions' (ibid.). In this respect, diaporas are sometimes celebrated as 'exemplary communities of the **transnational** moment' (Tololyan quoted in Collyer, 2011: 131). Yet the concept has a more analytical function than this.

CO-ORDINATES OF DIASPORA

The political sociologist Salman Sayyid (2000: 38) identifies some useful criteria that are frequently *implicit* in most discussions of diaspora, and which he tries to make more visible. This criterion includes the 'three co-ordinates: homeland, displacement and settlement'. He continues:

> [A] diaspora is constituted when communities of settlers articulate themselves in terms of displacement from a homeland. The homeland acts as horizon for the community, enabling it to construct its collective subjectivity. A diaspora is formed when people are displaced but continue to narrate their identity in terms of that displacement.

A perceived homeland is therefore central, as it is according to this site that distance is imagined, and boundaries – as with the case of **ethnicity** – are configured. As Sayyid recognises, however, the concept of diaspora has an elasticity that stretches beyond a real or imagined **nation** in exile after the process of **migration**, for the alternative view 'would only be partially adequate to account for the African diaspora' (ibid.). The latter, as Gilroy (1993) elaborated in his book *The Black Atlantic*, can take a much more diffuse and **hybrid** form, and develop over a long historical period. Gilroy's reading arguably owes something to Stuart Hall's (1990: 226) account of positionality, in so far as diasporic identities are frequently *positioned* 'by two axes or vectors, simultaneously operative: the vector of similarity and continuity; and the vector of difference or rupture'. In Hall's terms, the 'diaspora experience ... is defined, not by essence or purity, but by the recognition of a necessary heterogeneity and diversity; by a conception of "identity" which lives with and through, not despite, difference; by hybridity' (Hall, 1990: 235).

This discussion quickly signals how the contemporary meanings of diaspora have themselves moved some distance from how diaspora has previously been theorised. In offering a historical summary of these shifts, Brubaker (2005: 2) delineates current from earlier conceptualisations by differentiating between *classical*, *catastrophic* and *mobilized* diasporas. He summarises:

As discussions of diasporas began to branch out to include other cases, they remained oriented, at least initially, to this conceptual homeland, to the Jewish case and the other 'classical' diasporas, Armenian and Greek. When historian George Shepperson introduced the notion of the African diaspora, for example, he did so by expressly engaging the Jewish experience (Shepperson 1966; Alpers 2001; Edwards 2001). The Palestinian diaspora, too, has been construed as a 'catastrophic' diaspora, or in Cohen's (1997) term, a 'victim diaspora', on the model of the Jewish case. The concept of the trading diaspora – or in John Armstrong's (1976) terms, the 'mobilized diaspora' – was constructed on the model of another aspect of the Jewish, as well as the Greek and Armenian, experience. Chinese, Indians, Lebanese, Baltic Germans and the Hausa of Nigeria are among those often mentioned as trading diasporas.

The chief problem that Brubaker points to – and one that is consistent with ideas that emphasise fluidity in group formation and identity – such as that discussed in **super-diversity**, **transnationalism** and **hybridity** as well as Brubaker's (2002) broader work – is how the concept of diaspora can sometimes assume that a diasporic group is a coherent unit. This requires some explanation.

DIASPORAS AND GROUPS

In his account discussed earlier, Sayyid (2000: 38) argues that in the prevailing literature it is maintained that 'a precondition for diaspora is the articulation of a demotic ethnos (or, if you prefer, **nationalism**)'. That is to say that there is a prior existing identity that is deemed to be *continued* within and through a diasporic social formation. A number of authors (including Sayyid himself, albeit for different reasons) are very critical of what this implies. For example, in her discussion of the concept of diaspora, Anthias (1998: 557) challenges the way in which it is discussed, on the grounds that it distracts from the possibilities of 'cross-ethnic solidarities'. In her view this prioritises an imagined kinship with one's own group (and exacts a heavy toll in so doing). As a consequence, she maintains, the concept reproduces a certain form of essentialism that configures identity boundaries according to inflexible (even if re-imaged) culture (ibid.: 558). In the following ways, and quoting Sheffer (2003: 245), Brubaker (2005: 10) sees the issue as one of 'the definite article' where diasporas become 'bona fide actual entities' and are 'seen as possessing countable, quantifiable memberships'. Here he lists a number of weaknesses that the concept of diaspora might easily share with other concepts such as **nation** or **ethnicity**. He continues:

> Diaspora is often seen as destiny – a destiny to which previously dormant members (or previously dormant diasporas in their entirety) are now 'awakening' (Sheffer, 2003, p. 21). Embedded in the teleological language of 'awakening' the language, not coincidentally, of many nationalist movements are essentialist assumptions about 'true' identities. Little is gained if we escape from one teleology only to fall into another. (Brubaker, 2005: 13)

diaspora

29

This is an important corrective to uncritically treating diaspora as a self-evidently plural and anti-essentialist social formation. So how have those who have contributed to the literature on diaspora tried to address this?

DIASPORIC SPACE

What is interesting about both Anthias's and Brubaker's critique is that much of it has previously been anticipated and addressed by Avtar Brah (1996: 193), especially in her pioneering account *Cartographies of Diaspora: Contesting Identities*. In this important book, Brah proposes an idea of 'diasporic space', which places 'the discourse of "home" and "dispersion" in creative tension, inscribing a homing desire while simultaneously critiquing discourses of fixed origins'. Thus when Brubaker (2005: 13) argues that we need to move beyond a simplistic group-based idea of diaspora, in order to 'think of diaspora not in substantialist terms as a bounded entity, but rather as an idiom, a stance, a claim', he is in many respects consistent with Brah's original position. This is because the latter's theorisation of 'diaspora space' already moves us beyond a straightforward groupism (however that group is conceived, e.g. nation, ethnic group), in so far as she proposes 'diasporic space as a conceptual category [that] is "inhabited" not only by those who have migrated and their descendents, but equally by those who are constructed and represented as indigenous' (1996: 209). In this respect, Brah reminds us, 'not all diasporas sustain an ideology of return' (ibid.: 197). This is a simple but crucial observation that is frequently overlooked, and softens the criteria of diaspora which often has quite a high threshold, such as desire to return, strong groupism or a nation in exile. As Brah (1998) shows, in several ways these are strawman-like characterisations. The social anthropology of Pnina Werbner (2013: 410) is equally persuasive in elaborating this point when she describes multiple ways in which the British Pakistani diaspora create social formations in Britain:

> Pakistani diasporas have created three lived-in diasporic everyday 'worlds': the South Asian, with its aesthetic of fun and laughter, of vivid colours and fragrances, of music and dance; the Islamic, with its utopian vision of a perfect moral order; and the Pakistani, with its roots in the soil, in family, community and national loyalties, expressed also in competitive sports like cricket.

Since these diasporic spaces are simultaneously lived, sometimes coming together and at other times separated, like the strand of a DNA helix, we can observe how the concept of diaspora is intimately related to that of **transnationalism** and **hybridity**, and so retains a fluidity that is arguably under-emphasised in some accounts.

REFERENCES

Adamson, F. and Demetriou, M. (2007) 'Remapping the boundaries of "state" and "national identity": incorporating diasporas into IR theorizing', *European Journal of International Relations*, 13 (4): 489–526.

Anthias, F. (1998) 'Evaluating "diaspora": beyond ethnicity', *Sociology*, 32 (3): 557–80.

Brah, A. (1996) *Cartographies of Diaspora: Contesting Identities*. London: Routledge.

Brubaker, R. (2002) 'Ethnicity without groups', *Archives européenes de sociologie*, vol. XLIII, 2: 163–89.

Brubaker, R. (2005) 'The "diaspora" diaspora', *Ethnic and Racial Studies*, 28 (1): 1–19.

Clifford, J. (1994) 'Diasporas', *Cultural Anthropology*, 9 (3): 302–38.

Collyer, M. (2011) 'Diaspora', in S. M. Caliendo and C. D. McIlwain (eds) *The Routledge Companion to Race and Ethnicity*. London: Routledge.

Ember, M., Ember, C. R. and Skoggard, I. (2004) (eds) *Encyclopedia of Diasporas: Immigrant and Refugee Cultures Around the World. Volume I: Overviews and Topics; Volume II: Diaspora Communities*. New York: Springer.

Gilroy, P. (1993) *The Black Atlantic: Modernity and Double Consciousness*. London: Verso.

Hall, S. (1990) 'Cultural identity and diaspora', in J. Rutherford (ed.) *Identity: Community, Culture, Difference*. London: Sage.

Sayyid, B. (2000) 'Beyond Westphalia: nations and diasporas – the case of the Muslim *Umma*', in B. Hesse (ed.) *Un/settled Multiculturalism: Diasporas, Entanglements, Transruptions*. London: Zed Books.

Sheffer, G. (2003) *Diaspora Politics: At Home Abroad*. Cambridge: Cambridge University Press.

Werbner, P. (2013) 'Everyday multiculturalism: theorising the difference between "intersectionality" and "multiple identities"', *Ethnicities*, 13 (4): 404–19.

Equalities and Inequalities

Equalities and inequalities are obviously relational concepts, but they are also dynamic. In this sense what equality means in one time and in one context is rarely the same as what equality means in another time and in another context, especially where culture and history are included in our assessment of what makes something equal or unequal. The debate about equalities and inequalities therefore takes in novel challenges and questions as it relates to ethnic and racial minorities. For example, are there specific historical legacies or indeed current needs that affect ethnic and racial minorities disproportionately? What role does (or should) culture play in how we think about equality and inequality when discussing ethnicity and race? These are some of the issues that this concept will explore.

Most societies are characterised by not only divergent levels of wealth and associated opportunities, but also a historically specific treatment of some minorities that may have contemporary implications. For example, ethnic and racial minorities may descend from enslaved or indentured labourers (e.g. African Americans in the United States; they may have been migrant workers recruited for cheap labour (e.g. Turkish workers in post-war Germany who were recruited as part of a guest worker (*Gastarbeiter*) programme or South Asians in present day Saudi Arabia, but not afforded full citizenship); or they may be formally colonial subjects (e.g. as in Algerians in France or Pakistanis in Britain), amongst others. In these contexts the prevailing distribution of wealth and opportunities, the status quo, often disadvantages them. This is observable across a range of issues, especially those that touch on questions of direct and indirect disadvantage. Why, for example, are some ethnic and racial minorities consistently paid less and/or perform less well in education systems? In what ways can these be overcome through public policy? These are important questions in which we can recognise a continuing 'tension between equality and difference' (Scott, 1999: 1).

FOOT RACES AND STARTING LINES

Equality is a complicated concept and at a theoretical level there have been some robust debates, several of which are surveyed in the discussion of **multicultural- ism**, over whether approaches to equality in the context of difference need to be modified, including how and in what ways. As Kenny (2004: 32) describes, many people now 'accept that egalitarian principles do seem to require some distinct understanding of the particular needs and forms of exclusion experienced by social groups'. While this is not a unanimous view (O'Leary, 2006), it immediately encounters an appeal to wider 'social' characteristics that may affect some groups more than others.

One means of negotiating a path through a wide range of literatures is to begin with a basic analogy on which we can build a more complicated discussion. The one in mind is that of a foot race. In this analogy, if all runners are of comparable physical ability and start from the same line, it would be unfair to help one runner over another runner. But what if they do not commence together, with some runners starting behind others? Or what if we find that some runners are carrying injuries? Is it fair to expect them to compete in the same way? This scenario requires us to understand something of the participant's condition, their context or indeed their *identity*.

In his book *Taking Rights Seriously*, the American legal theorist Ronald Dworkin (1978) sets out an important observation that makes equality-based arguments more consistent with social context. He does so by elaborating a distinction between *equal treatment* and *treatment as an equal*. The former tends toward conceiving equality as *uniformity* while the second is able to take social *characteristics* into consideration. In the past this distinction has been used to argue that what are known as 'affirmative action' policies (e.g. quotas and targets in US college programmes for some ethnic and racial minority groups) are justified because those groups encounter unfair obstacles in society and which prevent them from competing *equally*. This is not a tendency that is solely relevant to ethnic and racial minorities, however, for as Scott (1999) elaborates, not dissimilar dynamics relating to the role of groups are evident in the historical struggles of workers from majority groups:

> The idea that all individuals could be treated equally has inspired those who found themselves excluded from access to something they and their societies considered a right (education, work, subsistence wages, property, citizenship) to claim inclusion by challenging the standards upon which equality was granted to some and denied to others. Democratic-socialist workers demanding universal manhood suffrage in France in 1848 insisted 'that there will not be a citizen who can say to another "you are more sovereign than I"'. (Ibid. 4)

While this is a political argument, it is also one that speaks to how for historical reasons ethnic and racial minorities can continue to face discrimination at a group level today. For example, in the US African Americans descend from enslaved peoples who were not permitted to receive formal education. Their offspring, even when free, found themselves at a comparative disadvantage with whites who enjoyed a rich tradition of receiving free and widespread education. Even where African Americans were able to secure education, they were often structurally prevented from taking this up and therefore making unhindered progress in society. As the discussion of **whiteness** shows, over generations this historical injustice has translated into a cycle of disadvantage reflected not only in education but across society in terms of social mobility and the penal system in particular.

GROUPS AND EXPERIENCES

It is for such reasons that Scott (1999) emphasises the role of groups, and sets out the 'conundrum of equality' for ethnic and racial minorities as she understands it in three stages:

1. Equality is an absolute principle and a historically contingent practice.
2. Group identities define individuals and deny the full expression or realization of their individuality.
3. Claims for equality involve the acceptance and rejection of the group identity attributed by discrimination. Or, to put it another way: the terms of exclusion on which discrimination is premised are at once refused and reproduced in demands for inclusion. (Ibid., 3)

What is being outlined here is a framing in which equality is meaningfully understood when placed within a proper context, historical and social, that takes into consideration the role and significance of groups. In a manner that supports the discussion of **ethnicity** and **race** considered throughout this book, Scott elaborates:

Group identities are an inevitable aspect of social and political life, and the two are interconnected because group differences become visible, salient and troubling in specific political contexts. It is at these moments – when exclusions are legitimated by group differences, when economic and social hierarchies advantage some groups at the expense of others, when one set of biological or religious or ethnic or cultural characteristics are valued over another – that the tension between individuals and groups emerges. Individuals for whom group identities were simply dimensions of a multi-faceted individuality, find themselves fully determined by a single element: religious or ethnic or racial or gender identity. (Ibid., 4)

This is why specific anti-discrimination measures have traditionally offered the most robust protections in proceeding through group-specific instruments to outlaw discrimination based not just on race and ethnicity, but also other identity groupings centering on gender, disability, age, sexual orientation and so forth, as well as sometimes insisting on the institutional monitoring of under-representation amongst such groups (Meer, 2008). In terms of race and ethnicity in particular, public policies have included the *categorisation* of people and groups, for example on the census categories or on ethnic monitoring forms (see **super-diversity**), as well as addressing embedded disadvantage by actively prohibiting prejudicial behaviour, or promoting opportunity of outcomes, or both. Being 'neutral' has also been an approach, typified by the non-discrimination promised in the French constitution, which deems equal treatment *as uniformity*. The Constitution of the Fifth Republic (1958) promises to 'ensure the equality of all citizens before the law without distinction of origin, race or religion'. This is in radical contrast to the kinds of affirmative action quotas and targets unevenly pursued in the United States mentioned above. What is notable is that affirmative action measures have developed in a way that places a specific emphasis on managing group relations.

Britain has perhaps borrowed something from an American approach, but in a manner that has also focused on how society can achieve fair treatment for different groups, something that reaches beyond how these groups might blend into society. This means that British anti-discrimination frameworks have tried to address the rights of distinct groups as well as their modes of interaction, and so are not merely concerned with the rights of individuals (Rudiger, 2007). As such, from the legal response to racial discrimination in particular flows one characterisation of what is commonly known as British multiculturalism (Modood, 2005, 2007). This includes how, under the remit of national legislation, the state has sought to integrate minorities into the labour market and other key arenas of British society through an approach that promotes equal access as an example of equality of opportunity. Indeed, it is nearly forty years since the introduction of a third Race Relations Act (RRA) (1976) cemented a state sponsorship of race equality by consolidating earlier, weaker legislative instruments (RRA, 1965, 1968).

This is an example, according to Joppke (1999: 642), of a **citizenship** that has amounted to a 'precarious balance between citizenship universalism and racial group particularism [that] stops short of giving special group rights to immigrants'. What it also suggests is that the institutionalisation of redress, against racially structured barriers to participation, can represent a defining characteristic in approaches to integrating minority ethnic and racial groups. This includes recognising how ethnic and racial 'inequality rests on presumed differences' that 'are not uniquely individualized, but taken to be categorical' (Scott, 1999: 8). The categorical here refers to a named identity grouping, a move that is not unproblematic. It is sometimes the case, for example, that too much emphasis is placed on internal strategies, hopes and aspiration, and too little on the external social context, such that we risk looking for structural explanations in agency at the costs of looking to the social system as a whole. This is especially the case in debates over differential success in ethnic minority labour-market participation or educational outcomes, in which the role of **ethnicity** can become 'mono-causal' (Gillborn, 2008). Moreover, do we risk boxing people into categories that those advocating **hybridity** and **super-diversity** would challenge? As Appaih (quoted in Minow, 1997: 56) argues:

> Demanding respect for people as blacks and as gays requires that there are some scripts that go with being an African-American or having same-sex desires. There will be proper ways of being black and gay, there will be expectations to be met, demands will be made. It is at this point that someone who takes autonomy seriously will ask whether we have not replaced one kind of tyranny with another.

So the concern here is that in trying to address a historical injustice, public policies that seek to take minority group categories into consideration *to address that historical disadvantage* begin to reify groups and essentialise their alleged properties. As the discussion of **intersectionality**, **ethnicity** and **mixedness** detail, it is important to register that the precise criteria of groups are always contested, but might helpfully be configured according to boundaries that shift over time. As we will find in later discussion, Modood (2005) offers some useful criteria *in addition* to identity which includes that of *disproportionality* in terms of the distribution of general negative societal characteristics such as unemployment, racial discrimination and poor health, amongst other inequalities.

RECOGNITION AND REDISTRIBUTION

The discussion of equality and inequality as it is related to ethnic and racial groups has increasingly come to rest in a prevailing debate between **recognition** (as elaborated later in this book) and redistribution. The latter is grounded in an egalitarian notion of justice which requires 'getting the privileged groups to share, by means of persuasion, pressure, or coercion, their resources with the poor and underprivileged' (Parekh, 2005: 199). In this regard redistribution 'primarily refers to the material resources which can be transferred from one group to another' (ibid.: 200), while **recognition** sees material resources as *interdependent* with those of status and identity. Redistribution has an old pedigree, Parekh reminds us, 'going back to the early Greek democrats, and includes influential Christian thinkers, millenarian movements, socialists, Marxists and egalitarian liberals' (ibid.). It is therefore a core concern that has become intimately established between related questions of equality, while recognition is often seen as a more peripheral project. Some writers have tried to bring matters of equality together under the two registers; thus Nancy Fraser (2004) in her dialogue with Axel Honneth eschews the dualism I have described on the grounds that equality needs both redistribution and recognition to be alligned.

To this end Fraser introduces the category of a 'bivalent collectivity' to bring socio-economic and cultural dimensions together. A bivalent collectivity includes groups that suffer both material maldistribution and cultural misrecognition, neither of which may be reduced to the other, because the injustice such a collectivity encounters emerges in both spheres. In Fraser's terms (1997: 16), 'People who are subject to both cultural injustice and economic injustice need both recognition and redistribution. They need both to claim and to deny their specificity.' In order to solve the redistribution–recognition dilemma Fraser (1997: 23) makes a distinction between two kinds of remedies for injustice, namely *affirmation* and *transformation*. By affirmative remedies for injustice she means remedies aimed at correcting inequitable outcomes of social arrangements without disturbing the underlying framework that generates them. By transformative remedies, she's concerned with correcting inequitable outcomes precisely by restructuring the underlying frameworks.

While this is a valuable addition to overcoming the recognition-redistribution dualism, which partly emerges out of how redistribution has been configured in dominant theoretical traditions (e.g. Rawls, 1999), it does not sufficiently register 'how no single language can adequately articulate the full range of diverse experiences of and insights into the structures of injustice' (Parekh, 2005: 207). Hence the solution proposed by Fraser risks normatively narrowing the ways in which recognition and redistribution can be configured and related, creating a hierarchy of some harms over others.

REFERENCES

Dworkin, R. (1978) *Taking Rights Seriously*. Cambridge, MA: Harvard University Press.

Fraser, N. (1997) *Justice Interruptus: Critical Reflections on the 'Postsocialist' Condition*. London: Verso.

Fraser, N. and Honneth, A. (2004) *Redistribution or Recognition? A Political–Philosophical Exchange*. London: Verso.

Gillborn, D. (2008) *Racism in Education: Coincidence or Conspiracy?* London: Routledge.

Joppke, C. (1999) 'How immigration is changing citizenship: a comparative view', *Ethnic and Racial Studies*, 22 (4): 629–52.

Kenny, M. (2004) *The Politics of Identity*. Cambridge: Polity.

Meer, N. (2008) 'The politics of voluntary and involuntary identities: are Muslims in Britain an ethnic, racial or religious minority?', *Patterns of Prejudice*, 41 (5): 61–81.

Minow, M. (1997) *Not Only For Myself: Identity, Politics and the Law*. New York: The New York Press.

Modood, T. (2005) *Multicultural Politics: Racism, Ethnicity and Muslims in Britain*. Edinburgh: Edinburgh University Press.

Modood, T. (2007) *Multiculturalism: A Civic Idea*. Cambridge: Polity Press.

O'Leary, B. (2006) 'Liberalism, multiculturalism, Danish cartoons, Islamist fraud, and the rights of the ungodly', *International Migration*, 44 (5): 22–33.

Parekh, B. (2005) 'Redistribution or recognition? A misguided debate', in G. Loury, T. Modood and S. Teles (eds) *Ethnicity, Social Mobility and Public Policy in the US and UK*. Cambridge: Cambridge University Press.

Rawls, R. (1999) *A Theory of Justice*, rev. edn. Cambridge, MA: Harvard University Press.

Rudiger, A. (2007) 'Cultures of equality, traditions of belonging', in C. Bertossi (ed.) *European Anti-discrimination and the Politics of Citizenship*. Basingstoke: Palgrave Macmillan.

Scott, J. (1999) *The Conundrum of Equality*, Paper Number 2, School of Social Sciences, Institute for Advanced Study, Princeton University.

Ethnicity

> *Ethnicity is a concept that describes the real or imagined features of group membership, typically in terms of one or other combination of language, collective memory, culture, ritual, dress and religion, amongst other features. It is therefore a looser definition than 'race', and the key distinction with other ways of conceiving groups is that it makes self-definition central.*

The *term* ethnicity – which as the introduction to this book outlines is different to a *concept* – has been around for a lot longer than its meaning in the social sciences (just as, say, **blackness**, **race** or **citizenship** have). Etymologically it is derived from the Greek word 'ethnos' (or 'ethnie' in plural) meaning a nation conceived as a unity of persons with common ancestry. Interestingly, in Greek usage, according to Ibrahim (2011: 12), it also expressed a negative inflection in so far as 'foreign barbarians were the *ethnea*, while they [Greeks] would commonly refer to themselves as a *Genos Hellenon* or 'the family of Hellenes'.

Perhaps the most relevant legacy in ideas of ethnicity from the Greek lineage was the distinction, and often conflation, of the *ethnos* with the *demos*. The former is an ethnic polity while the latter is polity made of one or more ethnic groups. In contemporary language this may range between an assimilationist social order that reflects the majority ethnic group, and a **multicultural** social order that accommodates, and so affords **recognition** to, plurality and difference. The *demos*, meanwhile, is a polity organised around features of democratic participation, state-hood and **citizenship**. As noted in the discussion of **citizenship**, there is a tension with the insider–outsider status that recurs across formulations of both the ethnos and the demos and, as the discussion of **nationalism** outlines, these categories are often understood to be mutually constitutive. This is both because and despite how, in the wider scholarly discussion of ethnicity in debates about groups and communities, 'it is almost de rigueur now in academic discourse to view ethnicity as socially and politically constructed' (May, 2001: 19). How did this become so?

SUBJECTIVITIES AND PRIMORDIALISMS

In an early account of **ethnicity**, Max Weber (1978 [1925]: 389) proposed that: 'We shall call "ethnic groups" those human groups that entertain a subjective belief in their common descent because of similarities of physical type or of customs or of both, or because of memories of colonization and migration ... it does not matter whether or not an objective blood relationship exist.' For Weber ethnicity therefore meant at least three things. First, it referred to the fact that common descent is less important than a *belief* in common descent. Second, the potential bases of this belief in common descent are multiple, varying from the physical resemblance to shared cultural practices to shared historical experiences, and so forth. Finally, an ethnic group exists wherever this distinctive connection – this belief in common descent – is part of a *foundation* of community.

Despite the broad influence of Weber on social science, this early *constructivist* account was to some extent offset by what would come to be known as *primordialist* readings of ethnicity. There are perhaps three main strands of this latter tradition. The first is often sourced to a German romanticism that precedes the Weberian formulation, and which in particular reacted against the dominance of rationalism in modernist thought by emphasising the role of inherited language, and in particular aesthetic features, in the alleged uniqueness of cultures (see Jenkins, 1997). This informs one strand of the discussion around the idea of **nationalism**. The second strand is more modern and adopts a socio-biological approach, and so portrays ethnic groups as extensions of self-choosing kinship groups, in a continuing process of human evolution (van den Berghe, 1979). The third strand, despite some characterisations, associates ethnicity least with its biological inheritance but instead conceives it as deeply rooted in primary and secondary socialisation. This reading is especially found in the works of Geertz (1973) amongst others, who undertook empirical research in immediately post-colonial societies. He argued that civil relationships, forged through democratic participation in public life, are often limited in societies marked by strong ethnic ties because they cannot overcome 'the assumed givens of social existence: immediate congruity and live connection mainly, but beyond them the giveness that stems from being born into a particular ... community, speaking a particular language ... following particular social practices' (ibid.: 259). In being deemed a 'given', of course, the explanatory role of *why* ethnicity (and not class or something else) is diminished, and this point is important because it also speaks to the role of cultural difference, which as we see below is not static, and does not always correspond with ethnic identity, and so should not be over-emphasised in a conception of ethnicity.

ETHNIC BOUNDARIES AND ETHNIC ASSERTIVENESS

One serious challenge to Geertz came in the work of the Norwegian anthropologist Fredrik Barth (1969), whose reading of ethnicity is arguably the foundation of the dominant contemporary formulation. Barth's argument revolves around two key points. The first is that the most *valid* thing to *measure* when studying ethnicity is how groups categorised themselves, namely how groups self-identify to one thing or another. This explicitly critiques some anthropological traditions which emphasised focusing on the cultural content of groups (cf. Levi-Strauss, 1994). The *subjective* dimension of recognition – an internal self-awareness – is therefore more important for Barth than the *objective* definition of the group which is designated by an external party. Second, and in shifting the emphasis away from the possible characteristics of a group – that is, taking us away from definitions of groups as heralding displays of particular traits or compromising particular behaviours in the classical anthropological sense – Barth (1969: 10–11) argued that we should focus upon the 'boundaries' between groups, and how these boundaries become sites of identity maintenance. By boundaries he did not mean that we should think of ethnicity in terms of 'separate people's, each with their culture and each organised in a society which can legitimately be isolated for description as an island to itself'. We should instead seek to understand how

> ethnic distinctions do not depend on an absence of mobility, contact and infor-
> mation, but do entail social processes of exclusion and incorporation whereby
> discrete categories are maintained *despite* changing participation and member-
> ship in the course of individual life histories. ... The features which are taken
> into account are not the sum of the objective differences, but only those which
> the actors themselves regard as significant. (Ibid.: 10, 14)

One interesting influence of this reading formulation is expressed in the work of Tariq Modood who shares something of this in his view of ethnicity, but also departs from Barth in emphasising the dialectical relationship between ethnic self-definition and group pride. In his research, this is evident in the projection of positive images and demands for respect, in a way that is capable of challenging negative attributions. Paradoxically, the vehicle for inclusion can sometimes invoke and repudiate the differences that have been denied inclusion in the first place. Key to this 'ethnic assertiveness', however, is the **recognition** of a group's *mode of being* rather than its *mode of oppression*. In other words, ethnic groups' identities should not be constructed beyond them by focusing on negative attributions alone.

What this view advocates is the space for ethnic minorities to draw upon internal resources to resist the external constraints of racial discrimination in creative ways. The methodological implications of listening to these internal voices is not only relevant to ethnographic work, however, but can be adopted in large-scale survey design. For example, in the ten-yearly Policy Studies Institute survey into the conditions of ethnic minorities in Britain, Modood et al. (1997: 291–338) investigated the question, 'How do ethnic minority people think of themselves?' Recognising the situational and contextual nature of the question, they worked on the understanding that expressions of ethnicity entail 'not what people do but what people say or believe about themselves'. Thus self-description is central to ethnicity, which includes expressions of what might be called an 'associational or communal identity', as well as cultural practices. Contrasting this with a designated ethnicity according to country of origin or heritage, they found that while people with African Caribbean ethnicities maintained that skin colour was the most important factor in terms of their self-description, for people with South Asian ethnicities it was religion that proved most important. Although they looked at various dimensions of culture and ethnicity such as marriage, language, dress – all of which 'command considerable allegiance' – they concluded that religion 'is central in the self-definition of the majority of South Asian people'. Thus when they asked South Asian respondents, 'Do you ever think of yourself as being black?' only about a fifth of over 1500 respondents gave an affirmative answer.

NEW AND OLD ETHNICITIES

In some ways an emphasis on the differentiated ethnic identity that recognises people's 'mode of being' feeds into the emergence of the 'new ethnicities' problematic. This sought to engage the shifting complexities of ethnic identities, specifically their processes of formation and change, and was given an authoritative voice in the work of Stuart Hall (1988, 1991). According to Cohen (2000: 5), the idea of new ethnicities seeks to capture the way in which 'identities had broken free of their anchorage in singular histories of race and nation', not least in the way that a single identity was meant to reference a common experience. At this earlier stage, 'ethnicity was the enemy' (Hall, 1991: 55) because it was conceived in the form of a culturally constructed sense that was problematic, in Hall's terms, because 'a particularly closed, exclusive, and regressive form of English national identity is one of the core characteristics of British racism today' (Hall, 1996 [1988]: 168). One response was the tendency to homogenise differences at the expense of more sociologically honest attempts to conceptualise the social relations of minorities:

> 'The Black Experience', as a singular and unifying framework based on the building up of identity across ethnic and cultural difference between the different communities, became 'hegemonic' over other ethnic/racial identities – though the latter did not, of course, disappear. (Hall, 1991 [1988]: 164)

With what Hall termed the 'end of innocence' surrounding the notion of an essential black subject, 'the politics of representation around the black subject shifts' enough for us to 'begin to see a renewed contestation over the meaning of the term "ethnicity" itself' (ibid.). Ethnicity, however, emerges in a different incarnation here than in the Barthian sense or in that of Modood.

The ethnicities in Hall's concept are found by 're-inscribing ethnicity outside of the discourses of the sociology of race and ethnic relations and the rhetoric of nationalism' (Solomos and Back, 1993: 137). This is because new ethnicities are more individualistic, choice based and 'consumed' in an interaction of the local and the global that displaces the 'centred' discourses 'of the West, putting into question its universalist character and its transcendental claims to speak for everyone, while being itself everywhere and nowhere' (Hall, 1996 [1988]: 169). In many ways the new-ethnicities project has been highly influential in propelling ways forward from theoretical standpoints that might once have seemed irreconcilable. At the same time, it successfully captured an intellectual movement that was already under way, specifically in resisting the master-builder attempts to conceptualise minority identity through already constructed (and then imposed) political objectives.

BOUNDARIES AND DRAWBACKS

As Hall's post-structuralist account illustrates, the precise criteria of ethnic boundaries are contested, but locating boundaries for ethnicity remains the most useful means of ordering the concept. In this regard, Modood (2005) lists the following. First, there is *identity* in terms of the public articulation of a specific self definition perhaps derived from a linguistic community or territory (Catalonian, Québécois, Welshness), real or imagined ancestry (African Caribbean), religion (Jewishness, Sikhism, Islam), or something else that has a subjective power. Second, there is *disproportionality* in so far as ethnic groups are marked by the disproportional distribution of general societal characteristics such as unemployment, racial discrimination, poor health or, more positively, academic aspiration and communal living. An illustration of this may be types of social and cultural capital that are created and sustained amongst minority ethnic groups (Modood, 2004). For example, in explaining disproportionately higher educational outcomes amongst poorer minority groups, Modood (2004: 95) points to the role of (i) family, (ii) norms and (iii) values:

(i) Parents, other significant relatives and community members share some general, but durable, ambitions to achieve upward mobility for themselves and especially for their children, and believe that (higher) education is important in achieving those ambitions, and so prioritize the acquisition of (higher) education.

(ii) They are successfully able to convey this view to the children, who to a large degree internalise it and even where they may not fully share it they develop ambitions and priorities that are consistent with those of their parents.

(iii) The parents have enough authority and power over their children, suitably reinforced by significant relatives and other community members, to ensure that the ambition is not ephemeral or fantastic, but the children do whatever is necessary at a particular stage for its progressive realization.

Third, there is *creativity* as far as some groups are associated with innovations in ways of living, be they styles of music, dress, cuisine, working practices and so forth. Fourth, there is *strategy*, since ethnic groups who are the subject of particular kinds of experiences might mobilise and challenge their treatment, illustrated by the Sikh turban campaigns, mobilisations for Black history or Kosher food. Fifth, *cultural distinctiveness* is often apparent amongst ethnic groups in the norms and practices surrounding such things as family relations, marriage rituals and mourning practices, amongst others.

Ethnicity is not an unproblematic concept, however, and suffers from the tensions associated with group categories discussed in **hybridity**. For example, where too much emphasis is placed on internal strategies, hopes and aspiration, and too little on the external social context, we risk looking for structural explanations in agency at the costs of looking to the social system as a whole. This is especially the case in debates over differential success in ethnic minority labour-market participation or educational outcomes, in which the role of ethnicity can become 'mono-causal' (Gillborn, 2008). This also repeats the charges of essentialism in a manner that under-emphasised how ethnicities can reflect a **mixedness**, or that when we talk about 'groups' we end up ignoring the internal diversity of such groups. This means that we risk overlooking how groups are constantly changing, developing and involve a variety of syntheses and mixing, so that we start to use ethnicity as people once used **race**.

REFERENCES

Barth, F. (1969) *Ethnic Groups and Boundaries: The Social Organisation of Culture and Difference*. Boston: Little, Brown & Co.

Cohen, P. (2000) *New Ethnicities, Old Racisms*. London: Zed Books.

Geertz, C. (1973) *The Interpretation of Cultures*. New York: Basic Books.

Gillborn, D. (2008) *Racism in Education: Coincidence or Conspiracy*. London: Routledge.

Hall, S. (1988) 'New ethnicities', reproduced in H. A. Baker Jr, M. Diawara and R. H. Lindeborg (eds) *Black British Cultural Studies: A Reader*. Chicago: University of Chicago Press.

Hall, S. (1991) 'The local and the global: globalisation and ethnicity', in A. King (ed.) *Culture, Globalization and the World System*. London: Macmillan.

Hall S. (1996 [1988]) 'New ethnicities', in H.A. Baker Jr, M. Diawara and R.H. Lindeborg (eds) *Black British Cultural Studies: A Reader*. Chicago: University of Chicago Press, pp.163–72.

Ibrahim, V. (2011) 'Ethnicity', in S. M. Caliendo and C. D. McIlwain (eds) *The Routledge Companion to Race and Ethnicity*. London: Routledge.

Jenkins, R. (1997) *Rethinking Ethnicity: Arguments and Explorations*. London: Sage.

Levi-Strauss, C. (1994) 'Anthropology, race, and politics: a conversation with Didier Eribon', in R. Borofsky (ed.) *Assessing Cultural Anthropology*. New York: McGraw Hill.

May, S. (2001) *Language and Minority Rights: Ethnicity, Nationalism and the Politics of Language*. Malaysia: Pearson Publishing.

Modood, T. (2004) 'Capitals, ethnic identity and educational qualifications', *Cultural Trends*, 13(2), Special Issue on Cultural Capital and Social Exclusion.

Modood, T. (2005) *Multicultural Politics: Racism, Ethnicity and Muslims in Britain*. Edinburgh: Edinburgh University Press.

Modood, T., Berthoud, R., Lakey, J., Nazroo, J., Smith, P., Virdee, S. and Beishon, S. (1997) *Ethnic Minorities in Britain: Diversity and Disadvantage: The Fourth National Survey of Ethnic Minorities*. London: Policy Studies Institute.

Solomos, J. and Back, L. (1993) *Racism and Society*. London: Macmillan.

van den Berghe, P. (1979) *The Ethnic Phenomenon*. New York: Elsevier.

Weber, M. (1978 [1925]) *Economy and Society: Volume 1*. London: University of California Press.

> *Euro-Islam describes a synthesis between Islamic conventions. What balance this synthesis takes, and how it occurs, is subject to dispute not only between proponents of Euro-Islam, but also those who reject the possibility of its development.*

Euro-Islam is a relatively recent addition to the repertoire of concepts concerned with race and ethnicity, and broadly describes the possibilities for Islam in Europe that Muslim migrants and subsequent generations herald. Beyond this there is little consensus amongst its main theoreticians. While the origins of the term Euro-Islam may be traced to a variety of sources, it is forthrightly claimed by the German Orientalist Bassam Tibi (2008: 156) that 'others use the notion "Euro-Islam" without a reference to its origins and often in a different, clearly distorted meaning'. More precisely, Tibi seeks to 'dissociate my reasoning on Euro-Islam from that of Tariq Ramadan, whom I consider a rival within Islam in Europe'. Its precise provenance therefore becomes less relevant than what it denotes, because although the concept may also be sourced to others (see Al Sayyad and Castells, 2002), Tibi squarely juxtaposes his account with that of Tariq Ramadan (1999), with whom this discussion might usefully begin.

EURO-ISLAM AS A MULTIDIRECTIONAL PROCESS

For the Swiss-born intellectual Tariq Ramadan (2004: 4), Euro-Islam describes a process that is already under way, in which 'more and more young people and intellectuals are actively looking for a way to live in harmony with their faith, participating in the societies that are their societies, whether they like it or not'. Ramadan describes this as the cultivation of a 'Muslim personality', one that is 'faithful to the principles of Islam, dressed in European and American cultures, and definitively rooted in Western societies' (2004: 4). He continues:

> While our fellow-citizens speak of this 'integration' of Muslims 'among us', the question for the Muslims presents itself differently: their universal principles teach them that wherever the law respects their integrity and their freedom of worship, they are at home and must consider the attainments of these societies as their own and must involve themselves, with their fellow-citizens, in making it good and better. (Ibid.: 5)

Ramadan is thus prioritising a scriptural inheritance that needs to be reconciled with current and future lived practice, in a manner that reflects 'a testimony based on faith, spirituality, values, a sense of where boundaries lie', something that 'reverses the perception based on the old concepts' (2004: 73). A key theological obstacle that Ramadan therefore seeks to overcome is that of the distinction between *Dar al-Islam* (abode of Islam) and *Dar al-Harb* (abode of war), a concern that is illustrative of his wider thesis. Muslims can recognise the 'abode of Islam', maintains Ramadan, by the fact that they are able to practise their religion freely and live their lives in a manner that is consistent with Islamic prescription. For Ramadan, this is a question of freedom of worship that is quite different from a question of the wider institutionalisation of Islam and/or non-practice of Islam in any given society. He elaborates this at length to contrast it with its anti-thesis, 'the abode of war', in which the legal system as well as the government are anti-Islamic. The important point for Ramadan is to recognise that this distinction does not turn on the distinction between Muslim and non-Muslim contexts, because it may well be the case that a majority-Muslim society, where the legal and political system prevents Muslims from living in accordance with their Islamic prescription, constitutes *Dar al-Harb*.

This reasoning leads to an interesting juxtaposition in that 'Muslims may feel safer in the West, as far as the free exercise of their religion is concerned, than in so-called Muslim countries' (2004: 65). The implication of this position is that the dichotomy between the two 'abodes' can no longer be sustained. The resolution to this, Ramadan suggests, rests in an exercise of critical interrogation in which European Muslims

> have no choice but to go back to the beginning and study their points of reference in order to delineate and distinguish what, in their religion, is unchangeable (thabit) from what is subject to change (mutaghayyir), and to measure, from the inside, what they have achieved and what they have lost by being in the West. (2004: 9)

To pursue this, Ramadan proposes that Islam can be appropriated in movements of reform and integration in new environments as long as the idea of the *alamiyyat al-islam* (the universal dimension of the teaching of Islam) is retained. Just as, he argues, the concepts of *dar al-islam* and *dar al-harb* 'constituted a human attempt, at a moment in history, to describe the world and to provide the Muslim community with a geopolitical scheme that seemed appropriate to the reality of the time' (2004: 69), in the current era what is proposed is the recognition of a third abode, *dar al-dawa* ('abode of prayer'). This is consistent with the ethic of Islam, he maintains, for 'Mecca was neither *dar al-islam* nor *dar al-harb*, but *dar al-dawa* and in the eyes of the Muslims, the whole of the Arabian Peninsula was *dar al-dawa*' (2004: 72). He summarises his position thus:

> I have investigated the tools that can give an impetus, from the inside, to a movement of reform and integration into the new environments. The power and effectiveness of the 'principles of integration', which is the foundation upon which all the juridical instruments for adaptation must depend, lie in

the fact that it comes with an entirely opposite perspective instead of being sensitive, obsessed by self-protection and withdrawal and attempts to integrate oneself by the 'little door', on the margin, or 'as a minority', it is on the contrary, a matter of integrating, making one's own all that people have produced that is good, just, humane – intellectually, scientifically, socially, politically, economically, culturally, and so on. (2004: 5)

EURO-ISLAM AS MUSLIM ADAPTATION

Ramadan's project might then be characterised as both *classicist* and *revisionist* in that he stakes out an ethical resource in Islamic scriptures to propose a qualitatively novel solution that is calibrated to contemporary – traditionally non-Muslim majority – societies. Yet it is precisely this project of reconciliation between Islamic doctrines and European conventions that is challenged by Bassam Tibi (2008: 177), the other key exponent of 'Euro-Islam'. For if Europe is no longer perceived as *dar al-harb*, and instead considered to be part of the peaceful house of Islam, he maintains, 'then this is not a sign of moderation, as some wrongly assume: it is the mindset of an Islamization of Europe'. He continues:

> In defense of the open society and of its principles, it needs to be spoken out candidly: Europe is not dar al-Islam (or, in the cover language of some, dar al-shahada), i.e. it is not an Islamic space but a civilisation of its own, albeit an exclusive one that is open to others, including Muslims. These are, however, expected to become Europeans if they want to be part of Europe as their new home. (2004: 159)

In Tibi's view, the burden of adaptation required to cultivate a Euro-Islam must necessarily rest heavier with Muslims than amongst the institutions and conventions that constitute European societies. That is to say that a civilisational notion of Europe, one that he traces back to the age of the Carolingians, must be the vessel in which Islam in Europe comes to rest. Tibi's formulation is principally driven by an anxiety over the disproportionate development of sizable Muslim communities in Europe, and the concomitant emergence of a Muslim consciousness (or in Ramadan's terms, 'Muslim personality'). This leads Tibi (2008: 180) to insist that without doctrinal reforms in Islam, that is, 'without a clear abandoning of concepts such as da'wa [prayer], hijra [migration] and shari'a, as well as jihad', there can be no Europeanisation of Islam. One source of Tibi's dualism centres on the relationship between religious doctrine and migration, especially with regards to the status on proselytisation, meaning that 'if da'wa and hijra combined continue to be at work, the envisioned "Islamization of Europe" will be the result in the long run' (2008: 177). This can only be averted in Tibi's view if Muslims acknowledge that the identity of Europe is not Islamic:

> It is perplexing to watch the contradictory reality of Europeans abandoning their faith while the global religionization of politics and conflict enters

Europe under the conditions of Islamic immigration ... The substance of the notion of Euro-Islam is aimed at the incorporation of the European values of democracy, laïcité, civil society, pluralism, secular tolerance and individual human rights into Islamic thought. (2008: 153, 157)

The direction of travel here, that is to say the focus on what needs to be revised, marks the key distinction here between Ramadan and Tibi. Hence the latter has elsewhere promoted the need for a European *Leitkultur* – a guiding culture or leading culture – characterised by values of 'modernity: democracy, secularism, the Enlightenment, human rights and civil society' (Tibi, 1998: 154). Of course how the concept of *Leitkultur* has been adopted varies profoundly and may in many instances not be endorsed by Tibi himself.

RE-LOCATING THE MUSLIM SUBJECT

Despite their differences, both accounts offer an interpretation of the Muslim subject that is theologically grounded but socially iterative. That is to say, that while differing profoundly in important respects, both Tariq Ramadan and Bassam Tibi anchor the development of a Muslim consciousness in Europe to a doctrinal innovation in Islam. Perhaps both authors therefore assume too linear a relationship between Islamic doctrine and Muslim identity in a way that minimises the role of the *social*, the implication being that – no less than with any text – Islamic scriptures offer guidance that is interpreted and applied by human agents in particular social contexts. As Omid Safi (2004: 22) reminds us: 'in all cases, the dissemination of the Divine teachings is achieved through human agency. Religion is always mediated.' The point is that the meaning of a text has to be understood in terms of not just interpretations but also social context. It is suggested here that the relationship between Islam and a Muslim identity might be better conceived as instructive but not determining, something analogous to the relationship between the categorisation of one's sex and one's gendered identity.

That is to say, one may be biologically female or male in a narrow sense of the definition, but one may be a woman or man in multiple, overlapping and discontinuous ways – one's gender reflects something that emerges on a continuum that can be either (or both) internally defined or externally ascribed. This allows that in addition to the scriptural conception, we could view Muslim identity as a quasi-ethnic sociological formation, which potentially allows a range of factors other than religion (such as ethnicity, race, gender, sexuality and agnosticism) to shape Muslim identities (Meer, 2010). 'Quasi' is used to denote something similar but not the same, because ethnic and religious boundaries continue to interact and are rarely wholly demarcated, hence the term 'ethno-religious' (see Modood, 1997: 337). Through such an approach we would be relocating the 'Muslim subject' in society and amongst Muslim populations.

REFERENCES

AlSayyad, N. and Castells, M. (eds) (2002) *Muslim Europe or Euroislam: Politics, Culture and Citizenship in the Age of Globalization*. Lanham: Lexington Books.

Meer, N. (2010) *Citizenship, Identity and the Politics of Multiculturalism*. Basingstoke: Palgrave.

Modood, T. (1997) 'Difference: cultural racism and anti-racism', in P. Werbner and T. Modood (eds) *Debating Cultural Hybridity: Multi-Cultural Identities and the Politics of Anti-Racism*. London: Zed Books, pp. 154–72.

Ramadan, T. (1999) *To be a European Muslim*. Leicester: Islamic Foundation.

Ramadan, T. (2004) *Western Muslims and the Future of Islam*. New York: Oxford University Press.

Safi, O. (2004) Introduction: 'The times they are a-changing', in O. Safi (ed.) *Progressive Muslims on Justice, Gender and Pluralism*. Oxford: Oneworld, pp. 147–62.

Tibi, B. (1998) *Europa ohne Identität, Die Krise der multikulturellen Gesellschaft*. Munich: Bertelsmann.

Tibi, B. (2008) *Political Islam, World Politics and Europe: Democratic Peace and Euro-Islam versus Global Jihad*. London: Routledge.

Health and
Well-being

Race and ethnicity have often been peripheral to the explicit study of health and well-being, even though categories of race and ethnicity have been implicitly informed by medical knowledge. Increasingly, however, we can observe a reframing amongst explanations (from biological to structural) that helps us to delineate how different kinds of health risks and status may correlate to different ethnic and racial categories. The important point is that these differences are rarely (if ever) a consequence of inherent group differences but instead a sociological reflection of these groups' broader experiences.

ETHNICITY AND HEALTH

The study of health in terms of ethnicity is an uneven activity across the health research landscape (Afshari and Bhopal, 2002). In the North American literature, it is often explored as health 'inequities' or 'disparities' (the more commonly used terms), especially between ethnic and racial groups (e.g. Raphael, 2000; Williams and Jackson, 2005; Griffith et al., 2006). Indeed, in the US the study of health in relation to categories of race and ethnicity is sometimes used as a proxy for the study of socio-economic status (Navarro, 1990).

In contrast in Britain, research on race and ethnicity has proliferated through **intersectional** approaches in recent years (Davey Smith, Charsley et al., 2000; Davey Smith, Chaturvedi et al., 2000; Chandola, 2001; Chaturvedi, 2003; Nazroo, 2006). This marks a departure from a period when medical researchers would conflate race and ethnicity or, where using 'ethnicity' alone, would inadequately define what is meant. An early critique of one illustration of this was put forward by Bhopal, Phillimore et al. (1991), who rejected the term 'Asian' to describe people with real and imagined ancestry from the Indian subcontinent, on the grounds that it conflates and collapses an extraordinary variety of health experiences and tendencies:

> The prevailing British use of the term 'Asian' is not a self-description by the peoples of the Indian subcontinent, but a label imposed by a society which has historically defined 'otherness' primarily in terms of colour, and continues to do so. Of course, 'Asian' is not a colour term in the strict sense; but its saliency comes from its place within a set of categories used to define those who are not 'white', and are therefore 'other'. The benefit, more apparent than real, of such labels as 'Asian' is to permit relatively simple generalizations about complex populations. ... Until more appropriate terminology is achieved, much research on ethnic minority groups will remain downright parochial, misleading and contradictory. (Bhopal, Phillimore et al., 1991: 244–5)

This has become a prevailing complaint that is sometimes used to look backwards as well as forwards. Hence we find that research undertaken in this area since the 1970s has been accused of over-emphasising 'ethnic' differences (Davey Smith, Charsley et al., 2000; Karlsen and Nazroo, 2000) and assuming that 'ethnic/race' variables represent true (and fixed) genetic or cultural differences between groups (Senior and Bhopal, 1994; Karlsen and Nazroo, 2000).

DISEASE AND CATEGORIES

As the discussion of **race** highlights, the relationship between medical knowledge and racial and ethnic categories has often been foundational, especially in supporting the idea of valid underlying biological differences between human populations. Yet the relationship between medical knowledge and race and ethnicity has developed into a broader account about how we think about health and well-being, and the kinds of differential outcomes that might be observed. For example, it is sometimes said the genetic condition of sickle cell anaemia is a predominantly 'black disease' (Platt et al., 1994), and so suggests that a discrete relationship exists between a racial category and a medical illness. Or, it is observed, that because there are higher levels of hypertension amongst African Americans than compared with white Americans (Lindhorst et al., 2007), a physiological explanation emerging from the group category is self-evident. A further example might be elevated levels of psychosis and poorer mental health amongst some ethnic and racial minority groups, something reflected in the over-representation of members of these groups in mental health institutions (Keating et al., 2003).

If we take each example in turn, we can see why we should be cautious about (and sometimes wholly reject) ideas of a causal relation between ethnic and racial categories and disease, and instead be willing to be guided by an understanding of the sociological conditions in the environment that frame and register such conditions. Beginning with sickle cell anaemia, it is clear that this results from genetic alteration in levels of haemoglobin protein in the red cells, which become brittle and sickle shaped. Yet on closer inspection we find that it correlates with a legacy of exposure to a particular kind of malaria (*falciparum*), to which people with sickle cell are actually more resistant. Since malaria is (or has been) a significant cause of death across continents, from West Africa to the Mediterranean coastline, as well as India, we can observe a historical gene–environment interaction – or a 'selection pressure' (in the process of natural selection) – which continues carrying this sickle cell gene even though it is sometimes harmful. As a consequence we find cases of sickle cell anaemia amongst a wider variety of population groups than may commonly be anticipated (Mohammed et al., 2006). Turning to higher levels of hypertension amongst African Americans than compared with white Americans, Gravlee (2009) illustrates in one study (outside the US) that there is an important relationship between social stigma and anxiety that affects hypertension. He makes a useful distinction between cultural and biological dimensions of skin colour in Puerto Rico. He does so in order to explore the relationship between biological and environmental indicators of race by, first, studying local ways of talking about skin colour and how skin colour shapes Puerto Ricans' exposure to racism and other social stresses. To measure this he developed a survey to compare blood pressure to the significance of colour, as local people understood colour. Strikingly, he found that the darker people were associated with higher blood pressure, in a way that supports the thesis that the *social aspects* of race, such as stigma and discrimination, can also have biological consequences – precisely an inversion of what is often presumed to be the case. What Gravlee points to outside the US is relevant for the US too, for recent studies show that perceptions of discrimination can increase levels of individual and social stress and anxiety (Lindhorst et al., 2007; Savoca et al., 2009).

The important observation is that different social and cultural environments between groups mean that different physiological outcomes will emerge, something that takes us to the last example of elevated levels of psychosis and poorer mental health amongst some ethnic and racial minority groups, something reflected in the over-representation of members of these groups in mental health institutions (Keating et al., 2003). What is interesting is that while African Caribbean groups in Britain are three to five times more likely to be diagnosed with severe mental health problems (and much more likely to be admitted for schizophrenia), they are much less likely to be diagnosed with neurosis. As Sharply (2001: 66) explains:

> [M]any of the factors suggested are associated, in the general population, with an increased risk of nonpsychotic disorders such as depression, anxiety and functional somatic symptoms rather than psychotic disorders (Goldberg

& Huxley, 1992). Yet UK-resident African-Caribbean people appear much less likely to receive a diagnosis of anxiety or depression from their general practitioner than non-Black attenders (Gillam *et al*, 1989).

Yet African Caribbeans tend to be over-represented in a number of secure institutions, special hospitals, prisons and medium secure units. So in terms of *incidence* – when these groups come into contact with formal agencies (rather than wider prevalence at large) – they fair significantly less well than other groups (Nazroo, 1998). In this respect and others, argue Karlsen and Nazroo (2006: 26), 'perhaps surprisingly, the effect of racism on social identity, social status and economic position are also often ignored'.

ETHNIC VARIATIONS

Despite all the criticisms, it is widely accepted that the majority of minority ethnic groups experience poorer health outcomes than many of their majority group counterparts (Nazroo, 1998). This should not mean, as Chaturvedi (2001) points out, that research which emphasises high rates of disease in minority ethnic groups implies the ethnic groups in question are a problem. For the moment, the important point is that there are serious concerns about the way in which the concepts of **ethnicity** and **race** are discussed and measured within health research. Some researchers believe the complexity of ethnicity and of its relationship to socio-economic position may, in the end, render it of limited use in studying health inequalities (e.g. Bradby, 2003). As Karlsen and Nazroo (2001: 26) elaborate:

> [A]spects of the relationship between ethnicity, social position and health are generally ignored in empirical health research. In particular, measures of social position often fail to account for the accumulation of disadvantage over the life-course – measuring socio-economic status only at one time point – and they typically ignore the role of ecological effects resulting from the concentration of ethnic minority groups in particular residential areas.

However, others argue, despite the difficulties in defining and measuring a concept as complex as ethnicity, it is no more challenging than measuring socio-economic position or social class and, furthermore, that understanding ethnic variations is crucial to determining the role of different exposures to disease risk, as well as providing important information for the targeting of public health interventions and resources (e.g. Chaturvedi, 2001). These various concerns and debates are only likely to be resolved when greater reflection on measuring and constructing *both* ethnicity and socio-economic positions are developed and utilised in health research (Davey Smith, Chaturvedi et al., 2000).

REFERENCES

Afshari, R. and Bhopal, R. (2002) 'Changing pattern of use of "ethnicity" and "race" in scientific literature', *International Journal of Epidemiology*, 31 (5): 1074.

Bhopal, R. S., Phillimore, P. and Kohli, H.S. (1991) 'Inappropriate use of the term "Asian": an obstacle to ethnicity and health research', *Journal of Public Health*, 13 (4): 244–6.

Bradby, H. (2003) 'Describing ethnicity in health research', *Ethnicity and Health*, 8 (1): 5–13.

Chandola, T. (2001) 'Ethnic and class differences in health in relation to British South Asians: using the new National Statistics Socio-Economic Classification', *Social Science and Medicine*, 52 (8): 1285–96.

Chandola, T., Britton, A., Brunner, E., Hemingway, H., Malik, M., Kumari, M., Badrick, E., Kivimaki, M. and Marmot, M. (2008) 'Work stress and coronary heart disease: what are the mechanisms?', *European Heart Journal*, 29 (5): 640–8.

Chaturvedi, N. (2001) 'Ethnicity as an epidemiological determinant – crudely racist or crucially important?', *International Journal of Epidemiology*, 30 (5): 925–7.

Chaturvedi, N. (2003) 'Ethnic differences in cardiovascular disease', *Heart*, 89 (6): 681–6.

Davey Smith, G., Charsley, K. et al. (2000) 'Ethnicity, health and the meaning of socioeconomic position', in H. Graham (ed.) *Understanding Inequalities in Health*. Buckingham: Open University Press.

Davey Smith, G., Chaturvedi, N., Harding, S., Nazroo, J. and Williams, R. (2000) 'Ethnic inequalities in health: a review of UK epidemiological evidence', *Critical Public Health*, 10 (4): 375–408.

Gravlee, C. R. (2009) 'How race becomes biology: embodiment of social inequality', *American Journal of Physical Anthropology*, 139 (1): 47–57.

Griffith, D. M., Moy, E., Reischl, T.M. and Dayton, E. (2006) 'National data for monitoring and evaluating racial and ethnic health inequities: where do we go from here?, *Health Education & Behavior*, 33 (4): 470–87.

Karlsen, S. and Nazroo, J. (2001) 'Identity and structure: rethinking ethnic inequalities in health', in H. Graham (ed.) *Understanding Inequalities in Health*. Buckingham: Open University Press.

Karlsen, S. and Nazroo, J. (2006) 'Defining and measuring ethnicity and "race": theoretical conceptual issues for health and social care research', in J. Nazroo (ed.) *Health and Social Research in Multiethnic Societies*. London: Routledge.

Keating, M., Stevenson, L., Cairney, P. and Taylor, K. (2003) 'Does devolution make a difference? Legislative output and policy divergence in Scotland', *Journal of Legislative Studies*, 9 (3): 110–39.

Lindhorst, J., Alexander, N., Blignaut, J. and Rayner, B. (2007) 'Differences in hypertension between blacks and whites: an overview', *Cardiovascular Journal of Africa*, 18 (4): 241–7.

Mohammed, A. O., Attalla, B., Bashir, F. M., Ahmed, F. E., El Hassan, A. M., Ibnauf, G., Jiang, W., Cavalli-Sforza, L. L., Karrar, Z. A. and Ibrahim, M. E. (2006) 'Relationship of the sickle cell gene to the ethnic and geographic groups populating the Sudan', *Community Genetics*, 9 (2): 113–20.

Navarro, V. (1990) 'Race or class versus race and class: mortality differentials in the United States', *The Lancet*, 336 (8725): 1238–40.

Nazroo, J. (1998) 'Rethinking the relationship between ethnicity and mental health: the British Fourth National Survey of Ethnic Minorities', *Social Psychiatry and Psychiatric Epidemiology*, 33: 145–8.

Nazroo, J. (ed.) (2006) *Health and Social Research in Multiethnic Societies*. London: Routledge.

Platt, O. S., Brambilla, D. J., Rosse, W. F., Milner, P. E., Castro, O., Steinberg, M.H. and Klug, P. P. (1994) 'Mortality in sickle cell disease: life expectancy and risk factors for early death', *New England Journal of Medicine*, 330 (23): 1639–44.

Raphael, D. (2000) 'Health Inequities in the United States: prospects and solutions', *Journal of Public Health Policy*, 21 (4): 394–427.

Savoca, M. R., Quandt, S. A., Evans, C. D., Flint, L. T., Bradfield, B. D., Morton, T. B., Harshfield, G. A. and Ludwig, D. A. (2009) 'View of hypertension among young African Americans who vary in their risk of developing hypertension', *Ethnicity and Disease*, 19: 29–34.

Senior, P. A. and Bhopal, R. (1994) 'Ethnicity as a variable in epidemiological research', *BMJ*, 309: 327–30.

Sharply, M. S. (2001) 'Understanding the excess of psychosis among the African-Caribbean population in England – review of current hypotheses', *British Journal of Psychiatry*, 178 (40): 60–8.

Williams, D.R. and Jackson, P.B. (2005) 'Social sources of racial disparities in health', *Health Affairs*, 24 (2): 325–34.

Hybridity

Hybridity is a concept that is ultimately concerned with different kinds of syntheses, be it of myriad cultural or sociological forms. Yet it seeks more than a description of empirical mixture; it can also be a normative (and so prescriptive) perspective on social and political relations.

At its simplest, hybridity is a concept that is most easily understood as the 'cultural logic' of globalisation, in so far as it 'entails that traces of other cultures exist in every culture' (Kraidy, 2005: 148). It has sometimes enjoyed a voguish status through the work of pioneering cultural theorists who were educated in the shadow of the 'cultural turn', especially in the humanities and social sciences, and is perhaps most definitively expressed in the writings of the cultural theorist Homi Bhabha (1994).

HYBRIDITY AS TRANSLATION

In his book *The Location of Culture*, Bhabha presents an account that rests in a post-colonial landscape, something that has deep and profound implications for the expression of culture, knowledge and ultimately power. In particular for Bhabha the emergence of hybridity challenges prevailing identity settlements, because it marks a moment of transition 'that nervously accompanies any mode of social transformation without the promise of celebratory closure or transcendence of the complex, even conflictual condition that attend the process' (Bhabha, quoted in Hall, 2000: 226). The task before us is to 'translate' what this heralds. Translation in this regard involves the 'movement of meaning' that alternates across several sites where 'the content or subject matter is made disjunct, overwhelmed and alienated' (Bhabha, 1994: 323). This is important because while the idea of hybridity intersects with the mixedness of populations (and so is sometimes related ideas of 'syncretism', 'creolisation' and 'mélange'), it is bigger than this because it frames what Hall (2000: 225–6) too describes as 'the cultural logic of *translation*', and so 'functions less as doctrine than as *repertoires of meaning*' (ibid.). What both Bhabha and Hall mean by this is that the only certainty about hybridity is the uncertainty that it unleashes. This formulation is to some extent inherited from cultural studies and, as Pieterse (2001: 221) shows in Figure 1, hybridity denotes a smorgasbord of 'cross-over, pick-'n'-mix, boundary-crossing experiences and styles'. Pieterse is especially useful at highlighting how the hybrid and non-hybrid are framed. Within the everyday expression of these, especially in an optimistic mode, hybridity is deemed to 'lubricate' and 'negotiate' a 'future free of xenophobia' (Papastergiadis, 1997: 261). In this sense, hybridity is a powerful counter to accounts of primordial, essential or exclusive identities, whether in ethnic, national, religious or racial settings.

Contra hybridity	Pro hybridity
Hybridity is meaningful only as a critique of essentialism.	There is plenty of essentialism around.
Were colonial times really so essentialist?	Enough for hybrids to be despised.
Hybridity is a dependent notion.	So are boundaries.
Asserting that all cultures and languages are mixed is trivial.	Claims of purity have long been dominant.
Hybridity matters to the extent that it is a self-identification.	Hybrid self-identification is hindered by classification boundaries.
Hybridity talk is a function of the decline of Western hegemony.	It also destabilizes other hegemonies.
Hybridity talk is carried by a new cultural class of cosmopolitans.	Would this qualify an old cultural class of boundary police?
'The lumpenproletariat real border-crossers live in constant fear of the border.'	Crossborder knowledge is survival knowledge.
'Hybridity is not parity.'	Boundaries don't usually help either.

Figure 1   Taken from Pieterse (2001: 225)

HYBRIDITY AS IDENTITY

Hybridity then can be deemed a subversive and dislocating force for entrenched categories (and so shares something with our discussion of **post-colonialism**). Gilroy (1993: 2) describes this as a 'theorisation of creaolisation, metissage, mestizaje, and hybridity ... a litany of pollution and impurity'. The latter observation is key, for Ashcroft et al. (1995: 183) maintain that hybridity 'and the power it releases may well be seen to be the characteristic feature and contribution of the post-colonial, allowing a means of evading the replication of the binary categories of the past and developing new anti-monolithic models of cultural exchange and growth'. In this respect hybridity becomes a resource that equips post-colonial societies with the means of transcending inherited cleavage and fissures. But there is also a methodo-logical critique here; one that slips into another kind of dogmatism which perceives all coherent ideas as a fiction. May (2001: 38–9) summarises this as follows:

> Out with the old singular, in with the new plurality – a plurality of cultures, knowledges, languages, and their continuous interspersion, where 'ethnic absolutism' has no place and 'where "race" will no longer be a meaningful

device for the categorization of human beings' (Gilroy, 1993b: 218). Within the discourses of hybridity and of postmodernism more broadly, the new social agents are plural – multiple agents forged and engaged in a variety of struggles and social movements (Giroux, 1997).

May then places hybridity within the register of postmodernism, where the idea of an essential self is decentred and multiplicity reigns. The ability to unsettle 'essential' identities here is key. Modood (2007: 89) describes a series of assumptions that anti-essentialist critique seeks to tackle, even from those seeking to defend ethnic and racial minorities. He summarises, 'it is said that the positing of minority or immigrant cultures, which need to be respected, defended, publicly supported and so on, appeals to the view that cultures are discrete, frozen in time, impervious to external influences, homogenous and without internal dissent.' Modood addresses this in his defence of using ethnic group categories by appealing to the ways in which all group categories are socially constructed, yet it is clear that people do have a sense of groups (to which they feel they belong or from which they are excluded). One of the reasons the hybridity-informed charge of essentialism needs to be treated with caution is that religious minorities, for example, often see and describe themselves as sharing a 'group' identity through such categories as 'Jewish', 'Muslim' or 'Sikh', amongst others. If we accept that their subjective self-identity cannot be ignored, and that this is no less valid than categories of 'working class', 'woman', 'black' or 'youth', it appears inconsistent to reject some groupist categories simply because they are subject to the same dialectical tension between specificity and generality to which all group categories are subject (ibid.). This is not to 'essentialise' or 'reify', however, since the category of 'Jew', 'Muslim' or 'Sikh' can remain 'as internally diverse as "Christian" or "Belgian" or "middle-class", or any other category helpful in ordering our understanding ... diversity does not lead to the abandonment of social concepts in general' (Modood, 2003: 100). The uses of hybridity therefore, just as it's focus of description, are far from settled in social science and human sciences.

REFERENCES

Ashcroft, B., Griffith, G. and Tiffin, H. (1995) *The Postcolonial Studies Reader*. London: Routledge.

Bhabha, H. (1994) *The Location of Culture*. London: Routledge.

Gilroy, P. (1993) *The Black Atlantic: Modernity and Double Consciousness*. London: Verso.

Hall, S. (2000) 'Conclusion: the multi-cultural question', in B. Hesse (ed.) *Un/Settled Multiculturalisms: Diasporas, Entanglements, Transruptions*. New York: St. Martin's Press/Zed Books.

Kraidy, M. (2005) *Hybridity, Or the Cultural Logic of Globalization*. Philadelphia: Temple.

May, S. (2001) *Language and Minority Rights: Ethnicity, Nationalism and the Politics of Language*. Malaysia: Pearson Publishing.

Modood, T. (2003) 'Muslims and the politics of difference', *Political Quarterly*, 74 (1): 100–15.

Modood, T. (2007) *Multiculturalism, a Civic Idea*. London: Polity Press.

Papastergiadis, N. (1997) 'Tracing hybridity in theory', in P. Werbner and T. Modood (eds) *Debating Cultural Hybridity*. London: Zed.

Pieterse, J. N. (2001) 'Hybridity, so what? The anti-hybridity backlash and the riddles of recognition', *Theory, Culture and Society*, 18 (2–3): 219–45.

Of all the concepts in this book, integration is one of the most salient in both every-day language and public policy agendas. It is frequently used to describe both a process under way as well as a social and political goal, for some integration is an uncritical basic requirement for the cohesion of society. To others it begs a prior question: integration into what? In other words, is the society unchanged by the integration of minorities, or should the burden of integration be shared by majority as well as minority groups? This discussion considers how integration is theoreti-cally conceived and politically used, and the ways in which it is a core concept in the study of race and ethnicity.

Few concepts sit so visibly at the centre of competing scholarly and political debates as integration. What is clear is that different actors and protagonists are convinced that integration serves their often diverging positions. Since all parties cannot be right, this would suggest that integration has more than one meaning in its contemporary usage.

TWO USES

'Integration is a concept both dazzling and treacherous', insist Saggar and Som-merville (2012: 6), such that 'policy makers must use and define it with care'. It is a warning that is rarely heeded, even though it describes a concept with a long history. A theoretical concern with integration is possibly as old as the earliest social scientific accounts of modernity, in so far as it goes to the heart of how social scientists have conceptualised the division of labour and the kinds of social relations that characterise modern societies. Especially relevant here is the migra-tion of people from communities of kin (*Gemeinschaft*) to wider communities of social relations (*Gesellschaft*). These were certainly the kinds of concerns that early social theorists understood the concept to relate to (Durkheim, 1893). Lat-terly, however, and especially as it was translated through the work of the Chicago school (e.g. Park, 1914, 1925, 1950), who utilised integration in their theorisation of **race relations**, the concept has come to describe post-**migration** relations. Despite the US influence, there is a tendency for European and US scholars to speak past each other when using the concept, which reminds us of Castles et al.'s (2002: 12) assessment that 'there is no single, generally acceptable definition, theory or model of immigrant … integration'. Nonetheless, from the perspective of the study of **race** and **ethnicity**, these authors sum up a common delineation that is useful for describing different approaches to theorising what a concept of integration can resemble, especially at it relates to cultural diversity. Here they offer two usages:

integration

55

Usage 1: The process through which immigrants and refugees become part of the receiving society. Integration is often used in a normative way, to imply a one-way process of adaptation by newcomers to fit in with a dominant culture and way of life. This usage does not recognise the diversity of cultural and social patterns in a multicultural society, so that integration seems to be merely a watered down form of assimilation.

Usage 2: A two-way process of adaptation, involving change in values, norms and behaviour for both newcomers and members of the existing society. This includes recognition of the role of the ethnic community and the idea that broader social patterns and cultural values may change in response to immigration. (Ibid.: 17–18)

Both these usages necessarily relate to other concepts in this book and what is especially relevant at this stage of the discussion is the re-emergence of a tension between unity and diversity, and how integration is sometimes understood as a means of overcoming this. This requires some explanation.

DIVERSITY AND INTEGRATION

Ethnic and racial diversity may be considered a form of pluralism, the fact of which – to borrow a phrase from John Rawls – emerges as self-evident in a world comprising at least six hundred languages, five hundred ethno-cultural groups and innumerable religions spread across nearly two hundred recognised sovereign states. By definition therefore 'diversity' is an inescapable feature of human societies, and 'can neither be wished out of existence nor suppressed without an unacceptable degree of coercion, and often not even then' (Parekh, 2000: 196). A large part of human history reflects the implications of coming to terms with this diversity throughout cycles of migration and patterns of settlement, whereupon the intermingling of diverse cultural, religious and ethnic mores renews and/or unsettles established social and political configurations. Here integration starts to become a normative debate that describes not only processes of change that occur amongst groups, but also what a principled position on that change should resemble. The challenge with concepts of integration is the extent to which it is underwritten by 'an assumption of universality' (Bhatia and Ram, 2009: 141).

As the discussion of several concepts has shown, especially **race relations** and **multiculturalism**, a key theoretical and policy challenge has been how to *integrate* diversity into the prevailing mode of membership (e.g. national identity). One view is that integration should proceed on the grounds of established configurations into which diverse cultural, religious and ethnic minorities should *assimilate*. That is to say that where minorities 'insist on retaining their separate cultures, they should not complain if they are viewed as outsiders and subjected to discriminatory treatment' (Parekh, 2000: 197). A more nuanced and elaborate version of this position limits the comprehensiveness of assimilation to the public sphere, into which minorities should assimilate in order to participate in the political cultures of a society, but not be prevented from retaining their diversity at the level of the family and some parts of civil society. The insistence here is upon a prescribed 'political culture, which includes its [society's] public or political values, ideals, practices, institutions, modes of political discourse, and self understanding' (ibid.: 200).

Some perceive this mode of integration – comprising at least partial assimilation – as presently ascendant across different contemporary societies, perhaps buoyed as a short-term panacea (and longer-term prophylactic) to the sorts of societal disunity allegedly associated with ethnic minority separatism in general, and Muslim alienation, estrangement and (ultimately) violent radicalism in particular. For example, according to Kostakopoulou (2010: 830) integration as partial assimilation is observable across Europe in

> policies for 'social cohesion', 'integration' and 'assimilation', including the offi-cial promotion of national identity, official lists of national values, language [and clothing] prohibitions in public transport, schools, universities and hospi-tals, compulsory language courses and tests for migrants, naturalisation cer-emonies and oaths of loyalty.

Such normative prescriptions for integration as comprising full or partial assimilation have not gone unchallenged, however, and indeed until relatively recently were in some instances viewed as less favourable than other modes of integration. This would include approaches deemed as **multicultural** and which recognise that social life consists of individuals and groups. Modood (2013) here has tried to elaborate a mode of multicultural integration where both individual and cultural groups be provided for in the formal and informal distribution of powers. 'This means that while individuals have rights, mediating institutions such as trade unions, churches, neighbourhoods, immigrant associations and so on may also be encouraged to be active public players and fora for political discussion and may even have a formal representative or administrative role to play in the state.' (Modood and Meer, 2012: 44).

INTEGRATION AS A VORTEX ISSUE

If we try to move away from a normative account to more applied analysis, we find that much of the problem with using integration is that it quickly becomes a 'vortex' issue, in so far as it 'may suck in view on a range of other issues such as trust in politicians, ability to influence decisions affecting local communities, provision of public services, and so on' (Saggar and Somerville, 2012: 5). This has profound methodological implications for thinking through what indicators are best suited to measure success and failure. As Castles et al. (2010: 113) elaborate:

> The very broadness of the integration process makes it hard to define in any precise way. Integration of newcomers to a society takes place at every level and in every sector of society. It involves a wide range of social players: public officials, political decision-makers, employers, trade union officials, fellow-workers, service providers, neighbours and so on.

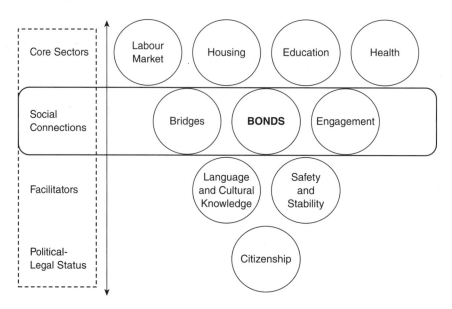

Figure 2   Indicators of integration

One means of illustrating this is in Figure 2, adapted from Ager and Strang (2008: 170), which shows how integration as a policy objective needs to take a number of interdependent spheres into account. To some extent this is reminiscent of a Weberian formulation that relates questions of class to those of status and party. These are conceived in Figure 2 as being those of labour-market participation and access to housing, health care and education.

Where there is much confusion, however, is that policy makers frequently drift from thinking about integration as structure, and thinking about integration as social connections (in terms of bridging, bonding and engagement). The two spheres are of course related – but the domain of social connections is where debates about common membership are more likely to be held, something that is consistent with Castles et al.'s formulation of Usage 2 outlined earlier. Here, the positive argument for thinking about integration as minimally a two-way process is that minorities 'do best, both in terms of psychological well-being and sociocultural outcomes, when they are able to combine their ethnic identity with a new national identity' (Kymlicka, 2012: 14). Indeed, others go beyond a two-way process but nonetheless stress that integration is in many ways a core objective of approaches to multicultural citizenship (Modood and Meer, 2013).

REFERENCES

Ager, A. and Strang, A. (2008) 'Understanding integration: a conceptual framework', *Journal of Refugee Studies*, 21 (2): 161–91.

Bhatia, S. and Ram, A. (2009) 'Theorizing identity in transnational and diaspora cultures: a critical approach to acculturation', *International Journal of Intercultural Relations*, 33: 140–9.

key concepts in race and ethnicity

Castles, S., Korac, M., Vasta, E. and Vertovec, S. (2002) *Integration: Mapping the Field*. London: Home Office.

Durkheim, E. (1893) *The Division of Labour*. New York: Free Press.

Kostakopoulou, D. (2010) 'Matters of control: integration tests, naturalisation reform and probationary citizenship in the United Kingdom', *Journal of Ethnic and Migration Studies*, 36 (5): 829–46.

Kymlicka, W. (2012) *Multiculturalism: Success, Failure and Future*. Washington, DC: Migration Policy Institute.

Modood, T. (2013) *Multiculturalism: A Civic Idea*. Bristol: Polity Press.

Modood, T. and Meer, N. (2012) 'Framing Multicultural Citizenship in Europe', in A. Triandafyllidou, T. Modood and N. Meer (eds), *European Multiculturalism(s): Cultural, Religious and Ethnic Challenges*. Edinburgh: Edinburgh University Press.

Parekh, B. (2000) *Re-thinking Multiculturalism*. Basingstoke: Palgrave.

Park, R. (1914) 'Racial assimilation in secondary groups with particular reference to the negro', *American Journal of Sociology*, 19: 606–23, reproduced in T. F. Pettigrew (ed.) (1980) *The Sociology of Race Relations: Reflections and Reform*. New York: Free Press.

Park, R. (1925) 'The city: suggestions for the investigation of human behaviour in the urban environment' in R. E. Park, E. W. Burgess and R. D. McKenzie (eds) *The City*. Chicago: University of Chicago Press.

Park, R. (1950) *Race and Culture*. Glencoe: Free Press.

Saggar, E. and Somerville, W. (2012) *Building a British Model of Integration in an Era of Immigration: Policy Lessons for Government*. Washington, DC: Migration Policy Institute.

Interculturalism

Interculturalism in the field of race and ethnicity is often understood as a mode of integration, one that stresses the importance of recurring features necessary for successful citizenship. These include communication, individual rights, unity and liberalism. Often these are considered missing in other modes of integration such as multiculturalism.

Interculturalism is a relational term that is often contrasted with (and proposed as a replacement to) **multiculturalism** (Bouchard, 2011; Cantle, 2012), and is now found in places as diverse as German and Greek education programmes; Belgian commissions on cultural diversity (see below); and Russian teaching on world cultures. A prominent symbolic example could be how 2008 was designated as the European Year of Intercultural Dialogue (EYID). It is worth stepping back, however, to consider what distinguishes these efforts from other established approaches concerned with recognising cultural diversity (see Meer and Modood, 2012; Modood and Meer, 2012, from which this discussion is taken). Is it merely the case, as Lentin (2005: 394) has suggested, that interculturalism is an 'updated version' of multiculturalism? If so, what is being 'updated'? If not, in what ways – if at all – is interculturalism different, substantively or otherwise, from multiculturalism? Here are potentially four.

COMMUNICATION BEYOND CO-EXISTENCE?

First, according to Wood et al. (2006: 9), 'communication' is the means through which 'an intercultural approach aims to facilitate dialogue, exchange and reciprocal understanding between people of different backgrounds'. But to what extent can this be claimed as either a unique or distinguishing quality of interculturalism when dialogue and reciprocity are foundational to most, if not all, accounts of multiculturalism?

According to some advocates, a difference is perceptible in the social or convivial 'openness' in which communication is facilitated. As Wood et al. (2006: 7) maintain:

> Multiculturalism has been founded on the belief in tolerance between cultures but it is not always the case that multicultural places are open places. Interculturalism on the other hand requires openness as a prerequisite and, while openness in itself is not the guarantee of interculturalism, it provides the setting for interculturalism to develop.

The 'openness' or 'closedness' that the authors have in mind is not an ethical or moral but a sociological concern related to – if not derived from – a spatial sense of community and settlement as discussed further below. What is striking, however, is the extent to which Wood et al.'s characterisation ignores how central the notions of dialogue and communication are to multiculturalism.

Take Charles Taylor's essay 'The Politics of Recognition' (1992), widely seen as a founding statement of multiculturalism in political theory, in which the Canadian philosopher characterises the emergence of a modern politics of identity based on an idea of 'recognition'. In it he emphasises 'dialogical' relationships and argues that it is a mistake to think people forge their identities 'monologically' (without dependence on others). As such he maintains that we are 'always in dialogue with, sometimes in struggle against, the things our significant others want to see in us'.

Another landmark text is Bhikhu Parekh's *Rethinking Multiculturalism* (2000). His argument is that cultural diversity has an intrinsic value precisely because it challenges people to evaluate the strengths and weaknesses of their own cultures and ways of life. He distinguishes his multiculturalism from various liberal and communitarian positions that may recognise that cultures can play an important role in making choices meaningful for their members, or host the development of the self for the members of that culture. Parekh's argument that cultures other than one's own have something to teach us, and that therefore members of minority cultures should be encouraged to cultivate their moral and aesthetic insights for humanity as a whole, is largely built upon a prescription of intercultural dialogue.

For both Taylor and Parekh, then, communication and dialogue are in different ways integral features to their intellectual and political advocacy of multiculturalism. The point is that to consider multiculturalists who draw upon these and similar formulations as being unconcerned with matters of dialogue and communication is to profoundly misread and mischaracterise their positions.

Whether it is at a philosophical or a political level, the leading theorists of multiculturalism give dialogue a centrality missing in liberal nationalist, human-rights or class-based approaches – and missed by interculturalist critics of multi-culturalism. The multiculturalists assume, however, that there is a sense in which the participants to a dialogue are 'groups' or 'cultures', and this leads us to a second point of alleged contrast with interculturalists.

FREE FROM CULTURAL GROUPS

It is said that the diversity of the locations that migrants and ethnic minorities herald from gives rise not to the creation of communities or groups but to a churn-ing mass of languages, ethnicities and religions all cutting across each other and creating a **super-diversity**. An intercultural perspective is better served to these sociological realities, it is argued, in a way that can be contrasted against a multi-culturalism that emphasises strong ethnic or cultural identities at the expense of wider cultural exchanges.

Is this description inconsistent with how groups actually feature in ideas of interculturalism and multiculturalism? We need to distinguish here between two different politics of interculturalism. Discourses of interculturalism in Europe tend to be relatively apolitical, offering civil-society-based local encounters and conviviality in everyday life to critique multiculturalism without explicitly offer-ing an alternative politics to it.

To find an explicit political interculturalism we need to turn to Quebec – and authors such as Alain-G. Gagnon and Gerard Bouchard, amongst others. Gagnon and Iacovino, for example, contrast interculturalism positively with multiculturalism: The interesting aspect for our discussion here is that they do so in a way that relies upon a formulation of groups, and by arguing that Quebec has developed a distinctive intercultural political approach to diversity that is explicitly in opposition to federal Canadian multiculturalism. Their positive argument for interculturalism can be expressed in the following five stages:

1. There should be a public space and identity that is not merely about individual constitutional or legal rights.
2. This public space is an important identity for those who share it and so quali-fies and counter-balances other identities valued by citizens.
3. This public space is created and shared through participation, interaction, debate and common endeavour.
4. This public space is not culture-less but nor is it merely the 'majority culture'. Everyone can participate in its synthesis and evolution, and – while it has an inescapable historical character – it is always being remade and ought to be remade to include new groups.
5. Quebec, and not merely federal Canada, is such a public space and so an object to which immigrants need to have identification with and integrate into, and should seek to maintain Quebec as a nation and not just a federal

province. (The same point may apply in other multi-national states, but there are different degrees and variations of 'multi-nationalism'.)

These interculturalists make a moral and policy case for the recognition of relatively distinct sub-state nationalisms. As such, they are less concerned with the diversity of the location that migrants and ethnic minorities are from, or the **super-diversity** that this is alleged to cultivate therein. Its emphasis on **multi-nationalism** does distinguish it from post-immigration multiculturalism (and post-immigration interculturalism), but not multiculturalism per se.

On the other hand, the less macro-level European interculturalism that focuses on neighbourhoods, classroom pedagogy, the funding of the arts and so on is not a critique of multiculturalism but a different exercise. Unfortunately, it is sometimes offered as, or used to play, an anti-multiculturalist role. It is politically deconstructive of the alleged essentialism of multiculturalism, but lacks a constructive politics of its own except for a celebration of cultural mixing and the local. It leaves an empty space where there should be national discourses, policies and belonging.

A STRONGER SENSE OF THE WHOLE

A third related way of framing interculturalism is that it speaks to the whole of society, while multiculturalism speaks only to and for the minorities within it. Thus it encourages resentment, fragmentation and disunity. This can be prevented or overcome through an interculturalism that promotes community cohesion on a local level and the subscription to national citizenship identities. As Alev (2007) and other commentators put it, through invocations of interculturalism that promote community cohesion on a local level, and more broadly through an interculturalism that encourages the subscription to national citizenship identities as forms of meta-membership:

> Interculturalism is a better term than multiculturalism. It emphasises interaction and participation of citizens in a common society, rather than cultural differences and different cultures existing next to each other without necessarily much contact or participative interaction. Interculturalism is therefore equivalent to mutual integration.

What such sentiment ignores is how all forms of prescribed unity retain a majoritarian bias that places the burden of adaptation upon the minority, and so is inconsistent with interculturalism's alleged commitment to 'mutual integration'. Much of the literature on national identity in particular has tended to be retrospective, to the extent that such contemporary concerns do not enjoy a widespread appeal (while the opposite could be said to be true of the literature on citizenship). It was this very assessment which, at the turn of the millennium, informed the Commission on Multi-Ethnic Britain's (CMEB) (2000) characterisation of British national identity as potentially 'based on generalisations [that] involve a selective and simplified account of a complex history'. Chaired by Bhikhu Parekh, it feared such an account would be one in which '[m]any complicated strands are reduced to a simple tale of essential and enduring national unity'.

The CMEB was alarmed at how invocations of national identity potentially force ethnic minorities into a predicament not of their making: one in which majorities are conflated with the nation and where national identity is promoted as a reflection of this state of affairs (because national identities are assumed to be cognates of monistic nations). By not easily fitting into a majoritarian account of national identity, or either being unable or unwilling to be reduced to or assimilated into a prescribed public culture, minority 'differences' may therefore become negatively conceived. The multicultural objective here was to place a greater emphasis upon the unifying potential of a renegotiated and inclusive national identity. In contrast to localist interculturalism, this is a genuine concern for a national citizenship, albeit perhaps a more pluralist one than Quebec-style interculturalism. While the latter point is welcomed by some commentators who had previously formed part of the pluralistic Left, bringing previously marginalised groups into the societal mainstream is, at best, greeted more ambivalently.

ILLIBERALISM AND CULTURE

The fourth contrast is that multiculturalism, unlike interculturalism, lends itself to illiberality and relativism, whereas interculturalism has the capacity to criticise and censure culture (as part of a process of intercultural dialogue), and so is more likely to emphasise the protection of individual rights. In Europe this charge assumes a role in the backlash against multiculturalism and is particularly evident in debates concerning the accommodation of religious minorities, especially when religion is perceived to take a conservative line on issues of gender equality, sexual orientation and progressive politics generally. (This is something that has arguably led some commentators who may otherwise sympathise with religious minorities to argue that it is difficult to view them as victims when they may themselves be potential oppressors.)

For these reasons, Muslim claims have been particularly characterised as ambitious and difficult to accommodate. This is the case when Muslims are perceived to be in contravention of discourses of individual rights and secularism, and is exemplified by the way in which visible Muslim practices such as veiling have in public discourses been reduced to and conflated with alleged Muslim practices such as forced marriages, female genital mutilation, a rejection of positive law in favour of criminal sharia law and so on. This suggests a radical 'otherness' about Muslims and an illiberality about multiculturalism, since the latter are alleged to license these practices.

This is problematic given that some of these practices are not religious but cultural. Clitoridectomy, for example, is often cited as an illiberal practice in the discussions we are referring to. It is, however, a cultural practice amongst various ethnic groups, and has little support from any religion; indeed, religious condemnation may be the most effective way of eliminating it. So to favour ethnicity and problematise religion is a reflection of a secularist bias that has alienated many religionists, especially Muslims.

Taken as a whole, the interculturalism versus multiculturalism debate is one strand of wider discussion on the proper ways of reconciling cultural diversity with enduring forms of social unity. Interculturalism, and other concepts such as cohesion and indeed integration, need to be allied to multiculturalism rather than presented as an alternative.

REFERENCES

Alev, F. (2007) 'Europe's future: make yourselves at home', The *Guardian*, 5 June. Available from: http://commentisfree.guardian.co.uk/fatih_alev/2007/06/europes_future_make_yourselves_at_home.html

Bouchard, G. (2011) 'What is interculturalism?', *McGill Law Journal*, 56 (2): 435–68.

Cantle, T. (2012) *Interculturalism*. Basingstoke: Palgrave.

Commission on the Future of Multi-Ethnic Britain (CMEB) (2000) *The Future of Multi-ethnic Britain*. London: Profile Books.

Gagnon, A. G. and Iacovino, R. (2007) *Federalism, Citizenship and Quebec: Debating Multinationalism*. Toronto: University of Toronto Press.

Lentin, A. (2005) 'Replacing "race": historizing the "culture" in the multiculturalism', *Patterns of Prejudice*, 39 (4): 379–96.

Meer, N. and Modood, T. (2012) 'How does interculturalism contrast with multiculturalism?', *Journal of Intercultural Studies*, 33 (2): 175–97.

Modood, T. and Meer, N. (2012) 'Assessing the divergences on our reading of interculturalism and multiculturalism', *Journal of Intercultural Studies*, 33 (2): 233–44.

Parekh, B. (2000) *Rethinking Multiculturalism: Cultural Diversity and Political Theory*. London: Palgrave.

Taylor, C. (1992) 'The politics of recognition', in A. Gutmann (ed.) *Multiculturalism and the Politics of Recognition*. Princeton: Princeton University Press.

Wood, P., Landry, C. and Bloomfield, J. (2006) *Cultural Diversity in Britain: A Toolkit for Cross-cultural Co-operation*. York: Joseph Rowntree Foundation.

Intersectionality

The concept of intersectionality has emerged from a tradition of black feminist critique. In important respects it has been taken up across the social sciences to help theorise an understanding of simultaneously held subject positions, and how these relate to social cleavages and identity categories.

The *term* intersectional refers to something which cuts into something else. The *concept* of intersectionality describes a cluster of theoretical positions which seek to revise the view that identity categories, and the web of social relations in which they are located, are experienced as 'separate roads' (Roth, 2004). While this necessarily takes in more than ethnicity or gender therefore, the provenance of the concept may be traced to a particular black feminist critique of the ways in which mainstream (white) feminism had historically ignored the intersections of race and patriarchy (hooks, 1984; Crenshaw, 1988, 1991). In one reading, intersectionality has compelled feminist researchers to explore how their 'moral positions as survivors of one expression of systemic violence become eroded in the absence of accepting responsibility of other expressions of systemic violence' (Collins, 2000: 247). Such critique has made conventional the view that women experience discrimination 'in varying configurations and in varying degrees of intensity' (Ritzer, 2007: 204).

From its origins in this critical mode, and despite the suggestion that 'it has not become a key concern for the many sociologists not directly working on gender issues' (Choo and Ferree, 2010: 129), important features of intersectionalist thought have been 'mainstreamed', such as being incorporated into equality agendas and research questionnaires. This is especially the case in the design of anti-discrimination policies that can simultaneously tackle more than gender and race intersections on their own, but include categories of age, disability, sexuality and religion as well (Meer, 2010). Resting at the centre of contemporary debates about intersectionality, however, as Yuval-Davis (2006: 195) reminds us, 'is conflation or separation of the different analytic levels in which intersectionality is located, rather than just a debate on the relationship of the divisions themselves'. It is to these delineations that we now turn.

STRUCTURAL OR POLITICAL INTERSECTIONALITY?

Some of the broad theoretical contours of intersectionality have been shaped by a relatively small number of authors who seek to bring different dynamics into focus (cf. Anthias and Yuval-Davis, 1983). From a perspective of Critical Race Theory in particular, Crenshaw (1988, 1991) initially proposed the concept of intersectionality 'to grasp the ways in which the interactions of gender and race limit black women's access to the US labour market, and how a lack of understanding of this intersection marginalizes black women and black women's experiences' (Walby et al., 2012: 227). In her own words, Crenshaw describes how intersectionality

> grew out of trying to conceptualize the way the law responded to issues where both race and gender discrimination were involved. What happened was like an accident, a collision. Intersectionality simply came from the idea that if you're standing in the path of multiple forms of exclusion, you are likely to get hit by both. (Crenshaw, 2004: 2)

Such discrimination, she maintained, could not be explained in terms of 'the traditional boundaries of race or gender discrimination as these boundaries are currently understood', because 'women of color can be erased by the strategic silences of anti-racism and feminism' (Crenshaw, 1991: 1244, 1253). So neither the category of 'black' nor the category of 'woman' is sufficiently capable of speaking to and redressing the discriminatory experiences of *black women*. To Crenshaw (1991: 1252), 'The failure of feminism to interrogate race means that resistance strategies of feminism will replicate and reinforce the subordination of people of color, and the failure of antiracism to interrogate patriarchy means that antiracism will frequently reproduce the subordination of women.' Of course Crenshaw was writing from the North American perspective which, as illustrated with the case of **whiteness**, has its own historical dynamics. The following passage is worth quoting at length for it captures a parallel set of complicated dynamics from a British perspective:

> In arguing that most contemporary feminist theory does not begin to adequately account for the experience of black women we also have to acknowledge that it is not a simple question of their absence, consequently the task is not one of rendering their visibility. On the contrary, we will have to argue that the process of accounting for their historical and contemporary position does, in itself, challenge the use of some of the central categories and assumptions of recent mainstream feminist thought. We can point to no single source for our oppression. When white feminists emphasize patriarchy alone, we want to redefine the term and make it more complex. (Carby, 1982: 213)

The first half of this passage advances a debate about **recognition**: as something distinct that can play a central role in a conception of equality. What is pioneering in Carby is that while this includes the issue of subjectivities, it also focuses attention on articulations of political relationships and not just matters of individual esteem or psychology, but in ways that link up with Crenshaw's argument. The latter therefore sought to eschew the conflation of *structural* intersectionality (which in her view focuses on inequality of social groups) and *political* intersectionality (which focuses on political agendas and projects). As an illustration of this, Walby et al. (2012: 227) describe how Crenshaw critiqued 'the invisibility of domestic violence against black women [which] focuses on two main actors – white women and black men'.

INTRA-CATEGORICAL, *ANTI*-CATEGORICAL AND *INTER*-CATEGORICAL

In some respects the approach of Crenshaw retains something of what Harding has termed the *additive approach* which promotes '"add women and stir" approaches to gender issues' (Harding, 1991: 212). In contrast, Yuval-Davis (2006: 200) encourages us to pursue what she terms a 'transversal politics'.

She elaborates: 'One cannot assume the same effect or constellation each time and, hence, the investigation of the specific social, political and economic processes involved in each historical instance is important' (2006: 200). What then are the analytical paths through which we can pursue this transversal?

With one innovation in conceptualising the category of intersectionality, McCall (2005: 1773–4) seeks to distinguish between three related strands. The first she describes as 'intra-categorical' which centres on 'particular social groups at neglected points of intersection ... in order to reveal the complexity of lived experience within such groups'. The objective here is to make group dynamics *visible* that were previously invisible. The second strand, 'anti-categorical', is 'based on a methodology that deconstructs analytical categories' (ibid.). This critiques the idea of internal coherence in a manner that seeks to challenge and guard against notions of identity as unchanging. Her final, 'inter-categorical' reading of intersectionality 'provisionally adopt[s] existing analytical categories to document relationships of inequality among social groups and changing configurations of inequality among multiple and conflicting dimensions' (ibid.). This latter formulation is her preferred means of reconciling identity and social structures. This, according to Choo and Ferree (2010: 134), allows McCall to stress the

> dynamic forces more than categories – racialisation rather than races, economic exploitation rather than classes, gendering and gender performance rather than genders – and recognize the distinctiveness of how power operates across particular institutional fields. Because of its interest in mutually transformative processes, this approach emphasizes change over time as well as between sites and institutions.

The *inter*-categorical approach thus is a means of accepting categories almost 'under erasure', in a manner that can harness their utility in knowledge of their limitations. This is not radically different to Iris Marion Young's (2000: 89) aspiration to 'retain a description of social group differentiation, but without fixing or reifying groups'.

UNITARY, MULTIPLE AND INTERSECTIONAL

The third cluster of theoretical readings of intersectionality find expression in Hancock (2007: 64, 67) who distinguishes intersectionality from 'unitary' and 'multiple' forms of social categories. In the first approach, 'only one category is examined, and it is presumed to be primary and stable'. In contrast, in the 'multiple' approach 'the categories are presumed to be stable and to have stable relationships with each other' (Walby et al., 2012: 228). In the 'intersectional' approach, meanwhile, 'more than one category is addressed; the categories matter equally; the relationship between the categories is open; the categories are fluid not stable; and mutually constitute each other' (ibid.). To some extent then, in this last usage, intersectionality is returned to its origins in so far as it corresponds to the argument that 'systems of race, social class, gender, sexuality, ethnicity, nation, and age form mutually constructing features of social organization' (Collins, 2000: 299). To avoid the additive tendency, however, we need to remind ourselves that different identity categories have a different ontological basis (Yuval-Davis, 2006). For example, in Werbner's (2013: 410) reading, 'identities of gender and **race** imply an essentialising definitional move on the part of wider, dominant society that subordinates and excludes'. In contrast, **ethnicity** is deemed to be 'an expression of multiple identities' which are 'positive, creative and dialogical'.

This reminds us of why the question of methodology cuts across empirical work on intersectionality. As Chang and Culp (2002: 485) ask, empirically 'how does one pay attention to the points of intersection?' Hitherto these questions have almost exclusively been pursued through qualitative and interpretive approaches, which identify future directions in lending the concept to comparative analyses yet to be undertaken (Nash, 2008). Equally interesting is the answer to Yuval-Davis's (2006: 202) question 'Do we have to be concerned that the list is limitless?' must surely be 'no'. This is because intersectionality has become 'both a normative theoretical argument and an approach to conducting empirical research that emphasises the interaction of categories of difference' (Hancock, 2007: 63–4).

REFERENCES

Anthias, F. and Yuval-Davis, N. (1983) 'Contextualising feminism: gender, ethnic and class divisions', *Feminist Review*, 15: 62–75.

Carby, H. (1982) '"White women listen!"' Black feminism and the boundaries of sisterhood, in Centre for Contemporary Cultural Studies (CCCS) *The Empire Strikes Back*. Birmingham: Hutchinson.

Chang, R. S. and Culp, J. M. (2002) 'After intersectionality', *University of Missouri–Kansas City Law Review*, 71: 485–91.

Choo, H. Y and Ferree, M. M. (2010) 'Practicing intersectionality in sociological research: a critical analysis of inclusions, interactions, and institutions in the study of inequalities', *Sociological Theory*, 28 (2): 129–49.

Collins, P. H. (2000) *Black Feminist Thought: Knowledge, Consciousness, and the Politics of Empowerment*. New York: Routledge.

Crenshaw, K. (1988) 'Race, reform, and retrenchment: transformation and legitimation in anti-discrimination law', *Harvard Law Review*, 101: 1331–87. Reprinted in (1989) *Critical Legal Thought: An American–German Debate*, edited by Christian Joerges and David M. Trubek. Baden-Baden: Nomos.

Crenshaw, K. (1991) 'Mapping the margins: intersectionality, identity politics, and violence against women of color', *Stanford Law Review*, 43 (6): 1241–99.

Crenshaw, K. (2004) 'Intersectionality: the double bind of race and gender', interview with Kimberlé Crenshaw, *American Bar Association*, Spring.

Hancock, A. M. (2007) 'When multiplication doesn't equal quick addition: examining intersectionality as a research paradigm', *Perspectives on Politics*, 5 (1): 63–79.

Harding, S. (1991) 'Comment on Hekman's "Truth and method: feminist standpoint theory revisited": whose standpoint needs the regimes of truth and reality?', *Signs*, 22 (2): 382–91.

hooks, b. (1984) *Feminist Theory: From Margin to Center*. Boston: South End Press.

McCall, L. (2005) 'The complexity of intersectionality', *Journal of Women in Culture and Society*, 30 (3): 1771–800.

Meer, N. (2010) 'The impact of European Equality Directives upon British anti-discrimination legislation', *Policy & Politics*, 38 (2): 197–215.

Nash, J. C. (2008) 'Re-thinking intersectionality', *Feminist Review*, 89: 1–15.

Phillips, M. (2005) *Londonistan*. London: Encounter Books.

Ritzer, G. (2007) *Contemporary Sociological Theory and Its Classical Roots: The Basics*. Boston: McGraw-Hill.

Roth, B. (2004) *Separate Roads to Feminism: Black, Chicana, and White Feminist Movements in America's Second Wave*. New York: Cambridge University Press.

Walby, S., Armstrong, J. and Strid, S. (2012) 'Intersectionality: multiple inequalities in social theory', *Sociology*, 46 (2): 224–40.

Werbner, P. (2013) 'Everyday multiculturalism: Theorising the difference between "intersectionality" and "multiple identities", *Ethnicities*, 13 (4): 404–19.

Young, I. M. (2000) *Inclusion and Democracy*. New York: Oxford University Press.

Yuval-Davis, N. (2006) 'Intersectionality and feminist politics', *European Journal of Women's Studies*, 13 (3): 193–204.

Islamophobia

> *Islamophobia is the suspicion, dislike or hatred of Muslim individuals or groups, viewing their real or assumed 'Islamicness' as a negative trait. It therefore reflects a racial and not just a theological logic, and can take a number of forms including attitudes, behaviours, discourse and imagery.*

The origins of the term Islamophobia have been variously traced to an essay by two French Orientalists (Dinet and Baamer, 1918), 'a neologism of the 1970s' (Rana, 2007: 148), an early 1990s American periodical (Sherridan, 2006), and, indeed, to a British political-sociologist (see Modood, 1991, quoted in Birt, 2006). What is less disputed is that the term received its public policy prominence with the Runnymede Trust's Commission on British Muslims and Islamophobia (CBMI) (1997) *Islamophobia: A Challenge for Us All*. Defined as 'an unfounded hostility towards Islam, and therefore fear or dislike of all or most Muslims' (ibid.: 4), the report conceived of eight argumentative positions to encapsulate its meaning, and through which the members of the commission sought to draw attention to their assessment that 'anti-Muslim prejudice has grown so considerably and so rapidly in recent years that a new item in the vocabulary is needed' (CBMI, 1997: 4).

These comprise: (1) Islam is seen as a monolithic bloc, static and unresponsive to change; (2) Islam is seen as separate and 'other' – it does not have values in common with other cultures, is not affected by them, and does not influence them; (3) Islam is seen as inferior to the West – it is seen as barbaric, irrational, primitive and sexist; (4) Islam is seen as violent, aggressive, threatening, support-ive of terrorism and engaged in a 'clash of civilisations'; (5) Islam is seen as a political ideology and is used for political or military advantage; (6) criticisms made of the West by Islam are rejected out of hand; (7) hostility towards Islam is used to justify discriminatory practices towards Muslims and exclusion of Muslims from mainstream society; and (8) anti-Muslim hostility is seen as natu-ral or normal.

This, of course, was before global events had elevated the issue to a promi-nence previously only hinted at, and which resulted in a second sitting of the commission which heard testimonies from leading Muslim spokespeople of how 'there is not a day that we do not have to face comments so ignorant that even Enoch Powell would not have made them' (Baroness Uddin, quoted in CBMI, 2004: 3).

CHALLENGES AND RESPONSES

What the commission perhaps did not fully anticipate was how the term would be criticised from several quarters for, amongst other things, allegedly reinforcing 'a monolithic concept of Islam, Islamic cultures, Muslims and Islamism, involving ethnic, cultural, linguistic, historical and doctrinal differ-ences while affording vocal Muslims a ready concept of victimology' (Ozanne, 2006: 28). For some, that the term does not adequately account for the nature of the prejudice directed at Muslims. Erdenir (2010: 29), for example, cham-pions the idea of 'Muslimophobia' over 'Islamophobia', because 'the former targets Muslims as citizens or residents of European countries rather than Islam as a religion'. To others, meanwhile, both terms would neglect 'the active and aggressive part of discrimination' (Reisigl and Wodak, 2001: 6) by conceiving discrimination as a collection of pathological beliefs, inferred through the language of '-phobias'. This more general complaint need not be specific to Islamophobia for, as Bleich (2011: 1586) observes, 'with parallel concepts such as homophobia or xenophobia, Islamophobia connotes a broader set of negative attitudes and emotions directed at individuals or groups because of their perceived membership in a defined category'. A more specific complaint is advanced in the late Fred Halliday's (1999) thesis and is worth examining because Halliday accepts that Muslims experience direct discrimination *as Muslims*. He nevertheless considers Islamophobia mislead-ing because:

> It misses the point about what it is that is being attacked: 'Islam' as a religion *was* the enemy in the past: in the crusades or the *reconquista*. It is not the enemy now ... The attack now is not against *Islam* as a faith but against

Muslims as a people, the latter grouping together all, especially immigrants, who might be covered by the term. (Halliday, 1999: 898, original emphasis)

So in contrast to the thrust of the Islamophobia concept, as he understands it, the stereotypical enemy 'is not a faith or a culture, but a people' who form the 'real' targets of prejudice. Halliday's critique is scholarly, empathetic and richer than many others, particularly more journalistic accounts. What it appears to ignore, however, is how the majority of Muslims who report experiencing street-level discrimination recount – as testimonies to the 2004 Runnymede follow-up commission (CBMI, 2004) bear witness – that they do so more when they appear 'conspicuously Muslim' than when they do not. Since this can result from wearing Islamic attire it becomes irrelevant – if it is even possible – to separate the impact of *appearing Muslim* from the impact of *appearing to follow Islam*. For example, the increase in everyday personal abuse since 9/11 and 7/7 in which the perceived 'Islamicness' of the victims is the central reason for abuse (see IRR, 2005), regardless of the validity of this presumption (resulting in Sikhs and others with an 'Arab' appearance being attacked), suggests that discrimination and/or hostility to Islam and Muslims is much more interlinked than Halliday's thesis allows (and, in all fairness to Halliday, may not easily have been anticipated at his time of writing).

Interestingly this relates to the characterisation of **antisemitism**. For example, a not dissimilar description of the logic may be found in Levey and Modood's (2009: 239) observation of 'shifts from inductive to deductive negative generalisations'. In the case of Muslims they maintain that where 'inductive negative stereotyping can be seen clearly in the security policies of "racial profiling", [in which] security services concentrate their attention on people who look or behave a certain way', this crystallises into negative deductions about Muslims that are then applied to Muslims in general. These delineations suggest that anti-Muslim sentiment – like antisemitism – is rarely a purely religious discrimination. The mixed compositions implied here are compelling and summarised by Amin (2010: 8):

> [A]s the scrutiny of Muslim bodies intensified after 9/11 and 7/7 in the so-called 'War on Terror', the 'phonotypical' evaluations – new upon old – returned to typecast the Asians ... along with Muslims elsewhere in Britain, as cultural aliens and national threats. Pinning new aversions such as anxiety, suspicion, fear and hate to local Muslims has relied ... on linking vicariously constructed phenotypes (including prayer caps, beards, baggy trousers, rucksacks, Yorkshire accents, loud music, shiny cars and shabby dwellings) to terrorism, radical Islam, sexual slavery, drug trafficking and cultural backwardness.

Instead of trying to neatly delineate social tendencies that are inextricably linked, therefore, we can understand Islamophobia as a composite of cultural racism that facilitates the racialisation of Muslim minorities (cf. Meer and Noorani, 2008).

INTERSECTIONAL ISLAMOPHOBIA: GENDER AND CIVILISATION

The visibility of Muslims, especially in terms of the display of what are sometimes termed 'contested signifiers' in terms of dress and appearance, is frequently the means through which this anti-Muslim feeling is turned into anti-Muslim behaviour (Meer et al., 2010). A good European-wide illustration may be found in the summary report on Islamophobia published by the European Monitoring Centre on Racism and Xenophobia shortly after 9/11. This identified a rise in the number of 'physical and verbal threats being made, particularly to those visually identifiable as Muslims, in particular women wearing the hijab' (Allen and Nielsen, 2002: 16). What is of particular note is that despite variations in the number and correlation of physical and verbal threats directed at Muslim populations amongst the individual nation-states, one overarching feature that emerged among the fifteen European Union countries was the tendency for *Muslim women* to be attacked because of how the *hijab* signifies an Islamic identity (ibid.: 35). This is precisely how in the concept of **racialisation** we can observe Miles (1989: 87) elaborate that the social dynamics of racism can in practice become mixed up with a host of different kinds of '-isms'. These frequently overlap in 'sharing a common content or generalised object which allows them to be joined together or interrelated, to be expressed in ways in which elements of one are incorporated in the other' (ibid.).

These assemblages are recognisable in the saliency and political force of the Eurabia panic, the widely received conspiracy theory, initially proposed by the polemicist Bat Ye'or (2001, 2005). This foretells the planned numerical and cultural domination of Europe by Muslims and Islam, where the latter comprise 'a negation of Christianity' (Miles, 1989: 19), and which has achieved significant traction and features prominently in the accounts of various best-selling authors. These include the late Italian intellectual Orianna Fallaci (2001, 2003), the German economist Thilo Sarrazin (2010), and the British polemicists Niall Ferguson (2004) and Melanie Phillips (2005), amongst many others. It also includes Mark Steyn (2006a), who has made the confident prediction that 'much of what we loosely call the Western world will not survive this century, and much of it will effectively disappear in our lifetimes, including many if not most Western European countries'.

Of course the predicted (inflated) levels of population growth have not gone undisputed, and indeed have been refuted by Carr (2006), Hawkins (2009), Jones (2005), Kuper (2007), and Laurence and Vaïsse (2006), amongst others, principally on the grounds that they both radically overestimate base figures and then extrapolate implausible levels of population growth. The demography panic has nonetheless achieved a degree of traction, and the same demographic fatalism is shared by Christopher Caldwell (2010) in his *Reflections on the Revolution in Europe* (subtitled *Can Europe Be the Same with Different People in It?*). These assessments have led Matt Carr (2011: 14) to note the ways in which 'Eurabia bears many of the essential features of the invented anti-Semitic tract, the *Protocols of the Elders of Zion*, in its presentation of European Muslims as agents in a conspiratorial world of domination'.

It is worth noting here how the visceral cultural response to the prospect of Turkish accession to the European Union, and the very notion of an 'Islamised Europe' ushered in through such a prospect, bears a remarkable similarity to Matar's (2009: 215) description of how the relationship between Ottoman and Habsburg empires was transformed into 'a cosmic conflict of Christianity against Islam, of the Christian cross versus the Muslim crescent'. Thus from the first decades of the sixteenth century onwards it became difficult to dislocate Islam and Muslims from an Ottoman 'threat' to Europe. In the present climate, this translates into roughly two-thirds of respondents in Western Europe (ranging from 59 per cent in Belgium to 70 per cent in Denmark) perceiving greater co-operation with the Muslim world as a threat (World Economic Forum, 2008: 139). It is in this context that the charter of *Cities Against Islamisation* has emerged to warn that the 'fast demographic increase of the Islamic population in the West threatens to result in an Islamic majority in Western European cities in a few decades'. In addition to the Eurabia literatures outlined earlier, we could include here Emmanuel Brenner's incendiary thesis on France's 'lost territories' – lost to its antisemitic Muslim inhabitants – that was warmly received in French intelligentsia (see Peace, 2009). This, therefore, feeds into the discussion of a 'new antisemitism' as discussed earlier.

REFERENCES

Allen, C. and Nielsen, J. S. (2002) *Summary Report on Islamophobia in the EU15 after 11 September 2001*. Vienna: European Monitoring Centre for Racism and Xenophobia.

Amin, A. (2010) 'Remainders of race', *Theory, Culture and Society*, 27 (1): 1–23

Birt, Y. (2006) 'Notes on Islamophobia', http://www.yahyabirt.co.uk/?p=48 (viewed 13 October 2013).

Bleich, E. (2011) 'What is Islamophobia and how much is there? Theorizing and measuring an emerging comparative concept', *American Behavioral Scientist*, 55 (12): 1581–600.

Caldwell, C. (2010) *Reflections of a Revolution in Europe: Can Europe Be the Same with Different People in It?* St Ives: Penguin.

Carr, M. (2006) 'You are now entering Eurabia', *Race & Class*, 48: 1–22.

Carr, M. (2011) 'The Moriscos: a lesson from history', *Arches Quarterly*, 4 (8): 10–17.

Commission on British Muslims and Islamophobia (CBMI) (1997) *Islamophobia: A Challenge for Us All*. London: Trentham Books.

Commission on British Muslims and Islamophobia (CBMI) (2004) *Islamophobia: Issues, Challenges and Action*. London: Trentham Books.

Dinet, E. and Silman Ben Inrahim, E. H. (1918) *The Life Mohammed: The Prophet of Allah*. Paris: Paris Books Club.

Erdenir, B. (2010) 'Islamophobia qua racial discrimination', in A. Triandyfillydou (ed.) *Muslims in 21st Century Europe Structural and Cultural Perspectives*. London: Routledge.

Fallaci, O. (2001) *The Force of Reason*. New York: Rizzoli International.

Fallaci, O. (2003) *The Rage and the Pride*. New York: Rizzoli International Publications.

Ferguson, N. (2004) 'The end of Europe?' American Enterprise Institute Bradley Lecture, 1 March, Washington, DC.

Halliday, F. (1999) 'Islamophobia reconsidered', *Ethnic and Racial Studies*, 22: 892–902.

Hawkins, O. (2009) 'Disproving the Muslim Demographics Sums'. Available at: www.bbc.co.uk/programmes/b00xw21x (accessed 25 January 2011).

Institute of Race Relations (IRR) (2005) *Islamophobia, Xenophobia and the Climate of Hate*. European Race Bulletin. London: IRR.

Jones, T. (2005) 'Short cuts: how to concoct a conspiracy theory', *London Review of Books*, July, 27 (20): 18.

Kuper, S. (2007) 'The crescent and the cross', *Financial Times*, 11 October, 7.

Laurence, J. and Vaïsse, J. (2006) *Integrating Islam Political and Religious Challenges in Contemporary France*. Washington, DC: Brookings Institution Press.

Levey, G. B. and Modood, T. (2009) 'Liberal democracy, multicultural citizenship and the Danish cartoon affair', in G. B. Levey and T. Modood (eds) *Secularism, Religion and Multicultural Citizenship*. Cambridge: Cambridge University Press.

Matar, N. (2009) 'Britons and Muslims in the early modern period: from prejudice to (a theory of) toleration', *Patterns of Prejudice*, 43 (3–4): 212–31.

Meer, N. (2012) 'Misrecognising Muslim consciousness in Europe', *Ethnicities*, 12 (2): 178–96.

Meer, N. and Modood, T. (2009) 'Refutations of racism in the "Muslim Question"', *Patterns of Prejudice*, 43 (3/4): 332–51.

Meer, N. and Noorani, T. (2008) 'A sociological comparison of anti-Semitism and anti-Muslim sentiment', *The Sociological Review*, 56 (2): 195–219.

Meer, N., Dwyer, C. and Modood, T. (2010) 'Embodying nationhood? Conceptions of British national identity, citizenship and gender in the "veil affair"', *The Sociological Review*, 58 (1): 84–111.

Miles, B. (1989) *Racism*. London: Routledge.

Ozannae, W. I. (2006) 'Review of confronting Islamophobia on educational practice', *Comparative Education*, 42 (2): 283–97.

Peace, T. (2009) 'Un antisemitisme nouveau? The debate about a "new anti-Semitism" in France', *Patterns of Prejudice*, 43 (2): 103–21.

Pew Global Attitudes Project (2008), 'Unfavorable views of Jews and Muslims on the increase in Europe', (Washington, DC: Pew Research Center), summary available online at http://pewglobal.org/reports/display.php?ReportID_262 (accessed 16 April 2009).

Phillips, M. (2005) *Londonistan*. London: Encounter Books.

Rana, J. (2007) 'The Story of Islamophobia', *Souls: A Critical Journal of Black Politics, Culture, and Society*, 9 (2): 148–62.

Reisigl, M. and Wodak, R. (2001) *Discourse and Discrimination: Rhetorics of Racism and Anti-Semitism*. London: Routledge.

Sarrazin, T. (2010) *Deutschland schafft sich ab*. Berlin: Anstalt.

Sheridan, L. (2006) 'Islamophobia pre and post September 11th 2001', *Journal of Interpersonal Violence*, 21 (3): 317–36.

Steyn, M. (2006a) 'European population will be "40 percent Muslim" by 2025', *Wall Street Journal*, 4 January, 17.

Steyn, M. (2006b) *America Alone: The End of the World as We Know It*. New York: Regnery Publishing

Werbner, P. (2005) 'Islamophobia: incitement to religious hatred – legislating for a new fear?', *Anthropology Today*, 21 (1): 5–9.

World Economic Forum (2008) *Islam and the West: Annual Report on the State of Dialogue*. Geneva: World Economic Forum.

Ye'or, B. (2001) *Islam and Dhimmitude: Where Civilizations Collide*. Madison: Dickinson University Press.

Ye'or, B. (2005) *Eurabia: The Euro Arab Axis*. Madison: Dickinson University Press.

Migration as a process has always been a feature of human societies, in all their variety, but it acquires a qualitatively novel status in modernity following the configuration of populations according to nation-states. Even though common motivations behind migration may be identified, alongside recurring social outcomes, a number of different 'ages' of migration shape the present landscape, and a series of contrasting theoretical tools are used in their analysis.

'Give me your tired, your poor, Your huddled masses yearning to breathe free, The wretched refuse of your teeming shore. Send these, the homeless, tempest-tost to me, I lift my lamp beside the golden door!' So begins the inscription at the foot of the Statue of Liberty. Taken from a poem entitled *The New Colossus* (Lazarus, 1883), it speaks of the millions of migrants who flocked to the United States through Ellis Island, and then the Lower East Side of New York, between the mid-eighteenth and early twentieth century. While migration has become a more complicated phenomenon than the sentiments betrayed in this poem, the core impulses (e.g. to seek out and create a better life for oneself and family), and the questions that these aspirations may raise (e.g. how to reconcile unity with perhaps novel diversity), remain in many respects the same.

The important point for scholars is that the phenomenon of migration cannot be explained as isolated to the choices of people. Instead, migration occurs in tandem with wider economic and social forces that can draw or push movement (e.g. labour recruitment or social conflict), or group networks that facilitate the process (e.g. established communities which support migrants), as well as political climates that may be hostile to some kinds of migration (e.g. unskilled) but favourable to others (e.g. skilled) – despite 'the line between preferences and discrimination' being 'a morally thin one that is easily crossed' (Weiner, 1996: 178).

The prevailing context for contemporary migration is that the majority of the world's population resides in 175 poorer countries relative to the wealth that is disproportionately concentrated in around twenty. In this context, and with levels of migration increasingly fluctuating and anxieties widespread, it is common to hear governments and other agencies favour 'managed migration' which, though meaning different things in different places, registers migration as an intractable feature of contemporary societies the world over. As Pécoud and de Guchteneire argue (2007: 5), 'migration is now structurally embedded in the economies and societies of most countries: once both sending and receiving countries become dependent upon migration, migration is almost impossible to stop.'

RECENT TRENDS IN MIGRATION

According to the International Labour Office (ILO) (2010), there are around 214 million international migrants (deemed as people living outside their country of origin or birth for twelve months). This makes up about 3 per cent of the global population but has implications that are far greater than the lives of these migrants. An important outcome, as Martin et al. (2006: 3) observe, is that 'the financial contributions of migrants to developing countries far exceeds official development assistance'. This is to the extent that 'many governments of emigration countries have recognized the development potential of their diasporas abroad and have taken steps to facilitate remittances' (ibid.), something that can include dual citizenship, absentee electoral voting and other 'special' non-resident status (e.g. the category of 'Non-Resident Indian' or 'NRI'). Migration therefore sits at the intersection of a series of questions concerning the relationship between societies and their citizenry.

In their widely cited discussion, Castles and Miller (1998: 8–9) identify five 'general tendencies' shaping current experiences. First, they point to the ways in which the *globalisation* of the scale and complexity of migration has increased (with respect to place of origin, destination, and indeed frequency of migration). Second, there has been an acceleration in terms of quantitative 'volume in all major regions at the present time' (ibid.: 8). Third, societies are witnessing increasing *differentiation*, with respect to the 'type' of migration, spanning labour seeking, refugee and settlement. Moreover, 'migratory chains which start with one type of movement often continue with others forms, despite (or often just because of) governments' efforts to stop or control the movement' (ibid.: 9). Fourth, there is a *feminisation* of migration that marks a contrast with previously male-led patterns of labour migration and subsequent family reunification, such that 'today women workers form the majority of movements' (ibid.: 9). Finally, there has been a *politicisation* of migration, not simply in a discursive sense with respect to popular opposition, but in terms of how 'domestic politics, bilateral and regional relationships and national security policies of states around the world are increasingly affected' (ibid.). What, however, are the sources of these tendencies and how do they contrast with what has preceded them?

THREE AGES OF *MASS* MIGRATION

As the discussion of **nationalism** outlines, the pattern of nation-states across the world is a relatively recent feature of a human history that is otherwise characterised by frequent movement and relocation of human populations. Indeed, a large part of human history reflects the implications of coming to terms with this diversity throughout cycles of migration and patterns of settlement, whereupon the intermingling of diverse cultural, religious and ethnic mores renews and/or unsettles established social and political configurations. However, Martin et al. (2006: 9–11) point to three 'ages' of *mass* migration that they understand as qualitatively different from previously smaller-scale patterns in human history. Their first age of

key concepts in
race and ethnicity

mass migration was touched upon at the outset, and saw roughly sixty million people travel from Europe to the Americas between the middle of the nineteenth and early twentieth centuries. As they summarise:

> Even though many of the migrants were birds of passage seeking higher wages to finance upward mobility at home, most settled in the New World, and a combination of rapid population growth and displacement from agriculture in Europe as well as a need for labour in the New World and the evolution of networks linking settled immigrants abroad to their communities of origin facilitated transatlantic migration. (Ibid.)

During this period the sources of migration fluctuated in moving between, initially, northern and Western Europe, before the large-scale movement of migrants from the Mediterranean (an internal shift that was deemed as regressive in the then-portrayal of southern Europeans as less civilised). Tightening of migration legislation, and then the Second World War, interrupted these flows before a second age of migration commenced in the post-war period. Instead of Europeans being catalogued at Ellis Island, however, this age is characterised, first, by guest workers in Europe (expected to return with their families to their countries of origin on completion of the employment), and whose recruitment reflected the ways in which in post-war Europe 'the Iron Curtain limited migration from the east' (ibid.). Much of the contemporary discussion around post-migrant integration and **citizenship** in Germany, Belgium and to a lesser extent France is informed by the legacy of this approach (Triandafyllidou, et al., 2012).

Outside of what became the European Union in the post-war period, large population movements and forced migrations, often associated with the end of European empires, were evident too (e.g. in Palestine, North Africa, Sub-Saharan Africa and Southern Asia). Perhaps the largest example came with the partition of India in 1947 and the creation of West and East Pakistan (the latter becoming Bangladesh in 1971 after a period of genocidal violence). The third age is more recent and global with many more countries becoming sites of origin, transit or destination, such that 'between 1975 and 2000, the number of international migrants doubled with the fastest growth between 1985 and 1995 when the stock of migrants rose by about six million a year in response to, among other things, the fall of Communism, wars and persecution in the ex-Yugoslavia' (Martin et al., 2006: 11).

The important point to remember is that 'pull' (as well as 'push') migratory trajectories are not reflections of choice and/or culture alone, but are instead profoundly shaped by institutional dynamics too. For example, the North American Free Trade Agreement (NAFTA) (linking some Latin and North American economies), Asia-Pacific Economic Cooperation (APEC), and the European Union (especially the Schengen Agreement) all contain procedures and mechanisms to facilitate migration. Yet it still remains the case, as Castles and Miller (1998: xi) observe, that 'the UN's main initiative on migration – the 1990 Convention on the Rights of All Migrant Workers and their families – has been ratified by only a handful of countries'. Hence the US and Mexico, while members of a common free trade agreement, are subject to a highly policed border to prevent people flows.

THEORISING MIGRATION

There are a number of theoretical schools that help us to conceptualise the study of migration, but following Castles and Miller (1998: 20–4) we might distinguish between three tendencies that find recurring expression in different strands.

First, there are general theories of *economic equilibrium* which predict that human movement can be studied according to either 'push' factors (e.g. lack of economic opportunities and low living standards) or 'pull' factors (e.g. demand for labour and the promise of work). What this maintains is that, conditions being suitable, the most economically impoverished will migrate in search of a better life. 'In the immigration market', maintains Borjas (1989, 461, quoted in Castles and Miller, 1998: 21), 'the various pieces of information are exchanged and the options are compared.' The methodological individualism inherent in this view assumes that people have mastery over their choices, in a manner that can overlook the ways in which the poorest are not able to migrate, because either they lack the means to do so, or they may be disadvantaged by prevailing admission criteria (e.g. language competencies, professional skill-sets and other training uncommon amongst the poorest). Equally, and as has already been touched upon, this view can encourage the false assumption that migration is an individual activity, and so ignore how it often relies upon established social networks and group forces, in ways that further down the line may function as social capital (Zhou, 1997; Modood, 2004).

Second, a more critical strand emerges in readings informed by *world systems* approaches (Wallerstein, 2004), which view migration as a means of 'mobilising cheap labour for capital' in a manner that 'perpetuates uneven development, exploiting the resources of poor countries to make rich countries even richer' (Castles and Miller, 1998: 23). This taps into the **racialisation** thesis, and especially Miles's (1989) work on migrant labour, but it also elevates the explanatory role of global capital and introduces international relations into the picture (e.g. the implications for German–Turkish relations as near-border sender and recipient countries). In this view, then, migration is a device of political economy, and migrants are objects of forces beyond their mastery. As such it serves as a useful corrective to individualistic and functionalist accounts. What it risks overlooking, however, is the *agency* of even low-status migrants, not as masters of their environment, but as subjects who make meaningful choices to settle, have families, form communities and renegotiate (through conflict and consensus) the terms of their migrant status. Here informal migrant networks too can serve as a powerful means of addressing risk. These outcomes often occur in hostile economic climates when market logics are inhospitable (e.g. recessions and outsourcing). It is also a view that does not satisfactorily account for non-labour-seeking migration, and so is insufficiently attuned to trends in the *differentiation* of migration.

A third, *migrations systems* approach seeks to plot a way through these positions by focusing on 'both ends of the flow and studying the linkages between the places concerned' (Castles and Miller, 1998: 24). In addition to both sending and receiving contexts, however, this approach also encourages us to consider and delineate both macro and micro features of migration, and how these interact together, in the following ways:

> Macro-structures refer to large-scale institutional factors, while micro-structures embrace the networks, practices and beliefs of the migrants themselves. The macro-structures include the political economy of the world market, interstate relationships, and the laws, structures and practices established by the states of sending and receiving countries to control migration settlement. (Ibid.)

Through a *migration systems* approach we are better able to explore a variety of non-orthodox or novel migration phenomena ranging from **transnationalism** to lifestyle migration. With the former, for example, the movement of people with a point of departure and arrival is complicated as an ongoing movement between multiple sites (Vertovec, 1999). This again returns us to the *globalised* nature of transportation in a way that also reflects advances in accessible communication technologies that are able to sustain these relationships. The latter meanwhile is different still, and reflects both the globalised and differentiated patterns of migration in so far as the impulse for movement remains a different way of living but is pursued by relatively affluent and empowered actors (O'Reilly and Benson, 2009). The latter highlights a persistent tendency that is yet to be satisfactorily addressed. This is 'a fundamental contradiction between the notion that emigration is widely regarded as a matter of human rights while immigration is regarded as a matter of national sovereignty' (Weiner, 1996: 171). For these reasons then the study of migration has to be alive to a series of social phenomena that are not easily explained by a singular theory or approach. Moreover, as the discussion of **racialisation** shows, there is a very real danger that the attempts by political actors to sound tough on migrants and migration feeds off and into a wider negative climate for visible minorities.

migration

REFERENCES

Borjas, G. J. (1989) 'Economic theory and international migration', *International Migration Review*, 23 (3): 457–85.

Castles, S. and Miller, M. J. (1998) *The Age of Migration: International Population Movements in a Modern World*. Basingstoke: Palgrave.

International Labour Office (2010) International labour migration – A rights-based approach. ILO: Geneva. Available here: http://www.ilo.org/public/libdoc/ilo/2010/110B09_59_engl.pdf. Accessed 10 November 2013.

Lazarus, E. (1883) *The New Colossus*. Washington, DC: Library of Congress.

Martin, P., Martin, S. and Weil, P. (2006) *Managing Migration: The Promise of Cooperation*. Oxford: Lexington Books.

Miles, R. (1989) *Racism*. London: Routledge.

Modood, T. (2004) 'Capitals, ethnic identity and educational qualifications', *Cultural Trends*, 13 (2): 50.

O'Reilly, K. and Benson, M. (2009) *Lifestyle Migration: Expectations, Aspirations and Experiences*. Farnham: Ashgate.

Pécoud, A. and de Guchteneire, P. (2007) 'Introduction: the migration without border scenario', in A. Pecou and P. de Guchteneire (eds) *Migration Without Borders: Essays on the Free Movement of People*. Paris: UNESCO Publishing.

Triandafyllidou, A., Modood, T. and Meer, N. (eds) (2012) *European Multiculturalism(s): Cultural, Religious and Ethnic Challenges*. Edinburgh: Edinburgh University Press.

Vertovec, S. (1999) 'Conceiving and researching transnationalism', *Ethnic and Racial Studies*, 22 (2): 447–62.

Wallerstein, I. (2004) *World-Systems Analysis: An Introduction*. Durham: Duke University Press.

Weiner, M. (1996) 'Ethics, national sovereignty and the control of immigration', *International Migration Review*, 30 (1): 171–97.

Zhou, M. (1997) 'Segmented assimilation: issues, controversies, and recent research on the new second generation', *International Migration Review*, 31 (4): 825–58.

Mixedness

> *Mixedness invariably describes something about our prevailing categories as much as new social processes. Often it is taken to mean a way of referring to inter-ethnic and inter-racial group mixing, but both of these phenomena are as ancient as human records; this is why it also describes a shift in our way of conceptualising variety in ethnic and racial identities.*

The concept of mixedness is a recent addition to the study of race and ethnicity. As the introduction registers, however, this does not mean that mixedness describes a new phenomenon. What the concept reiterates is that some ways of conceptualising ethnic and racial categories have a political significance that is not self-evident. Take the term 'mullato', for example, which 'refers to person of mixed white/European and mixed/African is commonly used (in Brazil "pardo" is used as a synonym for mulatto)'; or indeed the term 'mestizo' which 'describes an individual who is the product of white/European and indigenous/Indian ancestry' (Kivisto and Croll, 2012: 16). How valid are these categories and are they more or less constructed than others discussed elsewhere in this book? These questions are useful in helping us to explore how the status of mixedness is under constant construction as it relates to a variety of phenomena touched by ethnic and racial dynamics.

MIXEDNESS AS POPULATION CHANGE

Our first meaning of mixedness challenges singular ethnic and racial categories to better describe how we can conceptualise the mingling of human populations. For while the scale and frequency of human interaction has perhaps increased quantitatively with contemporary flows of mass **migration**, population mingling can be traced to the earliest human encounters. As Cornell and Hartman (1998: 238) argue: '[m]ultiethnicity – mixed ancestry – is an ancient phenomenon. Its history surely is as old as the history of interaction amongst distinct human peoples'. Pieterse (2001: 231), for example, points to the Babylonians, and how Alexander the Great 'compelled 7,000 of his soldiers to marry 7,000 Persian women'. This is important because it begins to mark out mixedness from **hybridity**, in so far as the former is 'layered in history, including pre-colonial, colonial and postcolonial layers' (ibid.). So it is not the fact of mixing (the social processes) that is novel, but our modern conceptions of ethnic and racial identity (the analytical description) that are unsettled by what mixedness heralds. Indeed, as Kivisto and Croll (2012: 16) describe, 'some nations, such as Brazil and a number of Caribbean countries, do not operate with a view of race that is constructed in binary terms, such that a person is either black or white. Instead, these nations recognize the reality of racial mixing and thus have constructed categories to account for this.'

An important illustration of the spatially contingent experience of mixedness, we might observe how the contemporary celebration of mixedness as the basis of Latin American nationalism can be traced to intellectuals such as Eugenio Maria de Hostos who emphasised the dynamic quality of *meztizo* identity (Ramos, 2001). For a long time, however, the contravening of supposed 'natural' racial categories – for example 'black' and 'white', or 'red' and 'yellow' – was not only treated as socially taboo, but was frequently legally prohibited in societies marked by varying processes of **racialisation**. 'Miscegenation', as it was described in many Western societies, was seen to go against the natural order of things. Thus, 'in Europe and the United States, mixed parentage was long viewed as a handicap. Social science in the early 20th century viewed persons of mixed parentage as psychologically disturbed and socially disruptive, and popular films and literature often portrayed interracial offspring as tortured souls' (Cornell and Hartman, 1998: 239). This was a stigma that drew justification from purportedly scientific rationalities, namely a 'belief in the degenerative consequences of racial mixing' (De Castro, 2011: 169).

MIXEDNESS AS RACIAL FORMATION

Another way of putting this is to say that prevailing modes of racial formation, in the manner described by Omi and Winant (1995), were often unable to deal with racial ambiguity in any other manner than to treat it as deviant. This is not to say there was not recognition of racial variance. There was. But this was treated as one or other derivative of 'pure stock' categorised as such by prevailing types of racial science. An illustration of this can be observed in Aspinall's (2009: 60) discussion of instructions provided to officials undertaking the 1890 US census. These researchers were told:

Be particularly careful to distinguish between blacks, mulattoes, quadroons and octoroons. The word 'black' should be used to describe those persons who have three-quarters or more black blood; 'mulatto', those persons who have from three eighths to five-eighths black blood; 'quadroon', those persons who have one quarter black blood; and 'octoroon', those persons who have one-eighth or any trace of black blood.

With the broader challenge to the coherence of fixed racial identities, however, race and ethnicity studies have been required to rethink the ways in which the **racialisation** of mixed categories has developed, in order to properly study 'mixed race' and 'multiracial' populations (Parker and Song, 2001; Rockquemore and Brunsma, 2002; Edwards et al., 2012). This once more takes in the socially constructed and politically contested nature of racial categories, in the manner that has seen both **race** and **ethnicity** debunked as natural or immutable categories. The elevation, then, of the subjective parameters in the construction of mixedness has been key. As Aspinall (2009: 56) describes, 'this important trend has led to an increased interest in the racial identifications of "mixed race" people, as well as the factors which shape and constrain the choices that "mixed race" people make' (see also **whiteness**).

One of the implications here has been the tendency for people with more than one ethnic or racial background to refuse 'to choose among them', seeking recognition instead that 'the mixing constitutes their perceived heritage' (Cornell and Hartman, 1998: 239). As such there are now mixed-race categories on social surveys and censuses that have previously recorded single racial and ethnic categories. This is at least one of the ways in which our understanding of mixedness relates to a further meaning, in so far as contestations over racial categories 'disturb those ideological maneuvers through which "imagined communities" are given essentialist identities' (Bhabha, 1990: 300).

REFERENCES

Aspinall, P. (2009) 'Does the British state's categorisation of "mixed race" meet public policy needs?', *Social Policy and Society*, 9 (1): 55–69.

Bhabha, H. (1990) *Nation and Narration*. London: Routledge.

Cornell, S. and Hartmann, D. (1998) *Ethnicity and Race: Making Identities in a Changing World*. Thousand Oaks, CA: Pine Forge Press (a Sage Publications company).

De Castro, J. E. (2011) 'Mestizos/Mestizas', in S. M. Caliendo and C. D. McIlwain (eds) *The Routledge Companion to Race and Ethnicity*. New York: Routledge.

Edwards, R., Ali, A., Caballero, C. and Song, M. (2012) *International Perspectives on Racial and Ethnic Mixedness and Mixing*. London: Routledge.

Kivisto, P. and Croll, P. R. (2012) *Race and Ethnicity*. New York: Routledge.

Omi, M. and Winant, H. (1995) *Racial Formation in the United States*. New York: Routledge.

Parker, D. and Song, M. (eds) (2001) *Rethinking 'Mixed Race'*. London: Pluto Press.

Pieterse, J. N. (2001) 'Hybridity, so what? The anti-hybridity backlash and the riddles of recognition', *Theory, Culture and Society*, 18 (2–3): 219–45.

Ramos, J. (2001) *Divergent Modernities: Culture and Politics in Nineteenth-Century Latin America*, trans. John D. Blanco. Durham: Duke University Press.

Rockquemore, K. A. and Brunsma, D. (2002) *Beyond Black: Biracial Identity in America*. Thousand Oaks, CA: Sage Publications.

> *Multiculturalism is an outgrowth of cultural diversity in any given society. The very fact of this diversity is much less controversial in most societies than the public policies the state may develop to support and recognise it. The latter represents a set of normative though dynamic responses. This can and has taken a number of forms across different societies responding to different kinds of diversity.*

The term multiculturalism can simultaneously describe a number of things. As a concept in the fields of **race** and **ethnicity** it is most widely understood to refer, first, to the fact of pluralism (Rawls, 1993) or cultural diversity in any given society (Parekh, 2000), and, second, to the reasonable accommodation of what that cultural diversity entails (Modood, 2007). While the fact of difference continues to raise much hostility and opposition (see **whiteness** and **racialisation**), in recent years it is the latter that has been the focus of political controversy, not only in itself, but in relation to what it more broadly deemed to represent. As Benhabib (2002: vii) has argued:

> Our contemporary condition is marked by the emergence of new forms of identity politics around the globe. The new forms complicate and increase centuries-old tensions between the universalistic principles ushered in by the American and French Revolutions and the particularities of nationality, ethnicity, gender, 'race', and language.

How can we think about multiculturalism as more than the fact of difference and, perhaps more importantly, why should we think of it in these terms?

A PHILOSOPHICAL RATIONALE

One way of answering this is to say that there is a profound underlying philosophical rationale against which we should measure our capacity for justice (see also the discussion in Modood and Meer (2014) on which this discussion draws). This begins by saying that in addition to appeals to freedom and equality, both of which informed the accommodation of class-based movements throughout most of the twentieth century, a further major idea established itself in the last quarter of that century (see **citizenship** and **equalities**). This idea contained the view that in order to satisfy the requirements of equal treatment and appeals to justice under conditions of cultural diversity, public policies and discourses should show sensitivity to the uniqueness of context, history, and identity of cultural minorities (Taylor, 1992). Such **recognition** tries to appeal to more than individuality as the terrain on which rights are afforded. As we will see there are ethical reasons for this shift (e.g. the ways

multiculturalism

83

in which autonomy can become more meaningful when groups are taken into consideration), as well as critical challenges to an implicit bias in the ways in which prevailing ideas of individuality may be conceived. As Scott (1999: 8) argues:

> The problem has been that *the individual*, for all its inclusionary possibilities, has been conceived in singular terms and typically figured as a white man. In order to qualify as an individual, a person has had to demonstrate some sameness to that singular figure. (The history of civil rights and women's rights has involved arguing about what this sameness might mean.) The difficulty here has been that the abstraction of the concept of the individual has masked the particularity of its figuration.

The broad implications of this idea are wide-ranging and multi-dimensional in posing questions for the cultural composition of national identities (Modood, 1992), the role and status of cultural groupings (Young, 1990), assumptions of public virtue (Parekh, 1994) and conceptions of membership or citizenship (Kymlicka, 1995). These issues are joined by a reinvigoration of debates surrounding the actual and ideal formulation of church–state relations and religion in the public sphere more broadly, especially with regard to Muslims and Islam in the West (Levey and Modood, 2009). Multiculturalism thus constitutes a powerful, if diverse, set of intellectual challenges with profound political ramifications.

POLITICAL PROVENANCE(S)

Over a number of publications, the political sociologist Tariq Modood (2007) has argued that the precise provenance of the label multiculturalism may be traced to the 1960s and 1970s in countries like Canada and Australia, and to a lesser extent in Britain and the United States. 'The policy focus was often initially on schooling and the children of Asian/black/Hispanic post-/neo-colonial immigrants, both in terms of curriculum and as an institution, to include features such as 'mother-tongue' teaching, non-Christian religions and holidays, halal food, Asian dress, and so on' (Modood and Meer, 2013: 113). From such a starting point, the perspective can develop to meeting such cultural requirements in other or even all social spheres and the empowering of marginalised groups.

Hence, the term 'multiculturalism' came to mean, and now means throughout the English-speaking world and beyond, the political accommodation by the state and/or a dominant group of all minority cultures defined first and foremost by reference to race or ethnicity, and, additionally but more controversially, by reference to other group-defining characteristics such as nationality, aboriginality, or religion. The latter is more controversial not only because it extends the range of the groups that have to be accommodated, but also because it tends to make larger political claims and so tends to resist having these claims reduced to those of immigrants (see Meer and Modood, 2012, and then Wievorka's 2012, response).

INTELLECTUAL CALIBRATIONS

To some commentators the staple issues that multiculturalism seeks to address, such as the rights of ethnic and national minorities, group representation and perhaps even the political claims-making of 'new' social movements, are in fact 'familiar long-standing problems of political theory and practice' (Kelly, 2002: 1). Indeed, some hold this view to the point of frustration:

> Liberals have had to recognise that they need to create a better account of what equal treatment entails under conditions of diversity. ... If we take a very broad definition of multiculturalism so that it simply corresponds to the demand that cultural diversity be accommodated, there is no necessary conflict between it and liberalism. . . . But most multiculturalists boast that they are innovators in political philosophy by virtue of having shown that liberalism cannot adequately satisfy the requirements of equal treatment and justice under conditions of cultural diversity. (Barry, 2002: 205)

The first part of Barry's statement is perhaps more conciliatory than might be anticipated from an author admired for his argumentative robustness and theoretical hostility toward multiculturalism, while the second part poses more of an empirical question. Beginning with the first part, Barry's view is by no means rejected by those engaged in the 'multicultural turn'. Modood (2007: 8), for instance, locates the genesis of multiculturalism within a 'matrix of principles that are central to contemporary liberal democracies', in a manner that establishes multiculturalism as 'the child of liberal egalitarianism, but like any child, it is not simply a faithful reproduction of its parents'. A more Hegelian way of putting this is to state that as a concept, multiculturalism is a partial outgrowth of liberalism in that it establishes

> a third generation norm of legitimacy, namely respect for reasonable cultural diversity, which needs to be considered on a par with the [first and second generation] norms of freedom and equality, and so to modify policies of 'free and equal treatment' accordingly. (Tully, 2002: 102)

Our interest is with the political implication of this 'third-generation norm of legitimacy' for a concept of citizenship, which includes the recognition that social life consists of individuals and groups, and that both need to be provided for in the formal and informal distribution of powers (Modood, 2013). What is being described is not a deontological activity. Third-generation norms of legitimacy are also born out of earlier political struggles for equality

(Young, 1990: 157). For example, radical feminists, starting with the motto 'The personal is political', began to challenge the distinction between the private and the public sphere, rejecting the idea that politics were confined to public institutions. In contrast to the liberal feminism of the nineteenth-century women's suffrage movement, who sought to open up the public sphere to women, this group of feminists sought to challenge the private/public distinction altogether, by seeking to gain respect for women's differences as women. They claimed that women's individual experience in personal relationships, school or work were all subject to male domination, which therefore rendered these spaces as important sites of political struggle. Kate Millett's *Sexual Politics* (1969) was a landmark in this view, and outlined how the domain of politics was no longer restricted to institutions in the public sphere but pervaded every aspect of individual and social life. A new political strategy emerged for feminists of consciousness-raising, where women would, through discussion with other women, analyse the seemingly personal problems of their everyday life as actual political problems (see Kauffman, 2001: 28). Similarly, the struggle for ethnic and racial equality began with the colour-blind humanism of Martin Luther King, but later shifted towards black pride and black nationalism (Modood, 2009: 485). As the discussion of **blackness** elaborates, the Black Panther Party had a ten-point programme (1966) that sought self-determination for the black community in America. Political claims were made on the basis of difference, such as seeking the right for blacks to be tried by a black jury (Austin, 2006).

Picking up the second part of Barry's earlier statement, to what extent then do we have an established 'canon' of multiculturalism as an intellectual tradition – one that persuasively distinguishes it from varieties of liberalism? It seems only wise at this stage to offer the intellectual health warning that multiculturalism as a concept is – like very many others – 'polysemic', such that multiculturalist authors cannot be held entirely responsible for the variety of ways in which the term is interpreted. This is something noted by Bhabha (1998: 31) who points to the tendency for multiculturalism to be appropriated as a 'portmanteau term', one that encapsulates a variety of sometimes contested meanings (see, for example, Meer and Modood, 2009). In this respect, the idea of multiculturalism might be said to have a 'chameleonic' quality that facilitates its simultaneous adoption and rejection in the critique or defence of a position (Smith, 2010). One illustration of this is the manner in which multiculturalism is simultaneously used as a label to describe the fact of pluralism or diversity in any given society, and a moral stance that cultural diversity is a desirable feature of a given society (as well as the different types of ways in which the state could recognise and support it). Some have turned to this variety in meaning and usage of the term as an explanation of the allegedly 'widely divergent assessments of the short history and potential future of multiculturalism' (Kivisto and Faist, 2007: 35). Either way, it is certainly the case that the political struggle for group-differentiated citizenship which became prominent in the 1960s and 1970s, in the form of feminist, anti-racist and gay liberation movements, brought group-based mobilisations, and what would become known as '*new social movements*' (NSMs), into normative conceptions of citizenship (Touraine, 1981; Melucci, 1989, 1996).

Nonetheless, the relationship to liberalism of this third strand of multiculturalism is a pertinent issue because it helps us to explore the ways in which public identity of multiculturalism is deemed unsatisfactory when compared with other responses to diversity, especially those perceived to be more conducive to models of social and political integration. For example, one view is that integration should proceed on the grounds of established configurations into which diverse cultural, religious and ethnic minorities should *assimilate*. That is to say that where minorities insist on retaining their separate cultures, according to this view they should not complain if they are marginalised or encounter discriminatory treatment. A more nuanced and elaborate version of this position limits the comprehensiveness of assimilation to the public sphere, into which minorities should assimilate in order to participate in the political cultures of a society, but not be prevented from retaining their diversity at the level of the family, and some parts of civil society. The insistence here is upon a prescribed political culture, which includes a society's public or political values, ideals, practices, institutions, modes of political discourse and self-understanding (cf. Parekh, 2000). Some perceive this mode of integration – comprising at least partial assimilation – presently ascendent, perhaps buoyed as a short-term panacea (and longer-term prophylactic) to the sorts of societal disunity allegedly associated with ethnic minority separatism in general, and Muslim alienation, estrangement and (ultimately) violent extremism in particular.

In contrast, multicultural integration is different from assimilation because it recognises the social reality of groups (not just of individuals and organisations). This reality can be of different kinds, for example a sense of solidarity with people of similar origins or faith or mother tongue, including those in a country of origin or a diaspora. 'Such feelings might be an act of imagination but may also be rooted in lived experience and embodied in formal organisations dedicated to fostering group identity and keeping it alive. This form of accommodation would also allow group-based cultural and religious practices to be fitted into existing, majoritarian ways of doing things. These identities and practices would not be regarded as immutable, but neither would there be pressure either to change them (unless a major issue of principle, legality or security was at stake) or to confine them to a limited community or private space' (Modood and Meer, 2013: 114). As Modood (2007) describes, multicultural integration therefore works simultaneously on two levels: creating new forms of belonging to citizenship and country, and helping sustain origins and diaspora. The result – without which multiculturalism would not be a form of integration – is the formation of 'hyphenated' identities such as Jewish-American or British Muslim (even if the hyphenated nature of the latter is still evolving and contested) (Modood and Meer, 2013).

These hyphenated identities are in this understanding a legitimate basis for political mobilisation and lobbying, not attacked as divisive or disloyal. The latter meaning derives from the fact that the ethnic assertiveness associated with multiculturalism has been part of a wider political current of 'identity politics' which first germinated in the 1960s and which transformed the idea of equality as sameness to equality as difference (Young, 1990); or, in a related conceptualisation, adding the concept of respect or 'recognition' to the older concept of equality as the equal dignity of individuals (Taylor, 1992). Black power and feminist and gay pride movements challenged the ideal of equality as assimilation and contended that a liberatory politics required allowing groups to assert their difference and to not have to conform to dominant cultural norms. Indeed, the attack on colour-blind, culture-neutral political concepts such as equality and citizenship, with the critique that ethnicity and culture cannot be confined to a private sphere but shape political and opportunity structures in all societies, is one of the most fundamental claims made by multiculturalism and the politics of difference. It is the theoretical basis for the conclusion that allegedly neutral liberal democracies are part of a hegemonic culture that marginalises minorities – hence the claim that minority cultures, norms and symbols have as much right as their hegemonic counterparts to state provision and to be in the public space, to be recognised as groups and not only as individuals.

KNOWN KNOWNS, KNOWN UNKNOWNS

The public policies that have resulted from political struggles for multicultural citizenship, and the relationship these bear to the social, economic and political advancement of minorities, is not an easy thing to measure. Some countries do not collect the appropriate kinds of data (e.g. ethnicity-specific statistics and monitoring) to be able to carry out this kind of research. Inevitably therefore we need to concentrate on what is available and where, and in a cross-national setting this is sometimes easier to assess through attitude surveys. Beginning with a more identity-centred approach, Berry et al. (2006) use the International Comparative Study of Ethnocultural Youth (which focuses on thirteen countries and takes in 5000 young people) to argue that polices and discourses of multiculturalism (e.g. plural national identities, equal-opportunity monitoring, effective anti-discrimination legislation and enforcement) encourage a more successful and deeply established integration in those settings. This is consistent with the wider summary by Kymlicka (2012: 48) who states that 'many studies have shown that immigrants do best, both in terms of psychological well-being and socio-cultural outcomes, when they combine their ethnic identity with a new national identity'. In the British case, this is supported by Heath and Roberts (2008: 2), who in their analyses of the UK Government's Citizenship survey, report: 'We find no evidence that Muslims or people of Pakistani heritage were in general less attached to Britain than were other religions or ethnic groups. Ethnic minorities show clear evidence of "dual" rather than "exclusive" identities.' They point instead to hyphenated identities, in showing that 43 per cent of Muslims belong 'very strongly' to Britain and 42 per cent say that they belong to

Britain 'fairly strongly', and taken together these figures are higher for Muslim respondents than they are for Christian ones and those of 'no religion'. This is now a widely accepted and repeated body of findings reiterated by Wind-Cowie and Gregory (2011: 41):

> Our polling shows that 88 per cent of Anglicans and Jews agreed that they were 'proud to be a British citizen' alongside 84 per cent of non-conformists and 83 per cent of Muslims – compared with 79 per cent for the population as a whole. (p. 39) ... This optimism in British Muslims is significant as – combined with their high score for pride in British – it runs counter to a prevailing narrative about Muslim dissatisfaction with and in the UK. While it is true that there are significant challenges to integration for some in the British Muslim community – and justified concern at the levels of radicalism and extremism in some British Muslim communities – overall British Muslims are more likely to be both patriotic and optimistic about Britain than are the white British community.

Elsewhere there is a robust debate on the position of minorities in the Netherlands, where the dispute centres on the role of a relatively closed labour market (for minorities) (Duyvendak and Scholten, 2011). Another study shows us that when we are able to control for other factors, when the same ethnic minority group (with the same pre-arrival characteristics) enters two different countries at the same time, the group who are in the multicultural context fares much better (Bloemraard, 2006). In her study, Bloemraard (2006) compared the integration of two Vietnamese groups in Toronto and Canada respectively, and then repeated this for Portuguese minorities. According to Kymlicka (2012: 46), in these cases Canada's proactive multicultural policies 'sent a clear message that Vietnamese [and Portuguese] political participation is welcome, and have also provided material and logistical support for self-organization and political representation of the community'.

THE BACKLASH AND BEYOND

The political theorist Bhikhu Parekh (2005: 349) has argued that 'when a writer attacks multiculturalism, we need to be on our guard, for he [sic] is likely to homogenise its different forms, equate it with one particular strand of it, and end up misunderstanding those who do not fit his simplistic version of it'. Since '9/11' and its aftermath it is Muslims as a group who come to be the focus of discourses about the failure of multiculturalism, and minorities in the West more broadly. Muslims in Western Europe, it is argued, are disloyal to European states and prefer segregation and socio-cultural separatism to integration; they are illiberal on a range of issues, most notably on the personal freedom of women and on homosexuality; and they are challenging the secular character of European political culture by thrusting religious identities and communalism into the public space. The last charge marks the most serious theoretical reversal of multiculturalism, as the non-privatisation of minority identities is one of the core ideas of multicultur-alism (Modood, 2007). Yet the emergence of Muslim political mobilisation has led some multiculturalists to argue that religion is a feature of plural societies that is uniquely legitimate to confine to the private sphere. This prohibiting of Muslim identity in public space has so far been taken furthest in France, where in 2004 Parliament passed, with little debate but an overwhelming majority, a ban on the wearing of 'ostentatious' religious symbols, primarily the hijab (headscarf), in pub-lic schools. This is accompanied by a 'multiculturalism is dead' rhetoric that has led to, or reinforced, policy reversals in many countries, even pioneering ones such as the Netherlands, and is most marked by the fact that a new assimilationism is espoused not just on the political right, but also on the centre-left and by erstwhile supporters of multiculturalism.

'As a matter of fact, in most if not all European countries there are points of symbolic, institutional, policy and fiscal linkages between the state and aspects of Christianity. Secularism has increasingly grown in power and scope, but a historically evolved and evolving compromise with religion is the defining fea-ture of European, especially North-western European secularism, rather than the absolute separation of religion and politics' (Modood and Meer, 2013: 115). **Secularism** today enjoys hegemony in Western Europe, but it is a 'moderate' rather than a 'radical' secularism (Modood, 2011). What this means is that while the appeal of multiculturalism as a public policy has suffered considerable political damage, the intellectual and policy argument that multiculturalism 'is a valuable means of remaking of public identities in order to achieve an equality of citizenship that is neither merely individualistic nor premised on assimila-tion' (Modood, 2005: 5), remains powerful and unlikely to be erased. Indeed, appeals to multiculturalism have emerged more diffusely in arguments in favour of **interculturalism**, inclusive national identities, community cohesion, and so forth. What needs to be kept in mind therefore is that multiculturalism is not concerned with silos – quite the opposite in fact; for it has both intellectually and politically been a concept concerned with synthesis, and politically has promoted the idea of integration as a mutual outgrowth of its constituent parts.

REFERENCES

Austin, C. J. (2006) *Up Against the Wall: Violence in the Making and Unmaking of the Black Panther Party*. Fayetteville: University of Arkansas Press.

Barry, B. (2002) 'Second thoughts; some first thoughts revived', in P. Kelly (ed.) *Multiculturalism Reconsidered*. Cambridge: Polity.

Benhabib, S. (2002) *The Claims of Culture: Equality and Diversity in a Global Era*. Princeton: Princeton University Press.

Berry, J. W., Phinney, J. S., Sam, D. L., and Vedder, P. (2006) 'Immigrant youth: acculturation, identity and adaptation', *Applied Psychology: An International Review*, 55 (3): 303–32.

Bhabha, H. K. (1998) 'Culture's in between', in D. Bennet (ed.) *Multicultural States: Rethinking Difference and Identity*. London: Routledge.

Bloemraard, I. (2006) *Becoming a Citizen: Incorporating Immigrants and Refugees in the United States and Canada*. Berkeley: University of California Press.

Duyvendak, W. G. J. and Scholten, P. W. A. (2011) 'The invention of the Dutch multicultural model and its effects on integration discourses in the Nertherlands', *Perspectives on Europe*, 40 (2): 39–45.

Gilroy, P. (2004) *After Empire: Melancholia or Convivial Culture?* Abingdon: Routledge.

Heath, A. and Roberts, J. (2008) *British Identity, Its Sources and Possible Implications for Civic Attitudes and Behaviour*. London: Department of Justice, HMSO.

Kauffman, L. A. (2001) 'The Anti-politics of identity', in B. Ryan (ed.) *Identity Politics in the Women's Movement*. London: New York University Press.

Kelly, P. (2002) 'Between culture and equality', in P. Kelly (ed.) *Multiculturalism Reconsidered*. Oxford: Polity.

Kivisto, P. and Faist, T. (2007) *Citizenship: Discourse, Theory, and Transnational Prospects*. London: Blackwell.

Kymlicka, W. (1995) *Multicultural Citizenship: A Liberal Theory of Minority Rights*. Oxford: Oxford University Press.

Kymlicka, W. (2012) 'Multiculturalism: success, failure, and the future', in Migration Policy Institute (eds) *Rethinking National Identity in the Age of Migration*. Bielefeld: Bertelsmann Stiftung.

Levey, G. B. and Modood, T. (eds) *Secularism, Religion and Multicultural Citizenship*. Cambridge: Cambridge University Press.

Meer, N. and Modood, T. (2009) 'The multicultural state we're in', *Political Studies*, 57: 473–9.

Meer, N. and Modood, T. (2012) 'How does interculturalism contrast with multiculturalism?', *Journal of Intercultural Studies*, 33 (2): 175–97.

Melucci, A. (1989) *Nomads of the Present: Social Movements and Individual Needs in Contemporary Society*. London: Hutchinson.

Melucci, A. (1996) *Challenging Codes: Collective Action in the Information Age*. Cambridge: Cambridge University Press.

Millet, K. (1969) *Sexual Politics*. Garden City, NY: Doubleday.

Modood, T. (1992) *Not Easy Being British*. London: Trentham Books.

Modood, T. (2005) *Multicultural Politics*. Edinburgh: Edinburgh University Press.

Modood, T. (2007) *Multiculturalism: A Civic Idea*. Cambridge: Polity Press.

Modood, T. (2009) 'Ethnicity and Religion', in M. Flinders, A. Gamble, C. Hay and M. Kenny (eds) *The Oxford Handbook of British Politics*. Oxford: Oxford University Press.

Modood, T. (2011) 'Moderate secularism, religion as identity and respect for religion', *Political Quarterly*, 81 (1): 4–14.

Modood, T. (2013) *Multiculturalism*. Cambridge: Polity.

Modood, T. and Meer, N. (2013) 'Multiculturalism', in *The Oxford Companion to Comparative Politics*. Oxford: Oxford University Press.

Parekh, B. (1994) 'Minority rights, majority values', in D. Miliband (ed.) *Reinventing the Left*. Cambridge: Polity Press.

Parekh, B. (2000) *Rethinking Multiculturalism: Cultural Diversity and Political Theory*. London: Macmillan; Cambridge, MA: Harvard University Press.

Parekh, B. (2005) *Rethinking Multiculturalism: Cultural Diversity and Political Theory*. Basingstoke: Palgrave Macmillan, 2nd edition.

Rawls, J. (1993) *Political Liberalism*. New York: Columbia University Press.

Scott, J. (1999) *The Conundrum of Equality*, Paper Number 2, School of Social Sciences, Institute for Advanced Study, Princeton University.

Smith, K.E. (2010) 'Research, policy and funding – academic treadmills and the squeeze on intellectual spaces', *British Journal of Sociology*, 61 (1): 176–95.

Taylor, C. (1992) 'Multiculturalism and "The Politics of Recognition"', in A. Gutmann (ed.) *Multiculturalism and 'The Politics of Recognition'*. Princeton: Princeton University Press.

Touraine, A. (1981) *The Voice and the Eye: An Analysis of Social Movements*. Cambridge: Cambridge University Press.

Tully, J. (2002) 'The illiberal liberal', in P. Kelly (ed.) *Multiculturalism Reconsidered*. Cambridge: Polity.

Wind-Cowie, M. and Gregory, T. (2011) *A Place for Pride*. London: Demos.

Wiverorka, M. (2012) 'Multiculturalism: a concept to be redefined and certainly not replaced by the extremely vague term of interculturalism', *Journal of Intercultural Studies*, 33 (2): 225–31.

Young, I. M. (1990) *Justice and the Politics of Difference*. Princeton: Princeton University Press.

Nationalism

> *Nationalism is more than a description of a political movement. It also describes a field of study concerned with the configuration of identity with contemporary state and society, including the provenance and implications of those identities, and so spans questions of sociology, history and politics.*

Nationalism, argues Hearn (2006: 11), is best conceived as 'the making of combined claims, on behalf of a *population*, to an *identity*, to *jurisdiction* and to *territory*'. This definition is put forward in a manner that emphasises the processes (e.g. 'making of') nationalism, rather than its objective content per se. Yet it is a definition that is also sensitive to how nationalism can entail a meaningful reflection of people's 'consciousness' too, and the dialectical interactions these may reflect. As such Hearn's definition is a useful means of delineating what is often portrayed as either 'natural' phenomena, or as something cynically engineered by elites. And yet there remain good reasons for Hall (1998: 1) to insist that 'no single, universal theory of nationalism is possible. As the historical context is diverse, so too must be our concepts.'

NATIONALISM AND THE STATE

The study of nationalism is complicated because of the ways in which it is coupled with a study of societies more broadly, and how this is related to the processes and structures of *the state* in particular. While the state can take a dynamic form (and so is not a monolithic entity), the *mass* state – as opposed to the *city* states described in the discussion of Athenian **citizenship** – is a product of modernity in so far as it came into being during a period of relatively rapid social, economic, political development (from the end of the fifteenth century onwards) (Gellner, 1983). One of the things this led to, and which is crucial for an understanding of nationalism, was the emergence of a *political body* – a government and wider bureaucracy – with enough authority to govern over a given territory, and in turn expect people in that territory to owe their allegiance to it (in contrast to, say, owing allegiances to a monarch or other ruler) (Smith, 1986). The point is that the state bases its very *legitimacy* (the very right to rule over populations) on being able to represent the people in it. While **citizenship** describes this relationship between people and the state – a relationship that grants certain 'rights' (such as voting, legal protection and free education) as long as citizens adhere to certain 'duties' (e.g. obey the law, pay taxes, even participate in jury service if asked, or undertake national military service where this is mandatory) – the modern type of state is also meant to be made up of people who share a similar language, culture and history. This is what makes it a *nation*-state, and an important part of a nation-state is a sense of national identity: an identity that reflects some of the characteristics shared across other people in *their* country, and which differentiates them from people in another country.

The criteria of national identity are not always easy to list and often end up being intuitive and psychological. Hearn (2006: 6–7) registers this and places it amongst other ways of conceiving nationalism (including nationalism as identity, ideology, a social movement, and historical process). That is to say, nationalism as a *feeling* in a manner that is intuitive, can be psychologically charged, or is at least emotionally 'non-rational' (ibid.). This, however, is not the only way of thinking about nationalism, and to take in a broad perspective it would be fruitful to begin with the first part of the concept – that of the *nation*.

WHAT IS A NATION?

The title of this section comes from a lecture given by the French writer Ernest Renan in the late nineteenth century. Renan could not understand how it was that Switzerland, which had three languages (French, German and Italian) and a variety of religions, could be a 'nation', when Tuscany (a region of Italy), which was much more homogeneous, was not. He wondered therefore how the idea of nationality differed from that of a nation. Renan's answer was that nations are not 'eternal entities' – by which he meant that they have a beginning and an ending. Like another French sociologist, Emile Durkheim, he argued that a nation is a large-scale solidarity, one made up of a desire to continue a common life:

> A nation is not therefore about objective criteria such as ethnic, linguistic, geographical bonds, but instead a belief in a common past as well as an ability to 'forget' which means that national identities are actually an outcome of imagined shared history. (Renan, 1990: 16)

So Renan emphasises the importance of a 'will to nationhood' that seeks a consensus (on historical memory) on which to rest present-day consent through a 'daily plebiscite'. This is the aim, and societies may well fall short of it, but nonetheless appeal, in Renan's terms, to consenting participation in a 'discourse on society that *performs* the problem of totalizing a people and unifying the national will' (Bhabha, 1994: 160–1).

Importantly, Renan makes a conceptual contrast with **ethnicity**, in a manner that has political implications that take us back to Hearn's definition discussed at the outset. Calhoun (1993: 229) elaborates this in his observation that a 'crucial distinction between ethnicities and nations is that the latter are envisioned as intrinsically political communities, as sources of sovereignty, while this is not central to the definition of ethnicities'. That is not to say that conceptions of the nation cannot (or do not) significantly overlap with ethnicity, that they are not, à la Hobsbawm (1991: 4), 'different, and indeed non-compatible, concepts'. Nor indeed should this suggest that all nations have sovereignty, but it is instead to open up the ways in which the ethnic basis of nationhood is often disputed. Those who hold this view are often grouped as 'modernists', and a trailblazing account was provided by Ernest Gellner's (1983) *Nations and Nationalism*. For him:

> It is not the case that the 'age of nationalism' is a mere summation of the awakening and political self assertion of this, that, or the other nation. Rather when general social conditions make for standardised homogeneous, centrally sustained high cultures, pervading ethnic populations and not just elite minorities, a situation arises in which well defined educationally sanctioned and unified cultures constitute very nearly the only kind of unit with which men willingly and often ardently identify with. (Ibid.: 55)

It is important to remember, however, that there are a variety of positions amongst modernists who may otherwise find agreement with Gellner, and who offer a different historical timing of the emergence of nationalism, as well as its key influences. Perhaps a core distinction concerns whether the creation of the modern state gave rise to nationalism (Gellner's position as above), or whether a modern cultural movement gave rise to a mass identity.

IMAGINED COMMUNITIES

A highly influential elaboration of the former view comes from the historical sociologist Benedict Anderson (1991) in his book *Imagined Communities*, which has emerged as a central account in the field. Anderson argues that nationalism emerged in Europe in the eighteenth century and *created* nations as 'imagined political communities' that are both 'limited and sovereign' (ibid.: 6). By this he means two things. First, it is imagined in so far as all members of even the smallest nation will never meet each other, and yet in the minds of each lives an image of their connection to each other. In this regard nations 'only fully realize their horizons in the mind's eye' (Bhabha, 1994: 293). Second, it is 'limited' because each nation has finite borders beyond which live other nations. Third, nations are 'sovereign' because they were created in an age of modernity when the ideas of rule by monarchies seemed less rational. Lastly, he argued that regardless of the actual inequality the nation is always conceived as a deep and horizontal comradeship. The latter passes over an often 'turbulent and contested history' to give an emphasis to 'tradition and heritage, above all on continuity so that our present political culture is seen as the flowering of a long organic evolution' (Schwarz, 1986: 155).

It is really important, however, not to confuse the term *imagining* with *fabrication* because Anderson argues that just because we imagine our social and political order as a 'national' one, this does not mean it is not 'real'. What he says is that ideas can become a powerful basis for social action. Indeed, it is worth bearing in mind that Gellner's (1983) position was also alive to this distinction. For the latter:

> The idea of man without a nation appears to impose strain on the modern imagination. A man must have a nationality as he must have a nose and two ears. All this seems obvious, though, alas, it is not true. But that it should come to seem so very obviously true is indeed an aspect, perhaps the very core, of the problem of nationalism. Having a nation is not an inherent attribute to humanity, but it has come to appear as such. (Ibid.: 6)

Anderson seeks to illustrate this with reference to his discussion of the relationship between national vernaculars and identity. To this end he identifies the emergence of the printing press – giving rise to what he called 'print capitalism' – as something which did more than anything else to allow people to imagine themselves as a nation. Why would this be important?

Well, first, it allowed for the development of commercial book publishing on a wide scale at a time when there was a serious decline in the use of Latin as the main European script. This meant that more and more regional languages – or 'vernaculars' – were used and provided the basis for a national language. This was particularly evident in the circulation of newspapers in which news stories were simultaneously consumed by an increasing number of reading masses who began to share the same language, and the widespread availability of these in the same language allowed the reader to have much in common with their co-reader. One implication is that these newspapers contained a 'calenderical symmetry' – by this he meant that because the date was at the top of newspapers it placed everybody in the country in the same time frame. The important thing to notice here is that he argues that nations and states are the result of a recent cultural artifact (so nationalism creates nations, not the other way around).

ETHNIES AND PRE-MODERNITY

Not everybody shares the view that nations are an outcome of a relatively modern imagined identity, however, and detractors often point to what they see as a key flaw in the modernist augment: why does nationalism persist in the modern (and modernised) world? The most prominent opposing view comes from a cluster of work around 'ethno-symbolism' which says that pre-modern ethnic ties have been important in creating ethnic cultures that forge a nation. For example, in his book

The Ethnic Origin of Nations, Anthony Smith (1986) argues that modernists, in their determination to reveal the invented or constructed nature of nationalism, ignore the continuing persistence of myths, symbols, values and memories over time, and the significance that these things can have for large numbers of people. He argues: 'the "roots" of these nations are to be found, both in a general way and in many specific cases, in the model of ethnic community prevalent in much of the recorded history of the globe' (ibid.: x). More precisely, he argues that modern nation-states have emerged out of a complex mixture of social and ethnic ties all the way back from pre-modern times. He calls these 'ethnies' which he says modernity has transformed but not erased. In so doing he seeks to link 'the consequences of modernity with an understanding of the continuing role played by cultural ties and ethnic identities which originated in pre-modern epochs' (Smith, 1995: 47).

The analogy he makes is that when it comes to thinking about nations we should regard the modern era as a scroll that has been re-used and on which are recorded the experiences and identities of different ethnic cultures in the past: the earlier influencing and being modified by the latter, to produce layers of collective cultures which we call 'the nation'. In Smith's view this would explain *which* populations are likely to start a movement of nationalism; *what* the content of this would be (role of memories, myths and symbols in languages, public holidays, sacred sites); and most importantly *why* nationalism is able to generate such widespread national appeal.

THE BAD AND THE BANAL

You may have already noticed that nowhere has this discussion of nationalism dwelt on the obviously bad kinds. You only need to think about some of the many conflicts that have scarred Europe in the last one hundred years. The Nazism of Hitler's Germany and the Holocaust, the Fascism of Franco's Spain and Mussolini's Italy – or even much more recently the ethnic cleansing of Muslims in Bosnia – are all illustrations of an extreme and terribly violent nationalism. Clearly very few academics would characterise these as other than what they are – racist movements that grasp and exploit part of a national story that supports their political cause. This is true of all the kinds mentioned above, the best known perhaps being Hitler's fantasy that the German people descended from racially superior 'Aryans' who had many mythical qualities but were principally white and Christian.

The reason for not dwelling on these types of nationalism is that they are today much less valid – though they have not gone away – and are difficult to sustain. But more importantly, by focusing on extreme nationalisms we push our own nationalism to the periphery of social life, making it something that happens elsewhere and not here, amongst us. In his book *Banal Nationalism* Michael Billig (1995) argues that we tend to think about *our* everyday nationalism as 'patriotism', something which is good and beneficial rather than irrational or dangerous. Reflecting on his account, Billig (2009: 349) states:

Banal nationalism attempted to look beyond the dialogues of conscious sense-making towards a psychology of the unnoticed. The flags hanging in the street, or attached to the lapels of politicians, carry no propositional message for the ordinary citizen to receive passively or consciously argue against. Yet, such symbols help us to maintain the everyday world as belonging to the world of nation-states.

He argues that this encourages the view that nationalism has gone away and then returns – that it is a latent force that manifests itself like a natural disaster which strikes spontaneously and unpredictably. This is referred to as the 'Sleeping Beauty' syndrome which only sees nationalism as sometimes spectacular but misses its more subtle manifestations and ignores how we all participate in sustaining it for different ends. Symbols in this way can act as 'border guards', and are 'linked to specific cultural codes and function to identify people as members or non-members of the specific national collectivity' (May, 2001: 61). Thus in *Why the French Don't Like Headscarves*, John Bowen (2006) says this is precisely what happens because even though the Muslim headscarves and mosque are not objectively more visible than other religious difference or the cathedral, they are subjectively shocking because they force French people to think about how *being* French is no longer – if it ever was – the preserve of white Christians. What the focus on headscarves also highlights is how central gender and women are to our 'banal nationalism'. If we stop and think about it the nation is often imagined as a big family, and the homeland as a vulnerable woman needing protection – the nasty aspect of this is that rape is frequently used as a weapon of war. Reflecting on this Nira Yuval-Davies (1997) has argued that gender is a key part of nationhood because women are often seen as biological reproducers of members of ethnic groups and, by extension, as reproducers of national groups. This means that while men are more likely to monopolise its political and military representation, it is women who come to 'embody' the nation as such (Meer et al., 2010).

REFERENCES

Anderson, B. (1983) *Imagined Communities: Reflections on the Origin and Spread of Nationalism*. London: Verso.

Anderson, B. (1991) *Imagined Communities: Reflections on the Origin and Spread of Nationalism*, 2nd edition. London: Verso.

Bhabha, H. (ed.) (1990) *Narrating the Nation*. London: Routledge.

Bhabha, H. (ed.) (1994) *The Location of Culture*. London: Routledge.

Billig, M. (1995) *Banal Nationalism*. London: Sage.

Billig, M. (2009) 'Reflecting on a critical engagement with banal nationalism', *Sociological Review*, 57 (2): 347–52.

Bowen, J. (2006) *Why the French Don't Like Headscarves: Islam, the State and Public Space*. Princeton: Princeton University Press.

Calhoun, C. (1993) 'Nationalism and Ethnicity', *Annual Review of Sociology*, 19: 211–39.

Gellner, E. (1983) *Nations and Nationalism*. Oxford: Blackwell.

Hall, J. A. (1998) 'Introduction', in: J. A. Hall (1998) (ed.) *The State of the Nation: Ernest Gellner and the Theory of Nationalism*. Cambridge: Cambridge University Press.

nationalism

Hearn, J. (2006) *Rethinking Nationalism*. Basingstoke: Palgrave.

Hobsbawm, E. (1991) *Nations and Nationalism since 1780*. Cambridge: Cambridge University Press.

May, S. (2001) *Language and Minority Rights*. Harlow: Longman.

Meer, N., Dwyer, C. and Modood, T. (2010) 'Embodying nationhood? Conceptions of British national identity, citizenship and gender in the "veil affair"', *The Sociological Review*, 58 (1): 84–111.

Renan, E. (1990) 'What is a nation?', in H. Bhabha (ed.) *Nation and Narration*. London: Routledge.

Schwarz, B. (1986) 'Conservatism, nationalism and imperialism', in J. Donald and S. Hall (eds) *Politics and Ideology*. Milton Keynes: Open University Press.

Smith, A. (1986) *The Ethnic Origins of Nations*. Oxford: Blackwell.

Smith, A. (1995) *Nations and Nationalism in a Global Era*. London: Polity Press.

Yuval-Davis, N. (1997) *Gender and Nation*. London: Sage.

Orientalism

Orientalism has come to be associated with the critique of Western scholarship, though it was once a respected mode of area studies, what we would today broadly understand as Middle Eastern studies. The critique was popularised through historical and literary criticism in the work of Edward Said in particular, but has been taken up across the social sciences in a way that is linked to post-colonial scholarship.

In its most benign form, Orientalism may be conceived as a mode of historical areas studies, not unlike Latinism or Hellenism, that is today broadly 'equated with Middle Eastern studies' (Samiei, 2010: 1145). The latter immediately departs from how the term 'Oriental' is frequently understood to describe East Asian cultures and territories. In contrast, as Samiei (ibid.) describes, 'the Orient in the nineteenth century usage of the word, meant the Arab world or generally the Middle East; it did not include India, China or the Far East'. This is important to remember: while some common discursive tropes may be observed in the description of Far East Asian and Middle East societies, the *scholarship* of Orientalism – and importantly the challenge to that scholarship – have centred much more on Muslim societies perhaps, in Edward Said's (1991: 59) terms, because 'for Europe, Islam was a lasting trauma'.

MUSLIM *SOCIETY*

An interesting and knowledgeable example of Orientalist scholarship from the recent past is Ernest Gellner's (1983) work contrasting Western societies with – in the title of his book – *Muslim Society* (in the singular). In this account Gellner takes the view that when it comes to discerning what kinds of authority are sovereign, there is a common (**secularism**-resistant) pattern of social organisation across different Muslim societies, born of Islam's alleged over-reliance on scripture, in contrast to Christianity's dualism (between church and state). This is a more complicated account than some for, as Zubaida (1995: 177) describes, it takes in a variety of social forces:

> Modernity for Muslims, according to Gellner, has not led to an erosion of their historic essence, but, on the contrary, to its renewal under new conditions. ... He then sets out to explain why this should be so. The social basis of the 'Low Culture' of the tribes has been eroded with the centralization of state power, urbanization and the associated processes of modernity. The newly urbanized, the new bourgeoisie, as it were, identify with the High Islam of the *ulama* [theologians and Islamic scholars] and the Norm. For them this is a sign of upward social mobility, education and learning.

What is interesting for the discussion of Orientalism is that similar trajectories are observable between rural and urban groups in non-Muslim societies. As discussed in the concept of **nationalism**, the dynamic between high and low (or mass) culture are elsewhere deemed to be integral to varying Western social formations that are not an obstacle to modernity, but an expression of a particular kind of modernity. Why then does Gellner deem Muslim social formations as so radically unfamiliar because they are expressed in a non-Western guise?

Part of the answer is that Islam has come to serve as a methodological tool in being contrasted with notions of Western conceptions of human progress. As we explore in the discussion of **secularism**, the narrative arc of Western social science has predicted that any given society's norms and values would move away from types of traditional rationality exemplified in religion, and coalesce on a more radical idiom, or new social solidarities, forged not by the promise of spiritual redemption but by material advancement. In this respect the idea that Islamic societies are anti-modern as measured by Western ideas of modernity becomes a circular argument, something that is itself 'a symptom of the limitations of Western sociology. Particularly in its classical shape' (Salvatore, 2013: 8).

A STYLE OF THOUGHT

It is this vein of critique that is most resolutely explored in Said's (1995 [1978]) *Orientalism*. Said's core thesis is that, through a body of scholarship and style of thought, probably from the eighteenth century onwards, the West created an idea of 'the Orient'. In his terms 'European culture was able to manage – even produce – the Orient politically, sociologically, militarily, ideologically, scientifically and imaginatively during the post-Enlightenment period' (Said, 1995 [1978]: 7). This is not only about proximity, namely being 'adjacent to Europe', but about 'a distribution of geopolitical awareness' expressed in 'aesthetic, scholarly, economic, sociological, historical, and philological texts' (Said, 1995 [1978]: 91). Beginning with the Napoleonic invasion, accompanied by detailed recording and cataloguing, through to the administration of colonialism, of nineteenth-century Egypt, Said distils key properties in the depiction of 'the Orient'. What he is trying to show is that *Orientalism* relies on a transaction between *semiotic* systems (e.g. texts) and political governance (e.g. colonialism).

Given how influential, indeed seminal, Said's account has been for our understanding of Orientalist inquiry, the description of the task he sets himself is worth quoting at length (and it is worth noting that the entire following paragraph reproduces just one single sentence!):

> [Orientalism] is an elaboration not only of a basic geographical distinction (the world is made of two halves, Orient and Occident) but also of a whole series of 'interests' which, by such means as scholarly discovery, philological analysis, landscape and sociological description, not only creates but also maintains; it *is*, rather than expresses, a certain *will* or *intention* to understand, in some cases to control, manipulate, even to incorporate, what is a manifestly different (or alternative and novel) world; it is, above all, a discourse that is by no means in direct, corresponding relationship with political power in the raw, but rather is produced and exists in an uneven exchange with power political (as with a colonial or imperial establishment), power intellectual (as with reigning sciences like linguistics or anatomy, or any of the modern policy sciences), power cultural (as with orthodoxies and canons of taste, texts, and values), power moral (as with ideas about what 'we' do and what 'they' cannot do or understand as 'we' do). (Said, 1995 [1978]: 91)

If there is a common thread that runs through these components of Orientalism, it is the relationship between *categories* and *geopolitics* – a relationship that social science inquiry cannot stand outside. This dialectical relationship is a rich repository for genealogical excavation, and returns to Said's observations that the 'Orient' is also the place of Europe's civilisation, and so the challenge of critical inquiry is to relate these historical and contemporary implications.

It is sometimes stated therefore that Said is applying the work of the French scholar Michel Foucault, something that Said himself robustly rejected. One can certainly see commonality in their respective approaches. Foucault was concerned with signposting shifts in moral, ethical and, ultimately, historical notions of legitimising power or authority (which he keenly observed as being exercised in conceptions of 'madness', 'sexuality', 'punishment', etc.), highlighting the degree to which the conditions behind a specific 'problem' often lie in its textual assumptions. This is outlined, amongst other places, in *The History of Sexuality* where he argues that power is a diffuse activity that emanates from every point in the social field, so is not a monolithic force, 'an institution, and nor a structure; neither is it a certain strength we are endowed with; it is the name one attributes to a complex strategical situation in a given society' (Foucault, 1979: 93). The power to represent is therefore everywhere and nowhere, 'exercised' by everybody and nobody. It is probably for these reasons that Said did not source his account to Foucault, and indeed argued that he would have produced a more limited account if he had. In his own words:

> The discovery I made about Foucault … was that, despite the fact that he seemed to be a theorist of power, obviously, and kept referring to resistance, he was really the *scribe* of power. He was really writing about the victory of power. I found very little in his work, especially after the second half of *Discipline and Punish* … so I completely lost interest. The later stuff on the subject I just found really weak and, to my way of thinking, uninteresting. (Said, 2005: 214)

Either way, one implication from Said's account is that European scholarship that has been 'elaborated within the confines of Western modernity' (Venn, 2003: 3) retains its ethnocentric anchorage. The objective of this complaint is not to devalue Western scholarship; it is instead to seek an understanding of its relationship to colonialism, and the ways in which 'they are already deeply implicated within each other' (Young, 1992: 243). A counter-Orientalist challenge, however, needs to do more than just reverse the complaint, for example argue that there is something inherent to European civilisations that has historically prevented it from incorporating difference into common life. This indeed is precisely what Turner (2007) has suggested, in his observation that European languages do not possess a word that inverts the term xenophobia (from the Greek word *xenos* meaning stranger), that is *xenophilia* (a fondness for the stranger). This leads him to the view that 'it appears there is little linguistic possibility for the love of strangers' (ibid.: 66). To develop a generalising theory, supplemented with some biblical references, would seem a implausible means of elaborating an account of Western civilisation. But it is precisely the type of Orientalist analysis that is to be found on account of Muslim societies, where there is a 'reluctance to attribute a transformative potential to non-Western social formations, with a corresponding devaluation of their religious and more broadly cultural traditions' (Salvatore, 2013: 8).

NEO-ORIENTALISM?

This is more than a series of historical debates, however, for Orientalism casts a long contemporary shadow over the present, and a current illustration of this finds expression in the language of civilisational struggle. As Said (1994: 1) describes:

> Appeals to the past are among the commonest of strategies in interpretations of the present. What animates such appeals is not only disagreement about what happened in the past and what the past was, but uncertainty about whether the past really is past, over and concluded, or whether it continues, albeit in different forms, perhaps.

For example, and in what has become an agenda-setting account, over two decades ago Buzan (1991) pointed to a novel pattern of international relations that he characterised as 'the clash of rival civilisational identities' (quoted in Al-Jabri, 1999: 67). In this early instantiation of what would later become known through other authors as the 'clash of civilisations' thesis, Buzan argued:

> In the case of Islam, this threat is compounded by geographical adjacency and historical antagonism and also the overtly political role that Islam plays in the lives of its followers. Rivalry with the West is made more potent by the fact that Islam is still itself a vigorous and expanding collective identity. (Ibid.)

Notice that the dialectic here is precisely that critiqued by Said, for the account more broadly helped to establish a view of a Muslim 'propensity towards violent conflict' (Huntington, 1996: 258), and plugged into a 'myth of confrontation' (Halliday, 1996) that portrayed Islam as 'an ancient rival against our Judeo-Christian heritage' (Lewis, 1993: 13). What follows on from these positions is a presumed 'oriental irrationality and the fanatical masses' (Lueg, 1995: 15).

In a recent study Morey and Yaqin (2011: 5) have explored the ways in which the Saidian critique of Orientalism can be adopted to understand how '[i]ntolerant images and pronouncements breed a kind of self fashioning that operates as the other half of a distorted dialogue'. With Muslims and Islam in mind, these authors tackle a variety of themes and recurrent argumentation which include the elaboration of intersections between masculinity and fanaticism e.g. in the omnipresent folk devil of 'Islamic rage boy' as 'probably the most immediately recognisable of all widely circulated Muslim stereotypes' (ibid.: 23), as well as the role of reading back in forms of cultural racism as inherent civilisational 'safe superiority, often deep-rooted and tenacious' (ibid.: 11) but also needing 'constant feeding and stoking' (ibid.). In pointing to evidence of a neo-Orientalism, their analysis shares something with others in critiquing the assumption that a 'conflictual *nature* in Islam, further strengthened by images of extremism, fanaticism and irrationality, compounds the discursive backwardness' (Poole, 2002: 45).

REFERENCES

Al-Jabri, M. A. (1999) '"Clash of civilisations": the relations of the future', in G. M. Munro (ed.) *Islam, Modernism and the West*. London: I.B. Tauris.

Buzan, B. (1991) 'New patterns of global security in the twenty-first century', *International Affairs*, 67 (3): 431–51.

Foucault, M. (1979) *The History of Sexuality, Volume One: An Introduction*. London: Allen Lane.

Gellner, E. (1983) *Muslim Society*. Cambridge: Cambridge University Press.

Halliday, F. (1996) *Islam and the Myth of Confrontation: Religion and Politics in the Middle East*. London: I.B. Taurus.

Huntingdon, S. (1996) *The Clash of Civilizations and the Remaking of the World Order*. New York: Simon & Schuster.

Lewis, B. (1993) *Islam and the West*. New York: Oxford University Press.

Lueg, A. (1995) 'The perceptions of Islam in Western debate', in J. Hippler and A. Lueg (eds) *The Next Threat: Western Perceptions of Islam*. London: Pluto Press.

Morey, P. and Yaqin, A. (2011) *Framing Muslims: Stereotyping and Representation after 9/11*. Cambridge, MA: Harvard University Press.

Poole, E. (2002) *Reporting Islam: Media Representation of British Muslims*. London: I.B. Tauris.

Said, E. (1991) *Orientalism*. London: Penguin.

Said, E. (1994) *Culture and Imperialism*. London: Vintage.

Said, E. (1995 [1978]) 'Orientalism', in B. Ashcroft, G. Griffith and H. Tiffin (1995) *The Postcolonial Studies Reader*. London: Routledge.

Said, E. (2005) *Power, Politics and Culture: Interviews with Edward Said*. London: Bloomsbury.

Salvatore, A. (2013) 'The sociology of Islam: precedents and perspectives', *Sociology of Islam*, 1 (1): 7–13.

Samiei, M. (2010) 'Neo-Orientalism? The relationship between the west and Islam in our globalised world', *Third World Quarterly*, 31 (7): 1145–60.

Turner, B. (2007) 'New and old xenophobia: the crisis of liberal multiculturalism', in S. Akbarzadeh and F. Mansouri (eds) *Islam and Political Violence – Muslim Diaspora and Radicalism in the West*. London: I.B. Taurus.

Venn, C. (2003) *The Postcolonial Challenge: Towards Alternative Worlds*. London: Sage.

Young, R. (1992) 'Colonialism and humanism', in J. Donald and A. Rattansi (1992) (eds) *'Race', Culture and Difference*. London: Sage.

Zubaida, S. (1995) 'Is there a Muslim society? Ernest Gellner's sociology of Islam', *Economy and Society*, 24 (1): 151–88.

Political Participation

Political participation is one of the most important arenas of citizenship, and this can be profoundly affected by ethnic and racial dynamics. For example, in terms of formal political engagement, ethnic and racial minorities may not be eligible for the franchise in electoral politics, or they may be less likely to exercise it even when they are. Equally, fair political representation assumes that ethnic and racial minorities will also be visible in mainstream politics, so move from being objects to participants in politics, and one question this raises is the extent to which these actors are also representative of minority as well as majority communities.

The political participation of ethnic and racial minorities is intimately related to their political rights and the scale of their political representation. Each of these issues sufficiently overlaps so that the focus can be described as being concerned with minority political engagement. This needs to take in a discussion of the broader discourses surrounding the inclusion of ethnic and racial minorities. Will Kymlicka (1995: 141), for example, has argued that the political representation of society has to consider the ways in which 'the historical domination of some groups has left a trail of barriers and prejudices that makes it difficult for historically disadvantaged groups to participate effectively in the political process'. This implies a relationship between political rights and the **citizenship** that is conferred to ethnic and racial minorities, and the routes this can take. If we focus on formal political participation, we can examine electoral matters in terms of voter registration and other factors informing voter activity.

THE FUNCTION OF POLITICAL RIGHTS

Full political rights (encompassing a range of entitlements beyond voting rights) are normally only secured if an immigrant becomes a citizen. It is important to bear in mind, however, that this describes the formal legal arrangements which are not necessarily taken up, or are inhibited by convoluted opportunity structures. This is particularly evident in the practical issues surrounding the formal political participation of some ethnic minorities in general, as described below, and is perhaps most starkly illustrated by the experiences of asylum seekers and refugees. This is usefully illustrated in the words of a practitioner in the areas of asylum and refugee migrant settlement.

Jonathon Ellis, Director of Policy and Development at the Refugee Council (UK), describes how the political participation of migrants who have applied for and achieved one or another status of indefinite leave, en route to seeking permanent residency and full citizenship, can be subject to a number of obstacles because 'there are barriers around information'. He continues:

> I think its mixed messages being set out around whether a country wants refugees to take on citizenship. For many people the cost of doing it is quite substantial, the cost of going through the process. For some people it's thinking about whether they actually want it in terms of their relationship with their own country [of origin], whether it's something they want to take on; the hope that they would return and how that might play in terms of going back ... [S]o it's a bizarre contradiction that you'd have people who for their very political activity were forced to leave [their country of origin], then not be politically active in this country! (Interviewed 3 September 2008)

Issues of 'newness' are not limited to asylum seekers and refugees, however, as there appear to be additional factors informing the non-participation of other ethnic and racial minorities. To take the British example, the status of new non-EU-member migrants, including asylum seekers and refugees, is complicated by the formal arrangements stipulated in the Representation of the People Act (1983 and 2000) which states that Irish and Commonwealth citizens are also entitled to vote in national elections. The right of Irish and Commonwealth citizens to vote in British elections is perhaps unusual compared to the arrangements amongst

European counterparts, and partly stems from the earlier Representation of the People Act 1918. This laid the ground to eventually extend the franchise to 'British subjects' which at the time included the people of Ireland – then part of the United Kingdom of Great Britain and Ireland – and all other parts of the British Empire. During de-colonisation, until they acquired one or other of the national citizenships of newly post-colonial countries, formerly British *subjects* continued to retain their British *status* which conferred a right to the franchise (see Lester, 2008). This was enshrined in the 1948 British Nationality Act which also granted freedom of movement to all formerly or presently dependent, and now Commonwealth, territories (regardless of whether their passports were issued by independent or colonial states) by creating the status of 'Citizenship of the United Kingdom and Colonies' (CUKC) (so although most of Ireland and the majority of the colonies became independent nations, their citizens retained the right to vote in British elections if they lived in the UK).

One outcome of this arrangement is that immigrants without leave to enter or remain, but who are Commonwealth citizens, are entitled to vote, while immigrants without leave to remain from non-Commonwealth countries are not eligible to vote. This means that any citizen of the fifty-three Commonwealth member states with its nearly two billion citizens can in theory, if residing in the UK, be registered on the electoral register. In practice, however, it is not uncommon to find that significant numbers of resident ethnic minorities bearing Commonwealth citizenship are unaware of this right and, moreover, do not register for the variety of reasons elaborated below (Mortimore and Kaur-Ballagan, 2006). This contradicts the specific arguments put forward by Migration Watch, a prominent lobby group which advocates radical limitations upon immigration to Britain, and which argues that Commonwealth citizenship categories are overly subscribed on the electoral register (Briefing Paper, 8.15, 12 April 2007).

The important fact to bear in mind is that compared to other European cases, Britain has one of the highest ethnic minority citizenry with a right to the franchise (Hansen, 2000: 3), and this can be very much part of the self-identity of civil society groups promoting ethnic minority political participation. As Ashok Viswanathan of Operation Black Vote (OBV) reminds us:

> Britain has an exceptional set of circumstances where many of them [black and ethnic minorities] have been in this country for a long time … and have had full citizenship rights, which can't always be claimed for people of African or Asian descent in Germany or in Spain or in other parts of Europe. (Interviewed 7 October 2008)

People from other European Union member states irrespective of immigration status, meanwhile, who are classed as citizens of the European Union (which would exclude some ethnic minorities such as visiting German-born Turks without leave to remain in Britain), may vote in local elections and in elections for devolved assemblies (Wales, Scotland, Northern Ireland, and the Mayor of London) but not in general elections. Conversely, British citizens living abroad can register as overseas electors and are eligible to vote in the UK and European Parliamentary elections for up to fifteen years after they have left the country.

POLITICAL PARTICIPATION AS THE FRANCHISE

The formal political participation of ethnic minorities by means of voting is, therefore, inevitably premised upon their levels of electoral registration. This is not an easy figure to ascertain, however, for as Fieldhouse and Cutts (2008: 336) note: 'obtaining reliable registration rates can be a difficult and imprecise process given uncertainty about the size of the eligible voting age population (because of census under coverage, temporary residency of foreign nationals, etc.)'. An obvious methodological implication of these contingent factors for our understanding is that if a section of the population is under-represented on the electoral register, the level of turnout will appear artificially high, and not necessarily offer the most reliable account of formal political participation. In some countries, such as Australia, it is a legal requirement both to be registered to vote and to exercise your franchise by casting your ballot during a general election. In contrast, while it is a legal requirement to be registered to vote if you are a resident British citizen, of whichever category, individuals have only been prosecuted for actively avoiding electoral registration in order to commit fraud (local authorities, instead of a national body, have responsibility for compiling and updating individual electoral registers). How, then, are levels of electoral registration affected by ethnicity dynamics associated with migration-related minorities?

First, it is widely accepted that young people are more likely not to be registered to vote than older people, and because the age profiles of minority communities often are *substantially* lower than those of majority groups, some ethnic minority communities are disproportionately affected by the lower levels of registration amongst younger voters (Russell et al., 2002a). Second, evidence suggests that fewer ethnic minority women register to vote than men, and OBV have conducted opinion surveys reporting that only 44 per cent of black and Asian women in the UK were registered (as compared to 60 per cent of black and Asian men) (OBV, 2001). Other factors affecting ethnic minority registration, not only disproportionately in relation to the wider population but also singularly, include an unfamiliarity with institutions and procedures or a 'newness', language difficulties, concerns over anonymity and confidentiality, fear of harassment, fear of officialdom, administrative inefficiency and anxieties over residence status (Anwar, 1990, 1996, 1998). There is also the issue of housing tenure since disproportionately high levels of some ethnic and racial minorities reside in social or rented housing which can lead to frequent movement and thus a requirement to continually re-register (Modood et al., 1997). Given the transitory nature of contemporary **migration** flows, it can only be assumed that these patterns of residence are being replicated, although we are yet to generate large-scale meaningful data on this (see Favell, 2008).

Anwar (1998) has thus argued that registration offices have not sufficiently developed their strategies to service ethnically diverse electorates, and what is interesting to note is that where research has expressly sought to ascertain *why* ethnic minorities are disproportionately not registered, rarely has it reported that they do not want to participate in politics. For example, Le Lohe's (1998) surveys found that only 0.9 per cent of all Asian respondents missing from the register did not want to participate in politics, and a study conducted by the Electoral Commission reported that less than 1 per cent of ethnic minorities who said that they did not vote in the 2001 general election did not do so because they were uninterested in politics (Purdham et al., 2002: 35).

The majority of this research is of course based upon attitudinal surveys of representative population samples, and there is clearly 'a need to do more research on what people do rather than what they say they do' (Purdham et al., 2002, quoted in Cutts et al., 2007: 398). The potential unreliability of such data is illustrated by Russell et al. (2002b) who refer to a MORI survey undertaken shortly after a general election in Britain that presented self-reported levels of turnout amongst ethnic minorities to be around 80 per cent and 70 per cent for whites, when in reality the turnout for the election as a whole was only 59 per cent. But until such data is created and made available we must work with the data that is already in existence.

SECURING REPRESENTATION

The important point is that the levels of registration amongst ethnic minority communities have increased with the confidence and sense of ownership they have in that society, albeit in varying degrees across and within different communities. Recent campaigns by OBV, which was set up in 1996 in order to increase the political participation of ethnic minorities, including in terms of voter registration, have had a considerable impact. This kind of activity convinces Raj Jethwa, Ethnic Minorities Officer for the London region of the Labour Party, 'that the reason for this [lower participation] is actually not to do with the fact that ethnic minority voters are less inclined to vote per se but we lack intermediary organisations to channel and assist this interest' (interviewed 13 September 2008).

These sorts of initiatives inherently concern matters of political participation and exemplify what Saggar and Geddes (2001: 28) describe as 'the transition from migrants and their descendents as "objects" of policy – as a public policy problem to be managed by tight immigration control and the paternalistic apparatus of race relations – to "actors" in the political process'. In 2004, MORI, on behalf of the Electoral Commission and the Hansard Society (2004), conducted an 'Audit of political engagement' and reported that only 30 per cent of ethnic minority respondents are satisfied with their MP, compared with 42 per cent of white people. These and other findings have informed organisations such as OBV's position that 'there is very much a symbiosis between those communities that vote and what would make them vote so there is a direct link between people seeing Black faces in high places and feeling that the democratic process is something that belongs to them and something that they want to take part in' (interview with Viswanathan, 2008). It is unsurprising then to learn that ethnic minority politicians are contacted by an ethnic minority electorate from outside their ward on the basis that they are more likely to respond to their concerns (Purdham, 2002). As Diane Abbott MP describes:

> I think that ethnic minority people think that I am their MP. Keith [Vaz MP], when he started had Asians coming to him from all over the Midlands with immigration problems. We've never run from being an ethnic minority MP, obviously you can't take all cases that come to you from over the country otherwise you wouldn't have time to do your own work, but I've never run from being an ethnic minority MP, it's a privilege. (Interview with author 2008)

As the first black female member of the British Parliament, it is perhaps unsurprising that Diane Abbott is widely known, and so attracts the attention of minority voters outside her constituency. At the same time it suggests that some ethnic and racial minority voters see in some ethnic and racial minority representatives some common experiences that are less apparent when there are fewer ethnic and racial figures in political life. This in many respects is their burden of representation, one that figures like Diane Abbott negotiate throughout their careers.

REFERENCES

Abbott, D. (2008) Interview with author.

Anwar, M. (1990) 'Ethnic minorities and the electoral process: some recent developments', in H. Goulbourne (ed.) *Black Politics in Britain*. London: Gower.

Anwar, M. (1996) *Race and Elections*. London: Routledge.

Anwar, M. (1998) *Ethnic Minorities and the British Electoral System*, CRER and OBV, University of Warwick.

Anwar, M. (2001) 'The participation of ethnic minorities in British politics', *Journal of Ethnic and Migration Studies*, 27 (3): 533–9.

Cutts, D., Fieldhouse, E., Purdam, K., Steel, D. & Tranmer, M. (2007) 'Voter turnout in British South Asian communities at the 2001 General Election', *British Journal of Politics and International Relations*, (9): 396–412.

Ellis, J. (2008) Interview with author.

Favell, A. (2008) 'The new face of East–West migration in Europe', *Journal of Ethnic and Migration Studies*, 34 (5): 701–16.

Fieldhouse, E. and Cutts, D. (2008) 'Mobilisation or marginalisation? Neighbourhood effects on Muslim electoral registration in Britain in 2001', *Political Studies*, 56: 333–54.

Hansard Society (2004) *Enhancing Engagement – Parliament and the Public: Research Study Conducted for the Hansard Society*. London: Hansard Society.

Hansen, R. (2000) *Citizenship and Immigration in Post-war Britain*. Oxford: Oxford University Press.

Jethwa, R. (2008) Interview with author.

Kymlicka, W. (1995) *Multicultural Citizenship*. Oxford: Oxford University Press.

Le Lohe, M. J. (1998) 'Ethnic minority participation and representation in the British electoral system', in S. Saggar (ed.) *Race and British Electoral Politics*. London: UCL Press.

Lester, A. (2008) 'Citizenship and the constitution', *Political Quarterly*, 79 (3): 388–403.

Migration Watch (2007) Briefing Paper, 8.15, 12 April.

Modood, T., Berthoud, R., Lakey, J., Nazroo, J., Smith, P., Virdee, S. and Beishon, S. (1997) *The Fourth National Survey of Ethnic Minorities in Britain: Diversity and Disadvantage*. London: PSI.

Mortimore, R. and Kaur-Ballagan, K. (2006) 'Ethnic minority voters and non-voters', paper for the EPOP Conference, University of Nottingham.

Operation Black Vote (OBV) (2001) *Black and Asian Voters Poll*. London: OBV.

Purdham, K. (2002) 'Democracy in practice: Muslims and the Labour Party at the local level', *Politics*, 21 (3): 147–57.

Rich, P. (1998) 'Ethnic politics and the Conservatives in the post-Thatcher era', in S. Saggar (ed.) *Race and British Electoral Politics*. London: UCL Press.

Russell, A., Fieldhouse, E. A., Kalra, V. and Purdam, K. (2002a). 'Black and minority ethnic disengagement and turnout', in *Constitution Unit's Special Conference on Political Participation*. London: UCL Press.

Russell, A., Fieldhouse, E. and MacAllister, I. (2002b) 'The anatomy of Liberal support in Britain, 1974–1997', *British Journal of Politics and International Relations*, 4 (1): 49–74.

Saggar, S. and Geddes, A. (2001) 'Negative and positive racialisation: re-examining ethnic minority political representation in the UK', *Journal of Ethnic and Migration Studies*, 26 (1): 25–44.

Viswanathan, A. (2008) Interview with author.

Post-colonialism

Post-colonialism describes both a historical formation – the state and nature of social and political relations after colonialism – and a mode of inquiry (namely a critique of power and knowledge production). The intellectual task is to understand how these interact and what their implications herald. The concept begins, however, by returning to colonial encounters which established patterns of social relations that would have implications long after their formal systems might have been discontinued.

One of the historical features of modernity has been the scope of European rule over the Global South. Since 1492 – for many the date which marks the 'beginning of the modern era' (Todorov, 1982: 5) – when Columbus landed in the Americas and the Catholic *Reconquista* captured the Iberian peninsula, Spanish, Portuguese, British, French, Dutch and Belgian Empires have in the subsequent centuries annexed and appropriated the resources (including human beings) of the entire African continent, and large parts of South and East Asia, Australasia, and Latin and Central America. How these empires went about this varies, for subsequent colonial rule took different forms. From the short-term plunder of the Spanish Conquistadors, indentured labour of the Congolese by the Belgians, to the creation of a compliant British Raj, and the settler societies and colonies of North America and Australasia, all offer different examples. As Doyle (1986: 45) puts it:

> Empire is a relationship, formal or informal, in which one state controls the effective political sovereignty of another political society. It can be achieved by force, by political collaboration, by economic, social, or cultural dependence. Imperialism is simply the process or policy of establishing or maintaining an empire.

Britain alone, at its height before the First World War, exercised a claim to a quarter of the planet's population. How could a small island in the North Sea have sustained such an expansive reign? The answer requires more than an audit of its military, especially naval, capacities. A better explanation rests in how the British Empire administered its imperial rule through 'varying constitutional and political arrangements' across a range of territories, and which were 'connected by a diverse set of strategic, cultural or historical links, rather than by allegiance to Crown or mother country' alone (Krieger, 2009: 590). One outcome of this was that even after decolonisation the implications of these 'interconnections lived on and in some ways intensified' (ibid.: 191).

POST OR PRESENT?

The concept of post-colonialism takes in a number of debates but principally turns on the interaction between political and cultural relationships forged, first, during colonialism and observed, second, in the aftermath of decolonisation. This is why the appellation 'post' can be misleading, for the challenge that post-colonial inquiry presents is not anchored in what happened *after* decolonisation, but instead on the form and content of colonialism, and its subsequent (indeed contemporary) implications.

Ashcroft et al. (1995: 2) thus maintain that 'all post-colonial societies are still subject in one way or another to overt or subtle forms of neo-colonial domination, and independence has not solved this problem'. In support of this view they point to the repositories of elites that were created or elevated under colonialism, and who have renewed and reproduced themselves following independence. This is alongside how social cleavages and hierarchies constructed during colonialism have blossomed instead of being deconstructed. Each of these examples relate to the internal legacies of given colonial relations, to which we can add the external legacies of political and economic exploitation that continue to hinder opportunities for development. As a concept, therefore, there is a continuing dialogue between colonialism and post-colonialism, one that foregrounds

> issues of power and significance, and even of timing [e.g. why did some Western powers come to prominence at certain times] ... technologies of

production and social control, of centres and margins: of metropolitan hubs like London and Paris, and peripheries and margins – like the colonies. (Hawley, 2011: 195)

Knowing how one feature connects to the other, however, rests on understanding the relationship between knowledge, representation and politics.

POLITICS, CULTURE OR BOTH?

There is a tendency to think of post-colonialism as a ubiquitous term, for it spans 'a remarkably heterogeneous set of subject positions, professional fields, and critical enterprises' (Slemon, 1995: 45). But what precisely does it have between its intellectual cross-hairs? Two important issues that it focuses on are, first, institutions (e.g. government departments and administrative bureaucracies) and, second, what we might call the semiotic field (e.g. discourse and text). How post-colonial theorists understand the interaction between the two is crucial but by no means straightforward. As Said (1994: 5) has argued:

> It is difficult to connect these different realms, to show the involvement of culture with expanding empires, to make observations about art that preserve its unique endowments and at the same time map its affiliation, but, I submit, we must attempt this, and set the art in the global, earthly context. Territory and possessions are at stake, geography and power. Everything about human history is rooted in the earth, which has meant that ... people have planned to have more territory ... At some very basic level, imperialism means thinking about, settling on, controlling land you do not possess, that is distant, that is lived on and owned by others.

One attempt to bring the cultural and political together may be found in *Masks of Conquest: Literary Study and the British Rule in India*, where Viswanathan (1995 [1989]) argues that the teaching of English literature in colonial India facilitated the entrenchment of a colonial social order. Namely, that 'the strategy of locating authority in these texts all but effaced the sordid history of colonialist expropriation, material exploitation, and class and race oppression behind European world dominance. Making the Englishman known to the natives through the products of his mental labour served a valuable purpose in that it removed him from the plane of ongoing colonialist activity ... and deactualised and diffused his material presence in the process. (Viswanathan, 1995: 436)

What Viswanathan is maintaining is that there was a relationship in colonial India, and on one we ought to focus, between knowledge production and power, which to some extent takes us back to the hierarchies of **race** discussed earlier. This is a thesis that is heavily informed by that of Edward Said's discussion of Orientalism but it is not the only way of configuring the relationship between coloniser and colonised. For, in related scholarship in the post-colonial canon, Bhabha (1994) tries to point to 'a constant intellectual, political and psychic negotiation between the colonizing and the colonized subject positions, so that variable hybrid moods, conditions and products emerge overtime ... shaping unstable – and always different – postcolonial conditions' (McLennan, 2006: 85).

ADDRESSING OR IGNORING THE POST-COLONIAL?

The academic study of **race** and **ethnicity** has been shaped by forces of knowledge construction historically meshed in 'the cultural mechanisms for the expression of colonial ideas and values' (Back and Solomos, 2009: 324). Yet there has clearly been a critical treatment of **race** and **racialisation**, amongst other concepts, in social science inquiry. Does this therefore mean that the social sciences have reconstructed themselves in the face of post-colonial challenges? Not so according to Bhambra (2007: 873) who, drawing on Holmwood (cited in Bhambra), distinguishes between the 'social' and the 'system' to argue that while the former has been receptive to particular critical readings, this has left intact general systems of thought. In her view this helps to explain how the social sciences have protected 'core categories of analysis from any reconstruction of what such recognition would entail' (ibid.).

So while there has been a surface-level reconstruction it has not penetrated the depths of our prevailing modes of thought and inquiry, one implication being that 'social theory elaborated within the confines of Western modernity' (Venn, 2003: 3) retains its ethnocentric anchorage. The objective of this complaint is not to devalue Western social theory. It is instead to seek an understanding of its relationship to colonialism, and the ways in which 'they are already deeply implicated within each other' (Young, 1992: 243). As Young continues:

> European thought since the Renaissance would be unthinkable without impact of colonialism as the history of the world since the Renaissance would be inconceivable without the effects of Europeanization. So it is not an issue of removing colonial thinking from European thought, of purging it... It is rather a question of repositioning European systems of knowledge so as to demonstrate the long history of their operation as the effect of their colonial other, a reversal captured in Fanon's observation: 'Europe is literally the creation of the Third World.' (Ibid.)

Recognising this as a matter of historical record would be a profound success for post-colonial critique, for it could begin to disrupt the binary narrative of the West and rest, progress and slowgress, in a manner that might 'open up to more pluralistic and cross-civilisational conceptions of society which are less ethnocentric and more suitable to meet global challenges' (Salvatore, 2013: 12).

REFERENCES

Ashcroft, B., Griffith, G. and Tiffin, H. (1995) *The Postcolonial Studies Reader*. London: Routledge.

Back, L. and Solomos, J. (2009) *Theories of Race and Racism*. London: Routledge.

Bhabha, H. (1994) *The Location of Culture*. London: Routledge.

Bhambra, G. K. (2007) 'Sociology and postcolonialism: another "missing" revolution?', *Sociology*, 41 (5): 871–84.

Doyle, M. (1986) *Empires*. Ithaca: Cornell University Press.

Hawley, J. C. (2011) 'The bittersweet taste of exile, as muse', in M. David and J. Munoz-Basols (eds) *Defining and R-Defining Diaspora*. Oxford: Interdisciplinary Press.

Krieger, J. (2009) 'After empire', in M. Fliners, A. Gamble, C. Hay and M. Kenny (eds) *The Oxford Handbook of British Politics*. New York: Oxford University Press.

McLennan, G. (2006) *Sociological Cultural Studies: Reflexivity and Positivity in the Human Sciences*. Basingstoke: Palgrave.

Said, E. (1994) *Culture and Imperialism*. London: Vintage.

Salvatore, A. (2013) 'The sociology of Islam: precedents and perspectives', *Sociology of Islam*, 1 (1): 7–13.

Slemon, S. (1995) 'Unsettling the Empire: resistance theory for the Second World War', in B. Ashcroft, G. Griffith and H. Tiffin (eds) *The Postcolonial Studies Reader*. London: Routledge.

Todorov, T. (1982) *The Conquest of America*. New York: Harper Perennial.

Turner, B. (2007) 'New and old xenophobia: the crisis of liberal multiculturalism', in S. Akbarzadeh and F. Mansouri (eds) *Islam and Political Violence – Muslim Diaspora and Radicalism in the West*. London: I.B. Taurus.

Venn, C. (2003) *The Postcolonial Challenge*. London: Sage.

Viswanathan, G. (1995) 'The beginnings of the English literary tradition in India', in B. Ashcroft, G. Griffith and H. Tiffin (1995) *The Postcolonial Studies Reader*. London: Routledge.

Young, R. (1992) 'Colonialism and humanism', in J. Donald and A. Rattansi (eds) *'Race', Culture and Difference*. London: Sage.

Race

> The idea of race as an objective or 'real' category is a myth. Instead it is widely accepted that race is a social construction that nonetheless has very real implications and outcomes. The idea of race has played a central role in shaping world history and continues to bear enormous relevance across contemporary societies.

The *idea* of race often makes for a dynamic *category*. That is to say racial categories have changed across the social and political contexts in which they are found (instead of being permanently fixed across any given society or throughout a society's history). For example, in his study of what the idea of race means in America, Omi (2001: 244) concludes that its expression 'has been and probably always will be fluid and subject to multiple determinations. Race cannot be seen simply as an objective fact, nor treated as an independent variable.' This is one reason why the idea of race as *objectively* real is today frequently derided as a myth (in the title of a book by Montagu (1942), it is in fact *Man's Most*

Dangerous Myth). Many academics therefore tend to treat it under erasure by presenting it in inverted commas in order to indicate that we are referring to a socially constructed category, based upon a problematic idea, instead of something that is self-evidently real in the world. Even those who do not repeat this practice agree with the thrust of the argument. This critical consensus, however, is relatively recent because for much of modernity race was deemed to be very real indeed.

HISTORY AND CATEGORISATION

As with other terms such as **ethnicity** and **nation**, **race** has an older pedigree than its modern usage may imply. In pre-modern societies for example, Christian symbolism portrayed 'white' as synonymous with purity, which in turn was contrasted with 'black' impurity. Yet a precise content to 'race' was at best ambiguous, and was certainly distinct to how it later became known (Banton, 1977). Amongst others, Michael Biddis (1979: 11) has charted the change in the meaning of race and observes that:

> Before 1800 race was used generally as a rough synonym for 'lineage'. But over the first half of the 19th race assumed an additional sense that seemed, initially, tighter and more scientific. This usage was evident, at its simplest, in the growing conviction that there were a finite number of basic human types, each embodying a package of fixed and mental traits whose permanence could only be eroded by mixture with other stocks.

So there is here a historical evolution that needs to be understood; namely, how and in what ways in the periods following colonial encounters between the European and non-European populations, say from the late fifteenth and sixteenth centuries onwards, did race begin to assume a powerful categorising role? This is an important context because the category was ascendant during a period in which an unprecedented magnitude of entirely new populations entered European consciousness (Gilroy, 1993). How this difference was understood and explained varied. For example, as well as making recourse to science, by the time the Atlantic slave trade was well under way, Christian theologians would seek religious justification from the Bible for hierarchies between **whiteness** and **blackness** as they were mapped onto colonised populations. This they did by pointing to the story of Canaan (Son of Ham) in the Book of Genesis (9:18–27), which told of a punishment to Canaan of servitude and blackness. This was important, as Garner (2011: 13) reminds us, because

> the frame of reference for educated Europeans until the Enlightenment was one in which: (i) the dominant idea about origins was that everyone was descended from Adam and Eve (*monogenisis*), and signs on the body were read as judgements of God, (ii) the idea of separate origins (*polygenesis*) was a minority one among biblical scholars, and responded to the obvious physical diversity of the human race.

Historically, therefore, racial classifications have been a reflection of prevailing power relations; and just as with theology, so it was the case with science. Walton and Caliendo (2011: 3) remind us of how in 1684 François Bernier, a French scientist, identified four groups of humans as 'Far Easterners', 'Europeans', 'blacks' and 'Lapps'. Developments in modes of classification were further coupled to what was understood as advancements in scientific inquiry, and so in 1775 five types of races were put forward by the German 'physiologist' Johann Friedrich Blumenbach. These comprised 'Caucasians' (Whites), 'Mongolians' (East Asians), 'Malayans' (South Asians), 'Negroids' (Black Africans) and 'Americans' (First Nations). Indeed, 'by the nineteenth century, there were dedicated searches for a universal definition of race that would be applicable across time and geographic location. Scientists went to work measuring bones and craniums in an attempt to justify racial distinctions on the basis of biology' (Walton and Caliendo, 2011: 4), the consensus being that physical appearance was an indication of something deeper, commonly reflecting cultural development and advancement.

A BIOLOGICAL CATEGORY

Some of the best-known work from this period sought to give the idea of race a deeper content by mixing science with a revisionist theology, and this mixture finds expression in the work of Robert Knox's (1850) *Races of Men* and Comte Author de Gobineau's (1853) *Essay on the Inequality of Men*. Others from this period, such as Pieter Camper and Franz Joseph Gall, measured facial angles as indications of what they perceived to be 'stature', 'beauty' and 'intelligence'. Such works both reflected and contributed to a mid-nineteenth-century concept of race that made four interrelated truth claims. First, both the physical appearance and social behaviour of individuals was an unalterable expression of biological type. So your race combined two categories which might describe both your appearance and your character, to serve as your social identity. Second, cultural variation was determined by differences in biological type, the former reducible to the latter. Third, biological variation was the origin of conflict between individuals and nations, both within societies but also in terms of what we would today understand as international relations. Fourth, races were endowed with different capacities according to a hierarchy, which meant some were inherently superior to others.

While comical from contemporary perspectives, this racial science was far from benign and would later give way to racial engineering in the eugenics movement, the selective 'breeding' of some humans and 'out-breeding' of others, in ways that included the Nazi aspiration for a 'master race' and the mass exterminations of human populations who did not correspond to an idealised 'Aryan' vision (see **antisemitism**). At the time, racial science went hand in hand with nineteenth-century social Darwinism, especially in the work of Herbert Spencer, who insisted that 'lesser' races ought to be dominated by advanced European counterparts. Much of this discourse informed and provided intellectual justification for the scramble for Africa and other colonial domination and exploitation by European powers. Indeed, some of the horrors of the Nazi death camps had earlier been trialled in Germany's African colonies with little outcry from other European powers (see **post-colonialism**). Of course Darwin himself was much more concerned with the dynamic process of biological change and adaptation, and in fact the logic of Darwinian Theory is that Europeans and Africans are intimately related (since human life began in Africa).

Having established all of this, it is striking that until 2003 medical reports were catalogued in PubMed/MEDLINE and in the Surgeon-General's Index Catalogue using nineteenth-century racial categories of Caucasoid, Mongoloid, Negroid and Austroloid. In one respect this is not surprising because race is often viewed as self-evident in cellular differences, that is, physiological variations such as skin colour or body forms, which are elevated to serve as a racial marker. Despite trying, however, science has been unable to persuasively link physical differences to variations in ability or intelligence or very much else, not least because phenotype, hair textures, and body forms vary – often dramatically – within populations of people designated to one race as much as between them.

This is no less the case with new scientific developments in genetics and especially the Human Genome Project, which has been identifying and mapping the sequence of human DNA since 1990. What this has proven is that while there can be a greater frequency of some sets of genes amongst some racial groups, those gene patterns are not limited to any given group. Indeed, current research supports Rose et al.'s (1985) argument that it is impossible to operationalise race in terms of human genetics. This can be illustrated if we think about how genetic inheritances interact with human environments, rather than focusing solely on race at a cellular level.

Gravlee (2009) illustrates this in one study where he makes a distinction between cultural and biological dimensions of skin colour in Puerto Rico. He does so in order to explore the relationship between biological and environmental indicators of race by, first, studying local ways of talking about skin colour and how skin colour shapes Puerto Ricans' exposure to racism and other social stresses. To measure this he developed a survey to compare blood pressure to the significance of colour, as local people understood colour. Strikingly, he found that the darker people were associated with higher blood pressure, in a way which supports the thesis that the *social aspects* of race, such as stigma and discrimination, can also have biological consequences – precisely an inversion of what is often presumed to be the case. The idea then of biologically distinct human races owes more to popular culture than consensus within science per se.

POST-RACE OR THE PARADOX OF RACE?

If there is no objective criterion with which to identify race, and that it is now scientifically accepted that variation amongst individuals within supposed racial groups is typically no greater than the variation between these supposed racial groups, how should we think about race? In many respects, this question takes us back to the beginning of the discussion and the observation made by Robert Miles (1982) that race is a belief and not a reality. He elaborates:

> I recognise that people do conceive of themselves and others as belonging to 'races' and do describe certain sorts of situations as being 'race-relations', but I am also arguing that these categories of everyday life cannot, automatically be taken up and employed analytically in an inquiry which aspires to objective or scientific status ... there is no scientific basis for categorising *Homo sapiens* into discrete races.

Some scholars have therefore argued that we should think in terms of the 'post-racial' nature of social and political conventions (cf. Parks and Hughey, 2011, and Kaplan, 2011), something perhaps symbolised in the election of a black US president. In this respect 'the wish for a post-racial politics is a powerful force, and rewards those that seem to carry its promise' (Vickerman, 2013: 8). As Goldberg (2013: 17) describes, this concept has an older pedigree:

> The notion of 'the postracial' can be traced genealogically and interactively to conceptions of 'colourblindedness' and the US civil rights movement, to anti-apartheid's 'nonracialism' (as articulated most clearly, for example, in the mid-1950s Freedom Charter), and broadly to the post World War II romance with racelessness.

Nonetheless, because of the history we have discussed, and despite the lack of a biological basis for the conception of distinct human races, race still wields enormous power as a social category. In many societies then the idea of race as a biological category remains a fixture in the popular discussion, or a basis for social action, a foundation of government policy and often a justification for distinctive treatment of one group over another. So some societies do take racial categories seriously, but equally some do for anti-racist reasons. In these cases it is widely known that races are not established natural forces but products of human perception and classification – they are social constructs. We invent categories of persons marked by certain characteristics, but these characteristics have no intrinsic meaning in or of themselves – on the contrary, we invest or give them meaning, and so in the process we create races.

To redress the traction of race, however, we sometimes encounter a paradox of race. That is to say that while race is a social construct it has real social and economic consequences. If we therefore choose to ignore race in public policy, we also ignore how racial categories are embedded in the routine practices of societies. So the paradox is that we need to recognise race to challenge it. In a number of countries this recognition has led to policies promoting equal access in such arenas as the labour market, education system and political **participation**, through state-level sponsorship of race equality agendas. These have often

race

117

comprised a broad remit spanning public and private institutions; recognition of *indirect* discrimination; imposition of public duties to monitor racial discrimination; and the creation of public bodies to promote these objectives. What this means is that while race has often been a means to deny equal dignity to those deemed as less developed, racial categories exist as social phenomena and are important because the assumption of race exists and has social implications. The researcher's task then is to remain vigilant to the social meanings attributed to such categories.

This is the inherent paradox in the use of race that researchers constantly grapple with, and it was probably first expressed by Huxley and Haddon (1935: 220) who argued against the use of race as a normative concept, though Du Bois (1939: 1) too argued that 'no scientific definition of race is possible'. In his words 'Race would seem to be a dynamic and not a static conception.' This has long been expressed in how many tend to utilise the term under erasure by presenting it in inverted commas so as to indicate that we are referring to a socially constructed category, based upon a problematic idea, instead of something that is self-evidently real in the world. Perhaps the simplest way to frame this is to say that social scientists tend to be interested in the dynamic and relational properties of race *as both a historical idea and social category*. Miles (quoted in Ashe and McGeever, 2011: 2017) describes this activity as differentiating between 'the idea of "race" and "race" as an analytical concept'. It is a sign of his continuing and profound influence that we invoke Miles in these debates even though he has not published new scholarship on this topic for many years (cf. Virdee, 2000; Kyriakides 2008; Meer, 2013). Either way, what we are left with is socio-historical understanding of race, something that is described by Omi and Winant (1986: 68–9) as a 'cluster concept' – a way of referring to a group of persons who share, and are thereby distinguished by, several properties 'disjunctively'.

REFERENCES

Ashe, S. D. and McGeever, B. F. (2011) 'Marxism, racism and the construction of "race" as a social and political relation: an interview with Professor Robert Miles', *Ethnic and Racial Studies*, 34 (12): 2009–26.

Banton, M. (1977) *The Idea of Race*. Boulder: Westview Press.

Biddis, M. (ed.) (1979) *Images of Race*. New York: Holmes & Meier.

Du Bois, W. E. B. (1939) *Black Folk Then and Now*. New York: Holt.

Garner, S. (2011) *Racisms*. London: Sage.

Gilroy, P. (1993) *The Black Atlantic*. London: Verso.

Gobineau, A. (Count Joseph Arthur de Gobineau) (1853) *The Inequality of Human Races*. Trans. A. Collins. London: William Heinemann.

Goldberg, D. T. (2013) 'The post racial contemporary', in N. Kappoor, V. Kalra and J. Rhodes, (eds) *The State of Race*. Basingstoke: Palgrave.

Gravlee, C. (2009) 'How race becomes biology: embodiment of social inequality', *American Journal of Physical Anthropology*, 139 (1): 47–57.

Huxley, J. and A. C. Haddon (1935) *We Europeans: A Survey of 'Racial' Problems*. London: Jonathan Cape.

Kaplan, R. H. (2011) *The Myth of Post-Racial America: Searching for Equality in the Age of Materialism*. Lanham: Rowman & Littlefield.

Knox, J. (1850) *The Races of Men: A Fragment*. London: Renshaw.

Kyriakides, C. (2008) 'Third way anti-racism: a contextual constructionist approach', *Ethnic and Racial Studies*, 31 (3): 592–610.

Meer, N. (2013) 'The role of race, culture and difference in antisemitism and Islamophobia', *Ethnic and Racial Studies*, 36 (3): 385–98.

Miles, R. (1982) *Racism and Migrant Labour*. Boston: Routledge & Kegan Paul.

Modood, T. (2005) *Multicultural Politics: Racism, Ethnicity and Muslims in Britain*. Edinburgh: Edinburgh University Press.

Montagu, A. (1942) *Man's Most Dangerous Myth: The Fallacy of Race*. New York: Columbia University Press.

Omi, M. (2001) 'The changing meaning of race', in N. Smelser, W. J. Wilson, and F. Mitchell (eds) *America Becoming: Racial Trends and Their Consequences*. Washington, DC: National Academy Press.

Omi, M. and H. Winant (1986) *Racial Formation in the United States*. New York: Routledge & Kegan Paul.

Parks, G. and Hughey, M. (2011) *The Obamas and a (Post-)Racial America?* Oxford: Oxford University Press.

Rose, S., Kamin, L. J. and Lewontin, R. (1985) *Not in Our Genes: Biology, Ideology and Human Nature*. New York: Pantheon Books.

Vickerman, M. (2013) *The Problem of Post-Racialism*. Basingstoke: Palgrave.

Virdee, S. (2000) 'A Marxist critique of black radical theories of trade-union racism', *Sociology*, 34 (3): 545–65.

Walton, C. F. and Caliendo, S. M. (2011) 'Origins of the concept of race', in S. M. Caliendo and C. D. McIlwain (eds) *The Routledge Companion to Race and Ethnicity*. London: Routledge.

Race Relations

Aace relations is a valuable concept in the study of race and ethnicity because its development and critique has forged a path for the field as a whole. Variously conceived as describing the outcomes of real or imagined relations, between groups with real or imagined differences, it has been a part of North American and British literatures and public policy in a manner that has shaped current approaches even where they depart from it.

In many respects race relations was the first contemporary social scientific concept concerned with the study of **race** and **ethnicity**, and although it is less frequently used as a core organising category in the field, it remains important to focus on for two reasons. First, it is not a static concept but instead has been dynamic and, throughout the twentieth century, has traversed different national contexts. Given this longevity it continues to find traction. Second, and perhaps more importantly, the intellectual and research trajectory of race relations has established a set of concerns, a problematic, which has structured the field. This means that subsequent concepts have directly and indirectly built upon (often by challenging) the inquiry forged by this concept.

ORIGINS

The idea of race relations has its intellectual origins in the work of sociologists and anthropologists who formed part of what has become known as the Chicago School. Working in the early part of the twentieth century, at a time of both European immigration to America as well as internal migration northward from the southern states, sociologists such as Robert Park (1920, 1925, 1950) set out to study race relations in terms of inter-group processes and 'adjustments', specifically with respect to conflicts over 'status-claims' and allocations of resources. One illustration of what this meant came in his examination of spatial segregation and immigration in the city of Chicago (as a site of urban immigrant settlement), which led Park (1980 [1914]: 36–7) to conclude that 'in our casual contact with aliens … it is the offensive rather than the pleasing traits that impress us. These impressions accumulate and reinforce natural prejudices.'

The emphasis here is clearly upon an interaction based on prejudice and conflict, and demonstrates an early attempt to analyse the ways in which race became a relevant social category where cultural and social meanings were attached to the physical traits of a particular social group. Informed by the broader aim of encouraging group contact and social interaction so that racial conflicts could be mediated or overcome, this perspective advanced a tradition of thinking about race in terms of social relations between people with different physical characteristics. To this Park (1950: 81) would come to give the name 'race relations' which he defined as 'the relations existing between peoples distinguished by marks of racial descent, particularly when these racial differences enter into the consciousness of the individuals and groups so distinguished'.

Park and the Chicago School have been criticised for characterising 'the race problem' as being one of 'integration and assimilation of minorities into the mainstream of a consensus based society' (van de Berge, 1967: 7). That is, Chicago School scholars squarely located the propensity for problems at the door of cultural differentiation. This is evident in what Park (1950: 82) describes as the 'cycle of race relations,' which moves between the four linear stages of 'contact, conflict, accommodation and assimilation'. The burden of adapting in this cycle is largely carried by the immigrant, wherein failure to assimilate into this 'functionalist consensus based view of society' is deemed regressive (van de Berge, 1967: 7). Equally, Park is sometimes read as endorsing the erroneous but commonly held view of **race** as biologically real (see **race**). Nevertheless, the formulations of the Chicago School were eagerly adopted elsewhere, not least in Britain.

BRITISH RACE RELATIONS

The initial post-war labour migration to Britain from former colonies in the West Indies and the Indian subcontinent between 1950 and 1962 was later accompanied by further immigration as families were unified. During this period a very British intellectual perspective on race relations was beginning to flourish through the work of Michael Banton (1955, 1959, 1967), Ruth Glass (1960), Shelia Patterson (1965) and E. J. B. Rose (1969), who were involved in the then government-sponsored Institute of Race Relations (IRR).

Their immediate impact was evident when the Labour government introduced measures to prevent discrimination against settled Commonwealth immigrants; it proceeded through the introduction of a Race Relations Act (1965). Why it was not, for example, called the 'Anti-Racism Act' is unclear (see **race**), but part of the rationale is undoubtedly the continuation of Park's assumption that the relations within which such discrimination occurs must be those of race relations.

Michael Banton's (1967) book, simply called *Race Relations*, is indicative of this way of thinking and serves as a useful illustration of how problematics in this period were being framed. This is because it shares with the Chicago School a view that race-relations research should be based upon two cornerstones: (i) patterns of interaction and (ii) cultural conflict. Where Banton deviated from the Chicago School, however, was in adopting a global *and* historical perspective to establish 'six orders of race relations'.

SIX ORDERS OF RACE RELATIONS

The first is called 'peripheral contact' and is characterised by interactions between groups that have little or no real influence upon one another, leading to minimal if any change in outlook within groups. An example of such peripheral contact can be found, according to Banton (1967: 68–76), in pygmies of the Ituri forest of central Africa, where goods are exchanged between groups by being left at a trading place independent of each group's settlement. Such interactions then require little intimate contact and mutual knowledge of customs, habits or language. The second order he termed as 'institutionalised contact', which is achieved when two 'societies' enter into contact 'principally through their outlying members' who live on the social boundaries of their respective groups, and so are most qualified to exchange with one another (ibid.: 99). This vanguard 'may occupy positions in both systems, and a new system of interrelationships develops between groups' (Kitano, 1980: 17). The third occurs as a result of 'acculturation' which, for Banton, heralds the 'coming together' or synthesis of different cultures. This might either encourage both groups to learn from one another or, depending upon the power relations between groups, lead to the cultural assimilation of the less-established group. The fourth order is described as an 'integrated order of race relations' (Banton, 1967: 73), in which racial distinctions are disregarded or only given 'minor' consideration. This facilitates interaction on most levels (including housing, schooling, employment, social relationships) so that 'race has less significance than the individual's occupation and his other status conferring roles'. After this there is the order of 'pluralism', which is understood by Banton as referring to 'separatism' amongst groups who live side by side, but wish to preserve their differences in culture, with a minimum of social interaction, integration or assimilation. Unlike the order of 'peripheral' contact, 'pluralism', for Banton, involves a knowing choice to self-segregate in order to maintain group boundaries, and is not a 'natural' but a forced order of race relations. His final order is that of 'domination', which can develop out of the idea of pluralism, when power relations between groups are radically unequal, and where, based upon racial criteria, members of one category are subordinate to the other and are responded to, not as individuals, but as representative of a category.

Banton's typology has been widely criticised from different quarters that seek to undermine both his starting point as well as the broader project of race relations as he sees it. With reference to the internal consistency of the schema itself, Philip Mason (1971: 60) has argued that Banton's definitions break down as soon as we begin to trace a progress from one race relations 'order' to another:

> Muslim rule in India was, I suppose, domination merging into pluralism, but what about British rule in India? This was, first, institutionalised contact with the servants of the East India Company acting as specialised go-betweens; later, it was paternalism perhaps the most perfect example of paternalism there has ever been. But it ended not in integration but in withdrawal. Again, in Rhodesia, in the Cape Colony, Mexico and Peru, there was first some control by the home government but independence meant ... something nearer to domination. It might, I suppose, be argued that the arrival of West Indians, Pakistanis, and Indians in Britain produced a situation in which acculturation was taking place, but with some doubt as to whether it would turn into integration or unequal pluralism.

Mason's point is that Banton ignores the 'shifting and intricate patterns' (ibid.) of minority–majority relations, because the lived experiences compromise his overly general formulations. This is not the most wounding of criticisms, however, and could equally be made against a great deal of theoretical work. A more important criticism is that Banton is so dependent upon anthropological work with tribal societies, that it encourages race-relations analysis to think of *racial differences in terms of cultural manifestations of difference* experienced in neat, bounded-units-as-groups. This is arguably why he mischaracterises the idea of 'pluralism', describing it as something closer to separate development or 'apartheid' (see **multiculturalism**). Third, Banton appears to conflate ideas of what constitutes a 'group' with 'society' and so is unable to comprehend the implication of different ethnic groups belonging to a single polity (see **ethnicity**).

This has obvious implications for the analysis of minorities in culturally heterogeneous societies and also for ideas of what constitutes a civic status amongst *the nation* in accounts of *the nation-state* (see **citizenship** and **nationalism**). Moreover, it is unclear as to what comprises a 'culture', a 'group' or a 'society' in his account above, since Banton uses these terms interchangeably and without clear definition.

STATUS AND PARTY

Some of these issues were addressed in John Rex's (1967, 1973, 1979, 1983, 1986) contribution to the race-relations problematic. Rex deviates from Banton in two important ways. First, he is keen to stress the socio-political rather than the anthropological context of 'relations' and, second, he adopts a less global and transhistorical approach:

> Race-relations ... refers to situations in which two or more groups with distinct identities and recognisable characteristics are forced by economic and political circumstances to live together in a society. Within this they refer to situations in which there is a high degree of conflict between the groups and in which ascriptive criteria are used to mark out the members of each group in order that one group may pursue one of a number of some hostile policies against the other. (Rex, 1983: 159–60)

For Rex, race relations ought to begin with an examination of 'structured conditions interacted with actors' definitions in such a way as to produce a racially structured social reality' (Solomos and Back, 1996: 6). In his empirical research on Sparkbrook (Rex and Moore, 1967) and Handsworth (Rex and Tomlinson, 1979) in Birmingham, Rex pursued this by investigating (i) the extent to which minorities had become incorporated into welfare-state institutions, and had access to housing, education and employment, and (ii) the impact of racial inequality upon 'the development of a "racialised" consciousness amongst both white and black working class' (Solomos, 1993: 20).

Although Rex was explicitly Weberian in his outlook, stressing the importance of status and party along with class, his conclusions from research in Birmingham draw upon a more Marxian style of class analysis in pointing to a 'truce' between the bourgeoisie and the white proletariat, furnished by the concessions gained through working-class movements such as trade unions and the Labour party. The minority ethnic groups of mainly Indians, Pakistanis, Bangladeshis (or Asians) and 'West-Indians', however, according to Rex and Tomlinson (1979), had fallen outside of these negotiations and remained subject to discrimination in all the areas that their white working-class counterparts had made gains (see **migration**).

What Rex and Tomlinson (1979) were keen to point to, however, was the emergence amongst West Indian and Asian communities of a type of 'underclass' which, for the former, would lead to 'a withdrawal from competition' and, for the latter, would result in 'a concentration on capital accumulation and social mobility' (Solomos, 1993: 20–1). Thus, they argued that 'the minorities were systematically at a disadvantage compared with their white peers and that, instead of identifying with working class culture, community and politics, they formed their own organisations and became effectively a separate, underprivileged class' (quoted in ibid.).

What remained integral to this tradition of race relations was of course that 'West Indian' and 'Asian' were the preferred terms to describe minority ethnic groups in Britain, and thus there were few concerted attempts to incorporate religion into these perspectives, either as an important component for self description or as a vehicle for the expression and mobilisation of collective minority interests. This is in spite of the activities of post-immigrant organisations and amalgamations such as the West Indian Standing Conference (WISC), Indian Workers' Association (IWA), and Pakistani Workers Association (PWA), which simultaneously mobilised against trade union and employment discrimination while seeking sponsorship and funding for churches, temples and mosques.

The absence of such a nuanced analysis was joined, at the time, by the charge from theorists of 'racialisation' that race-relations thinking failed to engage with any sustained analysis of questions of power, and was consequently 'atheoretical' and 'ahistorical'. Such charges have made race relations unfashionable and it is much less frequently utilised today – though there are remarkable similarities between its core prescriptions and those contained within ideas of community cohesion.

REFERENCES

Banton, M. (1955) *The Coloured Quarter: Negro Immigrants in an English City*. London: Jonathan Cape.

Banton, M. (1959) *White and Coloured: The Behaviour of British People Towards Coloured Immigrants*. New Brunswick: Rutgers University Press.

Banton, M. (1967) *Race Relations* London: Tavistock Publications.

Glass, R. (1960) *Newcomers: West Indians in London*. Michigan: University of Michigan.

Kitano, H. (1980) *Race Relations*. New Jersey: Prentice Hall.

Mason, P. (1970) *Race Relations*. London: Oxford University Press.

Mason, P. (1971) *Patterns of Dominance*. New York: Oxford University Press.

Park, R. (1980 [1914]) 'Racial assimilation in secondary groups with particular reference to the negro', *American Journal of Sociology*, 19: 606–23. Reproduced in T. F. Pettigrew (ed.) (1980) *The Sociology of Race Relations: Reflections and Reform*. New York: Free Press.

Park, R. (1920) 'Human migration and the marginal man', *American Journal of Sociology*, 33: 881–93.

Park, R. (1925) 'The city: suggestions for the investigation of human behaviour in the urban environment', in R. E. Park, E. W. Burgess and R. D. McKenzie (eds) *The City*. Chicago: University of Chicago Press.

Park, R. (1950) *Race and Culture*. Glencoe: Free Press.

Patterson, S. (1965) *Dark Strangers: A Sociological Study of the Absorption of a Recent West Indian Migrant Group in Brixton, South London*. London: Tavistock.

Patterson, S. (1969) *Immigration and Race Relations in Britain, 1960–1967*. London: Oxford University Press.

Rex, J. (1973) *Race, Colonialism and the City* . London: Routledge and Kegan Paul.

Rex, J. (1983) *Race-relations in Sociological Theory*. London: Routledge.

Rex, J. and Moore, R. (1967) *Race, Community and Conflict: A Study of Sparkbrook*. Oxford: Oxford University Press.

Rex, J. and Tomlinson, S. (1979) *Colonial Immigrants in a British City: A Class Analysis*. London: Routledge.

Rose, E. J. B. (1969) *Colour and Citizenship*. London: Institute for Race Relations.

Solomos, J. (1993) *Race and Racism in Britain*. Basingstoke: Macmillan Press.

Solomos, J. and Back, L. (1996) *Racism and Society*. Basingstoke: Macmillan Press.

van den Berge, P. L. (1967) *Race and Racism*. New York: Wiley.

Racialisation

> *Racialisation (or racialization) is an analytical concept that explores the dynamics of race and racism. Principally, this includes the social-historical processes through which people become members of racial groups. It is an addition to the concept of race in that it is more sensitive to explaining minority challenges to racial categories as well as how minorities can be cast in 'positive' racial terms.*

The *idea* of racialisation boasts a long pedigree, even if the term itself does not (Barot and Bird, 2001). Its early usage as a relatively benign analytical category is found in the work of Michael Banton, especially in his study of **race relations**. It was, however, Robert Miles (1982, 1984, 1986, 1988, 1989, 1993) who offered its most sustained and critical exposition. Different usages of racialisation converge, however, in understanding the processes by which racism creates racial difference, referring 'to the social and political processes whereby racially distinct groups are constituted' (Skinner, 2006: 460). An illustrative example is the recent historical experience of Irish migrants to the US, and the ways in which the 'Irish were frequently referred to as "niggers turned inside out"' while African Americans were termed 'smoked Irish' (Ignatiev, 1995: 41).

INTELLECTUAL PROVENANCES

An early idea of racialisation is described in the works of W. E. B. Du Bois (1868–1963) and Frantz Fanon (1925–61), each of whom intertwined psychological and social elements. In the former's case racialisation give rise to a sense of 'double consciousness' in which racial minorities (in his case African Americans) internalised the contempt of the majority and saw the world from two perspectives simultaneously – through their own eyes as well as how others saw them. In Fanon's case, racialisation was a European project which relieved colonisers of their guilt in seeking to convince both themselves – and non-European colonised peoples – that the latter were inferior and incapable of ruling themselves (sometimes referred to as 'The White Man's Burden', the title of a poem by the British Empire's celebrated writer Rudyard Kipling).

In Miles's (1989: 75) conception of racialisation he seeks to reflect the ways in which *racial processes* can attribute 'meaning to somatic characteristics' in a way that 'presumes a social psychological theory which explains the nature and dynamics of the process' (ibid.). This characterisation captures several of the core components of **antisemitism** and **Islamophobia**. As a Marxist, Miles anchored his conception of racialisation in an account of material relations, and an ideologically driven conflict born of the contradictory impulses inherent to circumscribed nationhood and labour migration (Miles, 1982: 170–3). What is important is that Miles never insisted that processes of racialisation must be premised upon a 'biological inherentism', which informed his resolve that scholars 'must not restrict the application of the concept of racialisation to situations where people distinguish one another by reference to skin colour' (ibid.: 121; see also the discussion of Miles in Modood (1996)). More specifically, he maintained that we should be studying the ways in which 'signifying processes' interact to 'construct differentiated social collectivities as races' (Miles, 1989: 79). To facilitate such inquiry, and because he recognised that the social dynamics of racism can in practice be mixed up with a host of different kinds of '-isms', such as nationalism and sexism and so forth, Miles (1989: 87) put forward a conceptualisation of 'racial articulations'. It has been argued elsewhere that this remains a valuable but overlooked formulation (see Modood, 2005: 14–18; Meer and Modood, 2010: 74–9).

HISTORICAL RACIALISATION

There is a longstanding methodological (and indeed philosophical) question as to whether 'the possession of a concept can predate the possession of a corresponding word' (Thomas, 2010: 1739). Without seeking to resolve this, if one is persuaded that language is both constitutive *and* reflective, we can see evidence of racialisation in the creation of racial categories through plantation slavery and Enlightenment-informed colonial encounters from the sixteenth century. Indeed, prior to this, both during the Spanish *Reconquista* and further back still, when Islam is first encountered in Europe, 'the Prophet Mohammed (with his Jewish parents and Nestorian/heretical teacher)' is embodied as a dark-skinned, satanic menace (Matar, 2009: 217). Racialisation then saturated cultural portrayals of religious minorities, endowing each with characteristics that offered 'reassurance that their difference could be easily identified by Christians' (Thomas, 2010: 1747).

In different ways both Nabil Matar (1999) and James Shapiro (1996) have provided a rich discussion of how ideas of *the* Moor and Jew featured in Elizabethan England, and in the period's most celebrated author we find illustrative depictions of each; namely, Shakespeare's characterisation of the tragically violent Othello, and the shrewd and sinister Shylock. While each are replete with redeeming qualities, and even by today's standards imbued with striking degrees of ambiguity, they nonetheless make sense as racialised affectations of their time.

In the case of the former, the moral panic over Moors in London is well documented. Popular depictions in which Muslims 'raged and lusted, killed their children or enslaved and brutalized Christians' (Matar, 2009: 219) were widely circulated. As Harris (2000: 35) reminds us, 'To Elizabethan Londoners the appearance and conduct of the Moors was a spectacle and an outrage, emphasizing the nature of the deep difference between themselves and their visitors, between their Queen and this "erring Barbarian"' (for more polysemic readings of the context of *Othello* see Lerner, 2000, and Soyinka, 2000). Thus, and complaining to the Lord Mayor of London that they were 'infidels, having no understanding of Christ or His Gospel', Queen Elizabeth expelled Turks from her realm (quoted in Jones, 1971: 20).

CONTEMPORARY RACIALISATION

This historical racialisation also has a contemporary cousin, as expressed by the celebrated novelist Martin Amis:

> They're also gaining on us demographically at a huge rate. A quarter of humanity now and by 2025 they'll be a third. Italy's down to 1.1 child per woman. We're just going to be outnumbered … There's a definite urge – don't you have it? – to say, 'The Muslim community will have to suffer until it gets its house in order.' What sort of suffering? Not letting them travel. Deportation – further down the road. Curtailing of freedoms. Strip-searching people who look like they're from the Middle East or from Pakistan. Discriminatory stuff, until it hurts the whole community and they start getting tough with their children. (Quoted in Dougary, 2006)

A number of key characteristics of racialisation are evident in Amis's statement. First, his attribution to all Muslims of pejorative group characteristics, specifically an irrational desire for violence. Second, the perpetuation of fears concerning a demographic challenge posed by Muslims to 'native' (non-Muslim) European populations. Third, the championing of discriminatory surveillance of people who 'appear' Muslim – 'strip-searching people who look like they're from the Middle East or from Pakistan' – on the grounds that there is an essential Muslim appearance and that it correlates with the risk of terrorism. Fourth, advocating a form of collective punishment according to which all Muslims must bear responsibility for the actions of the few (see **Islamophobia**). These are characteristic of a cluster of contemporary tropes.

POSITIVE RACIALISATION AND MODEL MINORITIES

As we have established, as long as racialisation does not need to be anchored in materialist conceptions of racism, what it facilitates is a focus on people, groups, and minorities who are the sites of racial inscriptions. What is no less relevant to this understanding is that racialisation so conceived provides us with a multi-directional (inclusive and exclusive) account. This connects to Tony Kushner's (2006: 211) argument that

> The racialisation processes in relation to the Jews have been in constant flux, pronounced often at time of crisis and less so in periods of greater stability. Moreover, it has been rare for *all* Jews to be racialised, or more accurately, for all Jews to be racialised negatively. It has been common, for example, to accept as 'one of us' what were perceived as westernized Jews as against the essentially 'oriental Jews' from the East.

In this manner racialisation can often divide minorities between *problem* and *model* groups. This is certainly reflected in spectacular 'events', such as international terrorism, but it also has relevance in more mundane debates. For example, in the US there are debates about the relationship between low African American IQ test scores compared with those of people with East Asian backgrounds. It is claimed that these and other alleged features, such as differences in family stability and aspiration for success, illustrate that there is an inherent quality to East Asian American communities that deems them to be considered a model group. These are contrasted positively against the qualities attributed to African American communities who are alleged to lack these features and so directly and indirectly disadvantage *themselves*. This is an argument that turns away from explanations in social structure and wider social relations, and turns on the capacity of individuals and communities.

INSTITUTIONAL RACISMS

Much of the discussion of racialisation has thus far suggested a relatively evident motive or source, be it individual attitude, prevailing stereotype, or indeed public policy. A politically contentious addition to this repertoire comes in with the idea of institutional racism (Murji, 2007). This concept was developed by the activist Stokely Carmichael (who later changed his name to Kwame Ture) and the political scientist Charles Hamilton in their book *Black Power*, where they described it in the following terms:

> Racism is both overt and covert. It takes two, closely related forms ... we call these individual racism and institutional racism. ... The second type is less overt, far more subtle, and less identifiable in terms of specific individuals committing these acts. But it is no less destructive of human life. The second type originates in the operation of established and respected forces in society, and thus receives far less condemnation than the first type. (Carmichael and Hamilton, 1967: 4)

Convention is the key here, to the extent that individual motives and objectives become much less relevant to the sustaining and proliferation of racialised outcomes. Carmichael and Hamilton were writing during a period of civil rights challenges to the American established practices that fell outside the letter of the law. For example, they argued that just because the American constitution guaranteed equal treatment as a citizen, this was far from honoured in various arenas of social and political life; not least in the treatment from police officers and the criminal justice system more broadly. Here they were not complaining about individuals who may or may not have been racist. Instead they argued that the criminal justice system had internalised and normalised a number of conventions that were not codified in a statute but instead were sanctioned by a prevailing cultural expectation that profoundly disadvantaged African Americans.

A word which relates to what is being described above is 'unwitting', and this is precisely how institutional racism came to be described in an inquiry into the London Metropolitan Police Service. This followed a long campaign by the parents of the black teenager Stephen Lawrence, who was murdered by a gang of white young men, and whose death was improperly investigated. In the official inquiry undertaken by Sir William Macpherson, and which came to be known as the Macpherson inquiry, the investigating judge found the police service guilty of 'unwitting racism', deemed an outcome of institutional racism, and so made a number of wide-ranging recommendations with a broad scope which then had implications outside the police force in a manner that related to the public sector more broadly. What is especially interesting is how a radically dissenting critique, in the form of black power activism, would give birth to a concept that would then become a commonsense (though not uncontested) feature of public discourse across the UK and beyond. As Scott and Marshall (quoted in Murji, 2007: 844) observe:

> In a remarkable episode in the history of ideas the concept of 'institutional racism' emerged in the context of a radical political struggle and the Black Power movement in the United States in the 1960s and then traversed three decades, two continents and the social class structure to be adopted by a member of the British nobility.

This is an interesting reading but it also limits anti-racist critique to peripheral arenas, and in so doing perhaps illustrates some of the challenges that the concept of racialisation more broadly faces in negotiating and achieving a greater salience (Meer and Nayak, 2013).

REFERENCES

Barot, R. and Bird, J. (2001) 'Racialisation: the genealogy and critique of a concept', *Ethnic and Racial Studies*, 21 (4): 601–18.

Carmichael, S. and Hamilton, C. V. (1967) *Black Power: The Politics of Liberation in America*. New York: Random House.

Dougary, G. (2006) 'The voice of experience', *The Times*. 17 September.

Harris, B. (2000) 'A portrait of a Moor', in C. M. S. Alexander and S. Wells (eds) *Shakespeare and Race*. Cambridge: Cambridge University Press.

Ignatiev, N. (1995) *How the Irish Became White*. New York: Routledge.

Jones, E. D. (1971) *The Elizabethan Image of Africa*. Charlottesville, VA: University Press of Virginia.

Kushner, T. (2006) 'Racialisation and "White European" Immigration to Britain', in K. Murji and J. Solomos (eds) *Racialisation: Studies in Theory and Practice*. Oxford: Oxford University Press.

Lerner, S. (2000) 'Wilhelm S and Shylock', in C. M. S. Alexander and S. Wells (eds) *Shakespeare and Race*. Cambridge: Cambridge University Press.

Macpherson Inquiry into the Matters Arising from the Death of Stephen Lawrence (1999) London: HMSO.

Matar, N. (2009) 'Britons and Muslims in the early modern period: from prejudice to a (theory of) toleration', *Patterns of Prejudice*, 43 (3/4): 213–32.

Meer, N. and Modood, T. (2010) 'The racialisation of Muslims', in A. K. Vakil and S. Sayyid (eds) *Thinking Through Islamophobia*. London: Hurst & Co.

Meer, N. and Nayak, A. (2013) 'Race, Racism and Contemporary Sociology', *Sociology*, DOI: 10.1177/0038038513501943.

Miles, R. (1982) *Racism and Migrant Labour*. London: Kegan Paul.

Miles, R. (1984) 'The riots of 1958: notes on the ideological construction of "race relations" as a political issue in Britain', *Immigrants & Minorities*, 3 (3): 252–75.

Miles, R. (1986) 'Labour migration, capital accumulation in western Europe since 1945', *Capital and Class*, 28 (1): 49–86.

Miles, R. (1988) 'Racism, Marxism and British politics', *Economy and Society*, 17 (3): 428–60.

Miles, R. (1989) *Racism*. London: Routledge.

Miles, R. (1993) *Racism After 'Race Relations'*. London: Routledge.

Modood, T. (1996) 'If races do not exist then what does? Racial categorisation and ethnic realities', in R. Barot (ed.) *The Racism Problematic: Contemporary Sociological Debates on Race and Ethnicity*. New York: Edwin Mullen Press.

Modood, T. (2005) *Multicultural Politics*. Edinburgh: Edinburgh University Press.

Murji, K. (2007) 'Sociological entanglements: institutional racism and beyond', *Sociology*, 41 (5): 843–55.

Shapiro, J. (1996) *Shakespeare and the Jews*. New York: Columbia University Press.

Skinner, D. (2006) 'Racialized Futures: Biologism and the Changing Politics of Identity', *Social Studies of Science*, 36 (3): 459–88.

Soyinka, W. (2000) 'Shakespeare and the living dramatist', in C. M. S. Alexander and S. Wells (eds) *Shakespeare and Race*. Cambridge: Cambridge University Press.

Thomas, J. M. (2010) 'The racial formation of medieval Jews: a challenge to the field', *Ethnic & Racial Studies*, 33 (10): 1737–55.

Recognition

> *The idea of recognition spans a range of phenomena, including the formation of individual psyches, the dynamics of political struggles and the nature of moral progress. In the fields of race and ethnicity it has become a cornerstone in debates about the best way to respond to people's desire to have their identities acknowledged.*

While sometimes conflated with related issues, especially concerning the politics of identity and difference, the politics of recognition has provided a distinctive and valuable perspective on the implications of a broad repertoire of sociological and political 'differences'. In the twenty or so years since the publication of Charles Taylor's essay 'The Politics of Recognition' (Taylor, 1992) and Axel Honneth's book *Kampf um Anerkennung* (Honneth, 1995), the concept of recognition has had a profound role in debates about **race** and **ethnicity**.

THE RANGE OF RECOGNITION

The idea of recognition has been employed not only as a normative concept of justice, but also as a means of understanding a range of phenomena, including the formation of individual psyches, the dynamics of political struggles, and the nature of moral progress (Seymour, 2010). As such, the politics of recognition has become a cornerstone in debates about the best way to respond to people's desire to have their cultural particularities acknowledged, and so has traversed a number of important issues: from the tension between individual freedom and group equality in multicultural societies, through the intersections between the multiple inequalities that permeate such societies, and the effects of recognition on individual psyche, to the nature of global justice. In short, the politics of recognition is characterised by lively debate about a range of important and topical issues (Thompson, 2006). The literature on recognition is therefore vast and overlapping, and so does not lend itself easily to categorisation into distinct bodies of thought. Nevertheless, it is possible to identify at least four 'traditions', albeit containing significant internal diversity and overlap.

PHENOMENOLOGY AND ETHICS

The first tradition may be traced to a Hegelian phenomenology that continues to compete with Kantian ethics in numerous areas of contemporary political theory. This is most obviously found in Hegel's *Phenomenology of Spirit* (especially in his allegory of the master and the slave) where he outlines a series of conflicts and their dialectical relationship to different kinds of recognition (Hegel, 1977). In examining reciprocal relations of power, he attempts to 'lift the veil' and reveal the processes mediating the transformation of a consciousness from dependence to one of self-consciousness and independence. Through this exercise, Hegel draws our attention to the manner in which a Hobbesian war of 'all against all' is unable to maintain the very individuality or independence upon which it is premised. This, indeed, stems from a question Hegel posed to himself, namely: how does a person come to conceive themselves as an independent being and/or when do they become conscious of themselves as such? In his answer, Hegel describes a process of objectification that suggests that we must first identify – outside of ourselves – some 'purposive intelligence' from which it follows that others are required to establish our own independent selfhood or identity. This is perhaps best captured in Binder's (1989: 1435) suggestion that Hegel attempted to show that 'freedom [has] to be conceived as some form of association rather than independence; and that it [has] to be mediated by politics rather than defended from politics'.

Besides stressing the primacy of the political, and through his 'devastating critique of the ideal of independence' (Binder, 1989: 1437), Binder's account traces back to Hegel the intellectual foundations of modern communitarian conceptions of freedom. This appropriation is observable in a number of places, including Michael Sandel's seminal critique of John Rawls and the work of Michael Walzer more broadly, but perhaps most obviously bears fruit in Charles Taylor's *Sources of the Self* where he states:

> I am a self only in relation to certain interlocutors: in one way in relation to their conversation partners who were essential to my achieving self-definition; in another in relation to those who are now crucial to continuing my grasp of languages of self understanding – and of course these classes overlap. A self exists only within what I call 'webs of interlocution'. (Taylor, 1989: 36)

CRITICAL THEORY AND RACE

Taylor's caution against a kind of modernist individualism re-emerges in a second tradition of recognition. While this is also informed by Hegel, it harnesses in addition influences from an idea of critical theory that is strongly oriented by vectors of emancipation and alienation. Here the issue of recognition comes to rest 'as a common denominator among many different struggles in which individuals and groups are engaged' (Seymour, 2010: 2). More precisely, it prioritises the notion of an 'original intersubjectivity of humankind' understood as communicative relations between embodied subjects, something that it fears is lost in a time when individualism or atomism has dominated the domain of ethics (Honneth, 1995: 29).

It would be uncontroversial to state that the chief exponent of this tradition has been Axel Honneth (1995), who anchors an account of recognition in a particular social ontology. This he partly retrieves from the early Hegel, to emphasise psychological features of recognition in the terms of self-confidence, self-respect and self-esteem – each of which he regards as a necessary condition of self-realisation. In other words, these three features jointly constitute the 'process of realizing . . . one's self-chosen life-goals' (1995: 174). This freedom from coercion facilitates the pursuit of a flourishing human life in a manner that forges links between the psychological, social and political realms (see Thompson, 2006). In this tradition we might also include certain approaches to social theories of **race** and **racialisation**, characterised in very different ways by Franz Fanon's *Black Skin, White Masks* (1967) and bell hooks' *Ain't I a Woman?* (1981). The kinds of recognition and misrecognition being referred to here were arguably first elaborated by W. E. B. Du Bois' description (in *The Souls of Black Folk*) of the 'peculiar sensation' common to African Americans comprising

> a double-consciousness, this sense of always looking at one's self through the eyes of others, of measuring one's soul by the tape of a world that looks on in amused contempt and pity. ... [T]hat nameless prejudice that leaps beyond all this, he stands helpless, dismayed and well-nigh speechless; before that personal disrespect and mockery, the ridicule and systematic humiliation, the distortion of fact and wanton license of fancy, the cynical ignoring of the better and boisterous welcoming of the worse, the all pervading desire to inculcate disdain ... (1999 [1903]: 15)

As Honneth puts it, experiencing such a denial of rational autonomy may lead those who Du Bois is describing to encounter 'social death' (1995: 135). In other words, such people may cease to be regarded – and may cease to regard themselves – as citizens who may rightly play an active part in the life of their political community (see Meer, 2011). In Du Bois' account, he is trying to reconcile the strivings for group recognition with more traditional accounts of **citizenship**, in an effort to identify a **multiculturalism** in which cultural and/or moral diversity would be considered an asset. Thus it has been argued elsewhere that Du Bois bequeaths to us a normative concept that can be appropriated in debates over multiculturalism, beginning with a rebuttal of narrow preferences for territorial and cultural congruencies (Meer, 2010: Chapter 2). As such, Du Bois perhaps bridges the second and third tradition of recognition scholarship, relating to what May et al. (2004) refer to as the 'multicultural turn' in social and political theory.

MULTICULTURAL TURNS

The multicultural turn is responding to the view that citizenship achieved through individual rights alone, based upon blindness to difference, can satisfy principles of social justice. What multicultural theories share in common is that they seek to go beyond the protection of the basic civil and political rights guaranteed to all individuals in a liberal-democratic state, and to extend some level of public recognition and support for ethno-cultural and ethno-religious minorities in order that they may maintain and express their distinctive identities (Banting and Kymlicka, 2006: 1). There must therefore be some change in what minorities are being asked to adapt to; hence Modood, for example, insists that 'when new groups enter a society, there has to be some education and refinement of . . . sensitivities in the light of changing circumstances and the specific vulnerabilities of new entrants' (2006: 61).

This view was powerfully elaborated by Iris Marion Young (1990) in her landmark *Justice and the Politics of Difference*. For Young, the requirement to assimilate is unjust because it 'always implies coming to the game after it is already begun, after the rules and standards have been set, and having to prove oneself accordingly' (1990: 165). Focusing upon individuals ignores how citizenship already fails to treat people equally, or where 'blindness to group difference disadvantages groups whose experience, culture and socialized capacities differ from those of privileged groups' (ibid.). Not being attentive to group differences can, therefore, lead to a form of oppression in itself and/or can contribute to further oppression because the injuries suffered from prejudice are not merely a result of the overt hostility from the majority, but also arise from minority invisibility in not being recognised or represented as a legitimate constituent of society. On this view, the most important orientation of a democratic state is not about granting various group rights or accommodations but about providing the 'mechanisms for the effective recognition and representation of the distinct voices and perspectives of those of its constituent groups that are oppressed or disadvantaged' (Young, 1990: 184).

DEMOCRATIC PARTICIPATION

In this way, Young can be seen also as a major exponent of the final 'tradition' that deserves note here, which allies questions of recognition with an approach of deliberative democracy. This 'democratic turn' represents a relatively new area of scholarship on recognition that has gained increasing prominence in recent years given the problems many have perceived with forms of group representation favoured by 'strong' versions of multiculturalism (see, for instance, Squires, 1999; Young, 2000; Benhabib, 2002). While differing in their accounts, what these perspectives share in common is the view that

> which individuals, minorities, and nations are to be recognized as members of a political association is not to be determined by a pre-emptive theory of recognition of any kind, but, rather, on the grounds of which claims for recognition can withstand the test of the exchange of public reasons. (Tully, 2004: 858)

Thus these accounts are oriented not towards the goals of struggles for recognition (that is, the specific accommodations of minorities or forms of recognition), but rather to the avenues through which struggles over recognition are carried out. The aim is to reconfigure the public sphere in such a way as to enable marginalised individuals and groups to themselves be the agents of the norms they are subject to. The intellectual roots here are informed directly by the Critical Theorists' demand for the intersubjective grounding of principles of justice in communicative reason, for instance found in Habermas's (1990) account. However, while earlier models of deliberative politics have been open to criticism that they are overly concerned with consensus and 'impartiality', which inevitably comes at the expense of those who are marginalised within society, more recent accounts expand the scope of democratic expression and deliberation. These include forms of non-formal democratic expression such as forms of cultural resistance and reinvention and different logics of reason-giving, greeting, storytelling and embedded speech (Young, 1997; Benhabib, 2002; Deveaux, 2003; Martineau and Squires, 2012).

THE EMERGENCE OF *MIS*RECOGNITION

In recent times we have also seen the advance of the concept of misrecognition, which departs from recognition in the following two respects. First, it allows us to register how minority religions provide politically valid categories of identity-related claims-making (alongside those of ethnic and cultural minority identities) in a manner that departs from an earlier kind of **secularism** in recognition theory. It points to the possibility of full civic membership irrespective of the particularity of one's ethnic or religious background; where, appropriating an argument by Habermas (2005), the burden of 'translating' religious reasons into common language is not placed on the shoulders of religious citizens alone and is not used to disqualify their contributions to public discourse. Second, because the concept of misrecognition adopts a more contextually sensitive approach we are better able to focus squarely on the specific strands and processes that make up political mobilisations. Misrecognition is not therefore a 'master concept', but an empirically sensitive instrument. In this respect misrecognition does not seek to bridge across psychological–political phenomena, but instead emerges as a civic–political concept in debates about formal participation and representation (see Dobbernack et al., 2014). Misrecognition can therefore play a central role in a politics of multicultural equality and equal respect. While this includes the issue of subjectivities, it also focuses attention on articulations of political relationships and not just matters of individual esteem or psychology.

REFERENCES

Banting, K. and Kymlicka, W. (eds) (2006) *Multiculturalism and the Welfare State*. Oxford: Oxford University Press.

Benhabib, S. (2002) *The Claims of Culture: Equality and Diversity in the Global Era*. Princeton: Princeton University Press.

Binder, G. (1989) 'Mastery, slavery and emancipation', *Cardozo Law Review*, 10: 1435–80.

Deveaux, M. (2003) 'A deliberative approach to conflicts of culture', *Political Theory*, 31 (6): 780–807.

Dobbernack, J., Meer, N. and Modood, T. (2014) 'Misrecognition and political participation: the case of the "Muslim vote" in the 2010 General Election', *British Journal of Politics and International Relations*. DOI: 10.1111/1467-856X.12033.

Du Bois, W.E.B. (1999 [1903]) *The Souls of Black Folk*, ed. H. L. Gates and T. H. Oliver. New York: Norton.

Fanon, F. (1967) *Black Skin, White Masks*, trans. C. L. Markmann. New York: Grove.

Habermas, J. (1990) *The Philosophical Discourse of Modernity: Twelve Lectures*, trans. F. Lawrence. Cambridge, MA: MIT Press.

Habermas, J. (2005) 'Concluding comments on empirical approaches to deliberative politics', *Acta Politica*, 40: 384–92.

Hegel, G. (1977) *Phenomenology of Spirit*, trans. A. V. Miller. Oxford: Oxford University Press.

Honneth, A. (1995) *The Struggle for Recognition: The Social Grammar of Moral Conflicts*, trans. J. Anderson. Cambridge: Polity.

hooks, b. (1981) *Ain't I a Woman? Black Women and Feminism*. Boston: South End Press.

Kymlicka, W. (1995) *Multicultural Citizenship: A Liberal Theory of Minority Rights*. Oxford: Oxford University Press.

Martineau, W. and Squires, J. (2012) 'Addressing the "dismal disconnection": normative theory, empirical inquiry and dialogic research', *Political Studies*, 60: 523–28.

May, S., Modood, T. and Squires, J. (2004) 'Ethnicity, nationalism and minority rights: charting the disciplinary debates', in S. May, T. Modood and J. Squires (eds) *Ethnicity, Nationalism and Minority Rights*. Cambridge: Cambridge University Press.

Meer, N. (2010) *Citizenship, Identity and the Politics of Multiculturalism: The Rise of Muslim Consciousness*. Basingstoke: Palgrave Macmillan.

Meer, N. (2011) 'Overcoming the injuries of double consciousness', in S. Thompson and M. Yar (eds) *The Politics of Misrecognition*. Farnham: Ashgate.

recognition

Modood, T. (2006) 'Obstacles to multicultural integration', *International Migration*, 44 (5): 51–62.

Phillips, A. and Saharso, S. (2008) 'The rights of women and the crisis of multiculturalism', *Ethnicities*, 8 (3): 291–301.

Seymour, M. (ed.) (2010) *The Plural States of Recognition*. Basingstoke: Palgrave Macmillan.

Squires, J. (1999) *Gender in Political Theory*. Cambridge: Polity Press.

Taylor, C. (1989) *Sources of the Self: The Making of the Modern Identity*. Cambridge: Cambridge University Press.

Taylor, C. (1992) *Multiculturalism and the Politics of Recognition*. Princeton: Princeton University Press.

Thompson, S. (2006) *The Political Theory of Recognition: A Critical Introduction*. Cambridge: Polity.

Tully, J. (2004) 'Approaches to recognition, power, and dialogue', *Political Theory*, 32 (6): 855–62.

Young, I. M. (1990) *Justice and the Politics of Difference*. Princeton: Princeton University Press.

Young, I. M. (1997) 'Difference as a resource for democratic communication', in J. Bohman and W. Rehg (eds) *Deliberative Democracy: Essays on Reason and Politics*. Cambridge, MA: MIT Press.

Young, I. M. (2000) *Inclusion and Democracy*. Oxford: Oxford University Press.

Secularism

> *Secularism can both describe and theorise a process or a preferred position, spanning the nature of religious and non-religious knowledge – analyses into the form, frequency and content of religious practice, and political concerns over how (and in what ways) religion is configured in relation to arenas of public life.*

The concept of secularism has acquired its meaning(s) over a set of long and complicated historical processes that are by no means at an end, and in recent years has been part of wider 'political revitalisation' concerning debates about religion in the public sphere (Habermas, 2007). Some trace the provenance of secularism to a desire to distinguish the rationale for public philosophies from religious injunction, an early expression of which may be found in the work of the Moorish philosopher Ibn Rushd (known in the West as Averroes). Others trace secularism to Latin traditions in which 'the adjective "secular" (from the Latin *saecularis*)' in the thirteenth century distinguished 'clergy living and working in the wider medieval world from "religious" clergy who lived in monastic seclusion' (Keane, 2002: 6). Either way, while the term secularism may owe its provenance to such conventions, there is no simple summary of what the concept of secularism has come to mean today.

CONTEMPORARY MEANINGS

In contemporary usage, secularism is a concept that can traverse metaphysical questions concerning the nature (and status) of religious and non-religious knowledge; sociological analyses into the form, frequency and content of religious practice; as well as political concerns over how (and in what ways) religion is configured in relation to arenas of public life (and the state more broadly). As such it is not always 'entirely clear what is meant by secularism' (Taylor, 1998: 31). One prevailing tendency, as Asad (2003: 13) describes, is to speak about a 'secular imaginary' where the vernacular landscape is populated by differentiating categories; for example 'spirituality' in contrast to 'scientific', 'sacred' in contrast to 'profane', and 'worship' in contrast to 'democracy', and so on.

SECULARISATION

If we steer away from live epistemological disputes for the moment (e.g. those concerning the nature of truth, divine knowledge and the robust challenge to that status) debates about secularism have often been related to the alleged trend or social processes of 'secularisation'. This maintains that the social role of religion has been undermined by at least three forces of modernisation, which may be described as: (1) social differentiation (increasing individualised role allocation within and across social systems), (2) societalisation (the cultivation of social – that is, non-religious – spaces), and (3) rationalisation (the critical revision of inherited traditions – what Weber (1967) would have termed traditional rationality) (Wallis and Bruce, 1994: 8). These comprise a set of empirical claims about the declining significance of religion which continue to be tested, disputed and revised on the basis of research data (Kaufmann et al., 2011). As Modood (2013: 169) summarises, however, there is a great deal of space *in between* the claims of religious decline where religion continues to flourish:

> To illustrate with the British case, church attendance of at least once a month has steadily declined from about 20 per cent in 1983 to about 15 per cent in 2008 amongst white people and with each younger age cohort (Voas and Crokett 2005; BRIN 2011; Kaufman, Goujon and Skirbekk, 2012). This is not to say that religion has disappeared or is about to, but for many it has become more in the form of 'belief without belonging' (Davie 1994), or spirituality (Heelas and Woodhead 2005), or 'implicit religion' (Bailey 1997). For example, while belief in a personal God has gone down from over 40 per cent in the middle of the twentieth century to less than 30 per cent by its end, belief in a spirit or life source has remained steady at around 35–40 per cent, and belief in a soul has actually increased from less than 60 per cent in the early 1980s to an additional 5–10 per cent today. (BRIN, 2011)

More broadly, the secularisation thesis is underpinned by a Western conception of religion that relies on 'a vocabulary related to Protestant Christianity as the prototype religion ... with levels of sincerity and interior conviction being the yardstick by which the more or less religious is measured – rather than levels of praxis or experience' (Johansen, 2013: 6). As we will come to later, this 'Christo-centric' tendency has led some to conclude that 'the dominant ideas about secu-larization ... were simply mistaken or mischievous' (Beckford, 2012: 3), perhaps because it has encouraged binary thinking (e.g. between secular/religious, mod-ern/pre-modern) which limits and reduces analysis to 'evidence of "a failure to modernize properly"' (Asad, 2003: 217). In addition, what the secularisation thesis has been less attentive to are some of the controversies concerning the relationship between state and society, and which return us to a focus on secular-*ism* rather then secular*isation*.

SECULARISM AND STATE

It has been argued that as a political position, some degree of secularism is viewed as 'a necessary pre-condition for the *exercise of democracy*', where 'democracy is government that is ultimately based on the idea of "the sovereignty of the people"' (Sayyid, 2009: 188). Sovereignty can of course be configured in different ways, but a useful summary of the development of this argument may be gained from Keane (2002: 7), and is worth quoting at length because it charts how secularism as a political position has been forged throughout modernity, and especially in relation to the development of nation-states.

> Secularisation requires that citizens be emancipated from the state and the ecclesiastical *diktat*; they should be free to believe or to worship according to their conscience and ethical judgements. Render unto Caesar the things that are Caesar's means: Caesar has no direct business in things that are not Caesar's. In practice, such religion freedom presupposes an open and toler-ant civil society within whose plural structures and space citizens are required to avoid bitterness and bloodletting so that each can enjoy freedom from others' dogmatic beliefs and codes of conduct. In other words, secu-larity requires citizens to agree to disagree about religion, which ultimately means, as Voltaire spelled out in *Traite sur la Tolerance* (1973), that there must be at least some civil spaces in which religion plays little or no role at all. (Keane, 2002: 7)

There is a lot here, and against the picture of this ideal-type – in which people willingly defer authority to an emancipating state, enjoy equally participatory civil space, and are protected through mutual tolerance – how democracies go about configuring such matters varies. In Europe, some states and religion have a formally *established* relationship which means that religion has a degree of legal and symbolic **recognition**, for example the Lutheran church in Denmark or Anglicanism in England. This contrasts with other conceptions of church–state relations; the US formally maintains a 'wall of separation', while separation in France has integral to it a certain idea of *laïcité*. The latter marks the political defeat of the Catholic Church (epitomised by the 1905 Act on the separation of church and state), which sought to push matters of faith and religion out of politics and policy into the private sphere. Some have argued that this settlement is illustrative of a wider tendency where secularism has been more 'aggressive' towards Catholicism than it has to Protestantism (Keru, 2009). Others have argued that the most appropriate frame through which to register such settlements can be understood as a distinction between 'radical' and 'moderate' modes of secularism (Modood, 1994, 2007).

In Modood's latter distinction, even while a state may be formally established, its civil society and mode of political organisation and practice are often secular, but in a manner that does not marginalise or vilify religion. Moreover, where there has not been complete separation, questions of parity and equal treatment present opportunities for new religious groups to seek what the formally recognised religion has. For example, in spite of maintaining a Protestant established Church of England, the superior status of the dominant Anglican Church has consistently been challenged by other Christian denominations, not least in Scotland where the religious majority is not Anglican but Presbyterian, and this has led to the creation of a Church of Scotland. Elsewhere in England and Wales, Protestant nonconformists have been vocal; and issues such as education have in the past encouraged many of these groups to 'stand out against the state for giving every opportunity to the Church of England to proselytize through the education system' (Skinner, 2002: 174). The cycles of nineteenth-century **migration** from Ireland to London, Glasgow and the north of England have considerably expanded the Roman Catholic presence in Britain. The turn of the twentieth century, meanwhile, witnessed the arrival of destitute Jewish migrants fleeing both the pogroms and economic deprivation in Russia (Meer and Noorani, 2008). Both groups have suffered racial discrimination and civil disabilities on the basis of their religious affiliation but in due course have come to enjoy some of the benefits initially associated with establishment settlement. This includes initially allowing the Catholic Church to set up schools alongside the state and then, in the 1944 Education Act, to opt into the state sector and receive similar provisions to those enjoyed by members of the established Church – a provision which was soon extended to other religious groups, notably Jewish minorities. Muslims, Hindus and Sikhs, who are the most recent and numerically significant addition to this plurality, have established themselves with varying degrees of success as part of the 'new cultural landscape' of Britain (Peach and Gale, 2003: 487–8).

One of the things this highlights is how, given its long and varied pedigree, secularism has relatively recently come to join a repertoire of concepts concerned with the study of race and ethnicity. That is to say that it has become relevant due to the salience of ethnic minority religious identities.

SECULARISM AND AUTONOMY

An arena in which religious identities and secularism have generated much debate has been education, and not least where this turns on the issue of autonomy. As we note in Keane (2002), in secularist thought, one of the most commonly held views of education is that it should cultivate the development of rational and moral autonomy. This position opposes all forms of religious schooling and strenuously argues that all autonomy-supporting societies *must* guard children from 'believers who wish to impose on them a non-autonomous conception of the good life' (White, 1990: 105). This is a central argument that is illustrated by the Humanist Philosophers' Group (HPG) (2001: 10), and it begins by charging faith schooling with 'indoctrination', characterised as limiting the autonomy of a child by implanting beliefs that neither empirical evidence nor rational argument might change. The implication of their broader perspective is that young people in religious schools are denied the opportunity to develop the competencies in making informed choices, specifically because such schools are predisposed to indoctrinate and proselytise. There are two very interesting and equally challenging responses to this argument.

The first begins by rejecting the *a priori* assumption that faith schools are necessarily out to indoctrinate and proselytise. This might potentially be viewed as an example of what McLaughlin (1992: 123) once described as one of *multiple* launch pads for autonomy, in which 'a legitimate starting point is from the basis of experience of a particular "world view" or cultural identity; a substantiality of belief, practice or value, as in (say) a certain sort of religious school'. This offers a more contextual comprehension of how a child's autonomy may be developed and is more comfortable with competing conceptions of education amongst different cultural constituencies within a **multicultural** context that is not hostile to the wishes of religious peoples. In this way it is plausible that faith schools could adopt an educational approach that is *relatively* neutral (Meer, 2009).

Children have to accept many things on trust in order eventually to progress to autonomy (and possibly reject those things later); religion could be treated no differently. The HPG rightly questions, however, whether indoctrination can ever be avoided, given the difficulty of teaching religion in such a way that children can grasp and appreciate it in any depth without necessarily accepting beliefs which are difficult, if not impossible, to revise or reject when one has reached an adult age. This is an important criticism which leads to a related debate about the nature of religious knowledge and the conditions under which it can be acquired. Espousing a 'Christian perspective' on this matter, Ahdar and Leigh (2005: 233) argue that religion:

> … need not involve hampering a child's autonomy regarding critical and independent thought. It is just that critical thought and the *right* use of reason ought to be undertaken from a base of faith first … This is autonomy, but not of the Enlightenment kind … The radically autonomous self cannot live the good life; reason is tainted by the Fall. We are back to a Christian paradox again. It is not a matter of fostering self-esteem but rather self-denial; lose oneself in God to truly find oneself.

What we should take from Ahdar and Leigh (2005) is the implication that unless a child acquires this knowledge at a sufficient depth of understanding, they will not be able to exercise valid consent anyway, so that from their perspective the goal of autonomy is already thwarted. Accordingly, the curriculum and environment of the religious school may be essential to the achievement of a level of understanding that makes informed consent (and thus autonomy) possible.

The second potential response to the charge of indoctrination has two parts to it but begins by making a relational argument which contests the assumption that secular schools can avoid indoctrination by being a-religious. For example, Aronson and Shapiro (1996) point to a sleight of hand in non-religious contexts where certain possibilities or options are only made available to adults because they have prioritised them to the exclusion of many others in childhood, such as developing skills in certain arts or sports. As Ahdar and Leigh (2005: 228) argue: 'The rigorous keeping of a child's future to maximize adult opportunities would, in effect, deprive the child of the possibility of becoming a professional ballerina or footballer. Could it not be argued that the same applies to religious upbringing?' A much stronger objection is made by Grace (2002: 14). However, who laments the degree of bad faith central to the charge of indoctrination against religious faith schools. This is because secular schools are not themselves ideologically free zones, and carry 'their own ideological assumptions about the human person, the ideal society' which 'characteristically permeate the ethos and culture of state-provided secular schools and form a crucial part of the "hidden curriculum"'.

This then rehearses the objection to viewing non-religious schooling as a neutral enterprise, and simultaneously invites the different and equally broad objection to modes of political integration that try to separate public and private spheres in some liberal-civic convention.

SECULARISM AND CITIZENSHIP

There is a genuine and problematic tension between espousing an HPG-type of radical autonomy argument against religious education while, simultaneously, holding the reasonable view that the education process should contribute to the cultivation of future 'good citizens'. This is epitomised by the state's interest in ascribing and inculcating liberal or civic virtues, a point famously set out in Rawls' (1993: 199) formulation as follows:

> Political liberalism ... will ask that children's education will include such things as knowledge of their constitutional and civic rights so that, for example, they know that liberty of conscience exists in their society and that apostasy is not a legal crime ... Moreover, their education should also prepare them to be fully cooperating members of society and enable them to be self supporting; it should also encourage the political virtues so that they want to honour the fair terms of social cooperation in their relations with the rest of society.

This sort of thinking has permeated the drive in Britain for citizenship education (QCA, 1998), which entails a clear desire to engender a particular 'civic morality' amongst young people through imparting knowledge of political functions and historic practices. This begs the question, however, as to when the impetus behind wanting to form 'good' or 'active' citizens will actually conflict with the growing autonomy of the child. To put it another way: 'At what point should he or she be free to reject liberalism and make mature, illiberal, choices of his or her own?' (Ahdar and Leigh, 2005: 231). The implication being that to make the objection to faith schools on the basis that they might curtail the child's autonomy can be inconsistent, given that the inculcation of any sort of civic morality can be subject to the same charge. Another way of stating it here would be to insist that education for citizenship must necessarily proceed with attention to the social, through the reciprocal balance of rights and responsibilities that confer upon its recipients a civic status that affords those pupils equal opportunity, dignity and confidence.

This embedded reading of autonomy can be interpreted as a critique of liberal perfectionist thinking that is often too abstracted from the lived relations and real world contexts in which Muslim schools seek to operate. It is an argument made by Parekh (2000: 202–3) when he contests the civic assimilationist approach, based upon a neat separation of public and private spheres, on the grounds that such a view fails to take account of institutions that encompass both.

POST-SECULARISM

The resilience of religion in posing the above questions (and others) has in recent years informed a growing body of literature which has set itself the task of charting the emergence of 'post-secularism'. Variously conceived as a challenge to a '200-year old hegemony of the secular Enlightenment over public discourse' (Neuhaus, 1982: 309), that 'something has happened' (Johansen, 2013: 4), post-secularism is in one respect at least criticism of the secularisation thesis discussed at the outset, in so far as the decline of religious practice was perhaps not best measured by the decline of attendance at Christian worship. As Johansen (2013: 10–11) describes:

> The term postsecular is here an attempt to grasp that the prediction about a steady decline in the role of religion as an inevitable consequence of processes of modernization has turned out to be untenable, forcing the secular states to reckon with the endurance of religion and thus to re-think their self perception.

In this regard post-secularism 'doesn't express a sudden increase in religiosity, after its epochal decrease, but rather a change in the mindset of those who, previously felt justified in considering religion to be moribund' (de Vries and Sullivan, 2006: 2–3). Yet this is more than a dispute over data and the interpretation of data. In many respects it takes us back to the discussion of multiple autonomies, or at least multiple launch-pads for autonomy that are not reducible to a model of the individualistic and Enlightenment-sanctioned ideas of legitimate reason. In this and other respects, post-secularism is potentially especially relevant to the salience of ethnic minority religious identities. The question that remains is whether this is best conceived as a departure *beyond* (as in post-)secularism, or instead a continuation of a kind of 'principled pragmatism' that has made liberal secularism so resilient over the years (Levey, 2009: 24).

REFERENCES

Ahdar, R. and Leigh, I. (2005) *Religious Freedom in the Liberal State*. New York: Oxford University Press.

Aronson, R.J. and Shapiro, J. (1996) 'Democratic autonomy and religious freedom: A critique of Wisconsin v. Yoder', in I. Shapiro, and R. Hardin (eds) *Political Order: NOMOS XXXVIII*. New York: New York University Press.

Asad, T. (2003) *Formations of the Secular: Christianity, Islam, Modernity*. Stanford: Stanford University Press.

Beckford, J. (2012) 'SSSR Presidential Address: public religions and the postsecular: critical reflections', *Journal for the Scientific Study of Religion*, 51 (1): 1–19.

British Religion In Numbers (BRIN) 'Census 2011 – Any other religion'. Availabe here: http://www.brin.ac.uk/news/2012/census-2011-any-other-religion/ (viewed 20 January 2014).

de Vries, H. and Sullivan, L. E. (2006) (eds) *Political Theologies: Public Religions in a Post-secular World*. New York: Fordham University Press.

Grace, G. (2002) *Catholic Schools: Misssion, Markets and Morality*. London: Falmer Press.

Guttman, A. (ed.) (1994) *Multiculturalism: Examining the Politics of Recognition*. Princeton: Princeton University Press.

Habermas, J. (2007) 'Religion in the public sphere', public lecture available at www.sandiego.edu (viewed 14 December 2012).

Humanist Philosophers' Group (HPG) (2001) *Religious Schools: The Case Against*. London: British Humanist Association.

Johansen, B. S. (2013) 'Post-secular sociology – modes, possibilities and challenges', *Approaching Religion*, 3 (1): 4–15.

Kaufmann, E., Goujon, A. and Skirbekk, V. (2011) 'The end of secularization in Europe? A socio-demographic perspective', *Sociology of Religion*, 73 (1): 69–91.

Keane, J. (2002) 'Secularism?', *Political Quarterly*, 71 (1): 5–19.

Keru, A. (2009) *Secularism and State Policy toward Religion: The United States, France and Turkey*. Cambridge: Cambridge University Press.

Levey, G. B. (2009) 'Secularism and religion in a multicultural age', in G. B. Levey and T. Modood (eds) *Secularism, Religion and Multicultural Citizenship*. Cambridge: Cambridge University Press.

McLaughlin, T. H. (1992) 'The ethics of separate schools', in *Ethics, Ethnicity and Education*, ed. M. Leicester and M. Taylor. London: Kegan Paul.

Meer, N. (2009) 'Identity articulations, mobilisation and autonomy in the movement for Muslim schools in Britain', *Race, Ethnicity and Education*, 12 (3): 379–98.

Meer, N. and Noorani, T. (2008) 'A sociological comparison of anti-Semitism and anti-Muslim sentiment.', *Sociological Review*, 56 (2): 195–219.

Modood, T. (1994) 'Establishment, multiculturalism and British citizenship', *Political Quarterly*, 65(1). Available online at: http://onlinelibrary.wiley.com/doi/10.1111/j.1467-923X.1994.tb00390.x/abstract.

Modood, T. (2007) *Multiculturalism: A Civic Idea*. London: Polity Press.

Modood, T. (2013) *Multiculturalism: A Civic Idea*. London: Polity Press, 2nd edn.

Neuhaus, R. J. (1982) 'Educational diversity in post-secular America', *Religious Education*, 77 (3): 309–20.

Parekh, B. (2000) *Rethinking Multiculturalism: Cultural Diversity and Political Theory*. New York: Palgrave.

Peach, C. and Gale, C. (2003) 'Muslims, Hindus, and Sikhs in the new religious landscape of England', *Geographical Review*, 93 (4): 487–8.

Qualifications Curriculum Authority (QCA) (1998) 'Education for citizenship and the teaching of democracy in schools – final report of the Advisory Group on Citizenship'. London: HMSO.

Rawls, J. (1993) *Political Liberalism*. New York: Columbia University Press.

Sayyid, S. (2009) 'Contemporary politics of secularism', in G. Levey and T. Modood (eds) *Secularism, Religion and Multicultural Citizenship*. Cambridge: Cambridge University Press.

Skinner, G. (2002) 'Religious pluralism and school provision in Britain', *Intercultural Education*, 13: 171–81.

Taylor, C. (1998) 'Modes of secularism', in R. Bharghava (ed.) *Secularism and its Critics*. New Delhi: Oxford University Press.

Wallis, R. and Bruce, S. (1994) 'Secularization: the orthodox model', in S. Bruce (ed.) *Religion and Modernization: Soiologists and Historians Debate the Secularization Thesis*. Oxford: Oxford University Press.

Weber, M. (1967) 'Science as a vocation', in H. H. Gerth and C. Wright Mills (eds) *From Max Weber: Essays in Sociology*. New York: Oxford University Press.

White, J. (1990) *Education and the Good Life*. London: Kogan Page.

Super-diversity

> *Super-diversity has emerged both as a description of empirical phenomena (the proliferation of diversities) and as a normative claim that increased pluralism (both associated with migration as well as wider changes in our understanding of identity categories) requires social scientists and policy makers to develop approaches to register this.*

As the discussion of **migration** details, around 3 per cent of the world's population (around 214 million people) are deemed to be living outside their country of origin or birth (see also **transnationalism**). While some will naturally take up residency or **citizenship** in their adopted countries, others will be prevented from doing so, or will not seek to for other reasons discussed in this book. Such diversity is not necessarily novel, however, and so joins that associated with more longstanding patterns of movement and settlement that is often many generations old. Metropolitan centres are in particular the sites of such diversity, illustrated by how in London, arguably one of the most diverse cities in the world, there are now 'people from some 179 countries' including 'populations numbering over 10,000 respectively from each of no less than forty-four countries; there are populations of over 5,000 from a further twelve countries' (Vertovec, 2007: 1029). The symbolism this allows can be very powerfully promoted as a form of **recognition**. In the successful London 2012 Olympic bid, for example, the idea of 'the world in one city' was deemed 'a key reason why London, one of the most multicultural cities in the world, was chosen to host the Games' (LOCOG, 2012: 1).

A CONCEPT FOR OUR TIME?

While few Western states have cities as culturally diverse as London, they nonetheless have others that boast myriad patterns of diversity born of post-colonial and migrant labour, as well as the kinds of circular **migration** and sub-state **nationalism** considered earlier. What the proponents of super-diversity wish to register is that in addition to this cultural diversity, prevailing identity categories are challenged by forces of intense diversity. Chief amongst the implications is **intersectionality**, which seeks to modify the view that identity categories, and the web of social relations in which they are located, can be understood through single identities (see also **interculturalism**).

Thus Vertovec (2007: 1025) has argued 'it is not enough to see diversity only in terms of ethnicity, as is regularly the case both in social science and the wider public sphere'. On the contrary, in an age of *subject* as well as cultural diversity – in which it is accepted that people may simultaneously be affected by a number of important social identities *in addition to ethnicity* – some have made the bolder claim that

> the very categorisations that we often rely on ... no longer seem to be able to tell us much about who people are, what lives they lead, who they identify with or what services they need from government and society. And the tick-box approach to identity seems to be missing out on growing numbers of people who fall outside or across standard classifications. (Fanshawe and Sriskandarajah, 2010: 5)

Super-diversity enters the frame here, through the argument that 'people do not identify around single identities and feel conflicted allegiances (if any allegiance at all) to predefined groups; activism around particular "strands" seems irrelevant to many people and may not even be that effective in addressing the true causes of inequality' (ibid.).

This is a bold statement. As the discussion of **ethnicity** elaborates, people do identify with groups, though they do so in a number of ways that may give emphasis to different subjective boundaries (which in turn may shift over time). Is it then plausible to suggest that group identities based around 'standard identifications' have withered away? Less persuasively, in their reading, Fanshawe and Sriskandarajah (2010) appear to retreat to a one-dimensional 'choice'-based view of social identity which, to take one example, ignores how processes of **racialisation** may create new groups not necessarily chosen by minorities themselves (though of course how a minority will respond to this process of racialisation will vary).

Super-diversity understood as the undermining of group categories, therefore, appears analytically simplistic, and so shares something with one way in which **interculturalism** is contrasted with **multiculturalism** (as a mode of political critique). No less important, however, is how some proponents of super-diversity understand and use the concept as a means to add to and broaden out (instead of eliminate) the role of standard group categories.

WHAT IS NEW THAT IS 'SUPER'?

Much in the concept of super-diversity hangs on what is in addition to *multiplicities* of ethnic categories, religions, languages and other cultural differences: those things conceived as novel that super-diversity is seeking to explain. Cantle (2012: 32), for example, maintains that 'super-diversity means that nation-states, as well as communities and individuals, have begun to think about their identity in much more nuanced and complex ways'. To help us understand this view, Vertovec (2007) identifies some core features from which three related characteristics stand out. Each, however, is arguably more about registering and taking seriously the implications of diversity rather than pointing to qualitatively new experiences of it. One, for example, turns on the following possibilities for methodological innovation:

> Research on super-diversity could encourage new techniques in quantitatively testing the relation between multiple variables and in qualitatively undertaking ethnographic exercises that are multi-sited (considering different localities and spaces within a given locality) and multi-group (defined in terms of the variable convergence of ethnicity, status, gender and other criteria of super-diversity). (Vertovec, 2007: 1046)

So a concern with super-diversity would be more responsive to space, multiplicity and flux than conventional registers of diversity. A question this raises is whether this is best pursued by *replacing* or *refining* existing approaches. For example, in one study of capturing super-diversity in survey and census questionnaires, the author concluded that the most viable approach would necessarily be 'paired with the traditional categorical question [e.g. what is your ethnic group?] *only where space on the schedule and human resources permit*' (Aspinall, 2012: 362, emphasis added). Notwithstanding the methodological discussion, being sensitive to super-diversity has implications for policy formulation in a number of respects – not least minority participation in governance regimes. Here channels of engagement and representation need to be alert to 'smaller, less (or not at all) organized groups' in addition to larger and well-established associations (Vertovec, 2007: 1047). This includes the danger that 'new immigrant populations are effectively "squeezed out" of local representative structures and consequently wield little power or influence' (Robinson and Reeve 2005: 35, quoted in Vertovec, 2007: 1047). It is a question of participation – which spans a range of sectors 'concerning the assessment of needs, planning, budgeting, commissioning of services, identification of partners for collaboration and gaining a broader appreciation of diverse experiences in order generally to inform debate' (ibid.: 1048).

What is striking, however, is that such an activity requires a significant governmental commitment that is facilitated by a wider political consensus that needs to be supportive of the kinds of comprehensive examination of super-diversity's implications for such things as public services. To a large extent, then, this depends on a deepening and enriching commitment to many of the core features of **multiculturalism**, for example tailoring social policies for the needs of different groups more precisely, and targeting them more accurately. This would allow agencies to take into consideration the

> 'plurality of affiliations' (recognizing multiple identifications and axes of differentiation, only some of which concern ethnicity), 'the coexistence of cohesion and separateness' (especially when one bears in mind a stratification of rights and benefits around immigrant categories), and – in the light of enhanced transnational practices – the fact that 'migrant communities, just as the settled population, can "cohere" to different social worlds and communities simultaneously'. (Zetter et al., 2005: 14, 19, quoted in Vertovec, 2007: 149)

In this way we might then understand super-diversity as allied concept to multiculturalism, as something that builds on the successes of the latter, expanding its public policy infrastructure on such things as equal opportunities and anti-discrimination, culturally specific **health** care provision and educational inclusion, as well as in valid data collection and public **recognition**. The important point is that super-diversity does not dispense with the challenges that **multiculturalism** is geared to tackling, but adds to them.

REFERENCES

Aspinall, P. (2012) 'Answer formats in British census and survey ethnicity questions: does open response better capture "superdiversity"?, *Sociology*, 46 (2): 254–364.

Cantle, T. (2012) *Interculturalism: A New Era of Cohesion and Diversity*. Basingstoke: Palgrave.

Fanshawe, S. and Sriskandarajah, D. (2010) *You Can't Put Me in a Box: Super-diversity and the End of Identity Politics in Britain*. London: IPPR.

LOCOG (2012) 'Diversity and inclusion', http://www.london2012.com/about-us/jobs/working-for-locog/diversity-and-inclusion/ (viewed 5 January 2012).

Vertovec, S. (2007) 'Super-diversity and its implications', *Ethnic and Racial Studies*, 30 (6): 1024–54.

Transnationalism

Transnationalism describes processes that sustain and re-invent post-migration communities with real and imagined points of origin, something made more frequent by late modern technologies and cross-national political spaces, each of which can work at once within and outside national registers.

The concept of transnationalism is closely linked to that of **migration** and related questions of **multiculturalism**, **interculturalism** and **super-diversity** – amongst others – surveyed elsewhere in this book. It is perhaps most closely associated with that of **diaspora**, though a useful distinction put forward by Faist (2010: 21) is a good means of separating the two. For the latter, a 'diaspora approaches focus on aspects of collective identity, while transnational approaches take their cue from cross-border mobility'. More succinctly put, 'transnational communities encompass diasporas, but not all transnational communities are diasporas' (ibid.).

Its meaning is very much signalled in its name, in so far as it refers to a phenomenon that in some way *transcends* the national, or more precisely is able to *span* two or more sites of the national. This it does in ways that herald important and often unintended consequences for a range of issues, from the configuration of families to the nature and content of political participation. So there are very material components of transnationalism that are sustained by cross-national traffic of different kinds of *capital*. These include, amongst others, 'money remittances, commercial ties between the country of origin, branches of religious organization that are set up in the new country, second homes in the country of origin, and mutual visits' (Van Oudenhoven et al., 2006: 647). Yet transnationalism is about more than 'things'.

THE CONDITIONS OF TRANSNATIONALISM

In the words of the political anthropologist Steve Vertovec (1999: 1–2, emphasis added):

> Transnationalism describes a *condition* in which, despite great distances and notwithstanding the presence of international borders (and all the laws, regulations and national narratives they represent), certain kinds of relationships have been globally intensified and now take place paradoxically in a planet-spanning yet common – however virtual – arena of activity.

The important points to take from this are that we are interested not only in numbers and motivations of people, but also the enduring relationships they give to, as well as the material and emotional 'things' that these shape and are shaped by. This is what is meant by 'condition'. More precisely, Vertovec usefully distinguishes between six conceptualisations of social and political (and economic) phenomena that come under its scope. These can usefully help organise our thinking here.

SOCIAL MORPHOLOGY AND CONSCIOUSNESS

The first he describes as *social morphology*, not least the ways in which transnationalism has facilitated the proliferation of ethnic **diasporas**, especially the ways in which these have been able to connect three tendencies. These comprise:

'(a) globally dispersed yet collectively self-identified ethnic groups, (b) the territorial states and contexts where such groups reside, and (c) the homeland states and contexts whence they or their forebears came' (Vertovec, 1999: 3).

These properties are very much in evidence in the Italian anthropologist Ambrosini's (2012: 276) argument, that transnational migratory processes are much more than a 'circulatory phenomena, where protagonists move, have homes, activities, and maybe even political citizenship in two (or more) different countries'. He elaborates:

> It is possible to be involved in transnational activities and relationships even without physically moving. The concept of a 'transnational social field' (Levitt and Glick Schiller 2004) expresses this wider idea of the different ways in which transnational dynamism can be articulated. Networks, activities and the ways of life of the involved migrants include both origin and destination societies, although in different ways and with variable intensity, and their lives cross national borders in one way or another, bringing both societies within a single social field (Glick Schiller et al. 1992). Country borders seem to be not only lines of separation but also fluid, moving spaces, crossed by multiple transits and connections (Morokvasic 2004, Sassen 2008). (Ibid.)

Diasporas of course vary and are not novel, and so by definition neither is this feature of transnationalism. But *as an imagined community* diasporas frequently challenge conventional accounts of group membership because they are not solely premised on concentrated settlements. On the contrary, they draw on a second feature of transnationalism. This concerns *types of consciousness* in which 'the awareness of multi-locality stimulates the desire to connect oneself with others, both "here" and "there" who share the same "routes" and "roots"' (Vertovec, 1999: 5). The kinds of things being described here find visible expression in solidarity movements or the ways in which what might be termed 'homeland politics' can be decantered into new social contexts. It is also the case that types of consciousness can imagine (from a distance) highly pressing issues in 'the homeland' in ways that depart from how they may be conceived there.

CULTURAL REPRODUCTION AND CAPITAL

The third of Vertovec's features of transnationalism turns on *modes of cultural reproduction*, in so far as 'transnationalism is often associated with a fluidity of constructed styles, social institutions and everyday practices' (1999: 6). Related concepts are here numerous, and include those such as 'hybridity', 'syncretism' and 'creolisation', amongst others, each of which is especially found in aesthetic forms in the creative spheres and industries, but also in a certain kind of urban mélange and multiculture (Gilroy, 2004). It is self-evident therefore why this mode of transnationalism hinges on processes of cultural interpenetration and intermingling.

The fourth is as an avenue of capital, which is important because 'the little players who comprise the bulk of transnational communities are making an ever greater impact' (Vertovec, 1999: 8). This returns us to the discussion of **migration**, and the finding that remittances amount to considerably more than development aid. Conversely, as Mitchell (1997: 106) observes, 'the interest of the state in attracting the investments of wealthy transmigrants widens the possibilities for new kinds of national narratives and understandings'. For example, world cities, and especially London and New York, have in recent years attracted a strata of migrant that occupies some of the highest positions in international commerce and industry.

POLITICAL ENGAGEMENT AND SPACE

A fifth feature of transnationalism is as a site of political engagement, not least as 'social movements which occupy a particular political space ... but not necessarily a *specific* space' (Mandaville, 2003: 16). In his account, Vertovec ties this to Beck's (1998: 29) reading that 'there is a new dialectic of global and local questions which do not fit into national politics, and only in a transnational framework can they be properly posed, debated and resolved'. Illustrations here could be transnational activism and aid work: Greenpeace, Amnesty International, WaterAid and *Médecins Sans Frontières* are all established examples. Others may include virtual lobbies or indeed the solidarity movements and participants (sometimes from intermediate countries) as witnessed in the Arab Spring (Dabashi, 2013).

Further still, and perhaps not immediately apparent to Beck or indeed Vertovec, we might include Islamist transnational politics. One thinks here of Islamist movements that have travelled outwards, and been relocated, from their provenance in the Muslim Brotherhood (MB) from Egypt in 1928, or Jamat-e-Islami from northern India of the 1930s. The point with either example is that there is some semblance of a framework in which the public sphere is globalised and participatory. The implications of this are brought out in Mandaville's (2003: 46) assessment that we can 'think of transnationalism as possessing certain emancipatory qualities which allow us to move towards a political imagination beyond the categories of the territorial state'.

This is certainly one expression of Muslim transnationalism, and Mandaville (2009) sets it in the context of four prevailing – and often overlapping – forms. Instead of focusing on the religious framings, Mandaville provides a useful discussion of some core social and political expressions of Muslim transnationalism. The first concerns Muslim 'people flows' in so far as the physical movement of Muslims to Europe has created 'an infrastructure of conduits and networks through which other forms of Muslim transnationalism can flow' (ibid.: 494). This is a direct outcome of significant Muslim settlement and community formation. The second is expressed in organised social and political movements 'whose agendas and organisational structures transcend nation-state boundaries (although some of them, importantly, operate at the behest, or with the financial support, of state authorities)' (ibid.: 494–5). While this may be organised in some sense, it is highly dispersed across social fields and political landscapes. The third prevailing form relates to the creation of transnational public spheres, 'enabled by the proliferation of new media and information and communication technologies' (ibid.: 495). This is a highly dynamic development and might be one illustration of Fraser's (1992) 'subaltern-counterpublics' in which Muslim media sources 'represent an expanding social field characterized by more than contested authority and by more than proliferating voices or blurred boundaries; central to this expanding public sphere of Islam are new media and interest profiles they advance' (Anderson, 2003: 888).

This takes us to Vertovec's (1999: 13) final feature of transnationalism, and relates to the *(re)construction of 'place' or locality*, much of which centres on making a home from home through the 'creation of trans-local understandings'. In an earlier account from Hannerz (1992: 47), this process was understood as recognition that culture is 'the social organization of meaning'. The fuller implication of this reading facilitates a 'reconstruction' of place, via culture, and returns us to Appadurai's (1996: 13, my emphasis) insistence that a focus on 'the dimensionality of culture *rather than its substantiality* permits out thinking of culture less as a property of individuals and groups and more as a heuristic device that we can use to talk about differences'. In many respects, then, what is detailed by six features of transnationalism may be succinctly found in Walker's (1993: 14) cautionary summation that

> what is at stake in the interpretation of contemporary transformations is not the eternal presence or imminent absence of states. It is the degree to which the modernist resolution of state–time relations expressed by the principle of state sovereignty offers a plausible account of contemporary political practices.

The continuing debate, therefore, centres on the extent to which theoretical questions have been sufficiently answered.

REFERENCES

Ambrosini, M. (2012) 'Migrants' entrepreneurship in transnational social fields: research in the Italian context', *International Review of Sociology*, 22 (2): 273–92.

Anderson, J. (2003) 'New media, new publics: reconfiguring the public sphere of Islam', *Social Research*, 70 (3): 887–906.

Appadurai, A. (1996) *Modernity at Large: Cultural Dimensions of Globalisation*. Minneapolis: University of Minnesota Press.

Beck, U. (1998) 'The cosmopolitan manifesto', *New Statesman*, 20 March, 28–30.

Dabashi, H. (2013) *The Arab Spring: The End of Postcolonialism*. New York: Zed Books.

Faist, T. (2010) 'Diaspora and transnationalism: what kind of dance partners?' In R. Bauböck and T. Faist (eds) *Diaspora and Transnationalism: Concepts, Theories and Methods*. Amsterdam: Amsterdam University Press.

Fraser, N. (1992) 'Rethinking the public sphere: a contribution to the critique of actually existing democracies', in C. Calhoun (ed.) *Habermas and the Public Sphere*. Cambridge, MA: MIT Press.

Gilroy, P. (2004) *After Empire: Conviviality of Postcolonial Melancholia?* London: Routledge.

Hannerz, U. (1992) *Cultural Complexity: Studies in the Social Organization of Meaning*. New York: Columbia University Press.

Mandaville, P. (2003) *Transnational Muslim Politics: Reimagining the Umma*. London: Routledge.

Mandaville, R. (2009) 'Muslim transnational identity and state responses in Europe and the UK after 9/11: political community, ideology and authority', *Journal of Ethnic and Migration Studies*, 35 (3): 491–506.

Mitchell, K. (1997) 'Different diasporas and the hype of "hybridity"', *Environment and Planning D: Society and Space*, 15: 533–53.

Van Oudenhoven, J. P., Ward, C. and Magoret, A.-M. (2006) 'Patterns of relations between immigrants and host societies', *International Journal of Intercultural Relations*, 30: 637–51.

Vertovec, S. (1999) 'Conceiving and researching transnationalism', *Ethnic and Racial Studies*, 22 (2): 1–24.

Walker, R. B. J. (1993) *Inside/Outside: International Relations as Political Theory*. Cambridge: Cambridge University Press.

Whiteness

*As a category in the fields of **race** and **ethnicity**, whiteness is predominantly conceived in terms of the advantageous material and symbolic resources it confers in relation to non-white racial categories. Locked more into a white–black dualism in the US literature, in Europe it is coming to be discussed with greater complexity, for example alongside class, youth and place, and how whiteness is negotiated differently by different white groups.*

The study of whiteness is a relatively recent area of scholarship, even though many of the questions it addresses are inherently intertwined with issues of **race** and **racialisation**, as well as other concepts discussed elsewhere in this book. However, and perhaps peculiarly within the fields of **race** and **ethnicity**, whiteness as a concept sits at an intersection between historical privilege and identity, something that has a contemporary dynamic but which is not universally shared in (or can be distant to) how many white people experience their identities. That is to say that 'whiteness as a site of privilege is not absolute but rather cross-cut by a range of other axes of relative advantage and subordination; these do not erase or render irrelevant race privilege, but rather inflect or modify it' (Frankenberg, 2001: 76). Moreover, in thinking about whiteness there is often a tension between its study from contexts marked by historical segregation (e.g. the US and South Africa) and elsewhere where whiteness has either (i) functioned (at least formally) as a banal repository of white majority conceptions of the given identity of societies (Hage, 1998; Hewitt, 2005) (see also **nationalism**), or (ii) ordered social relations in colonial states occupied overseas (see **post-colonialism**). What each reading shares in common, however, is that while whiteness was once 'seen as both invisible and normative, as being a state of "racelessness", this is increasingly recognised only as *appearing* to be the case' (Rhodes, 2013: 52).

WHITE OR WESTERN?

Beginning with the last issue, Fenton and Mann (2010: 143) offer three conceptions of how whiteness and the majority in the West are intertwined or mutually constituting. The first is in conceptions of whiteness as supremacist and so most obviously racist, the second is as a non-ethnic national identity, perhaps best reflected in notions of 'banal nationalism' (Billig, 1995), while the third is as a cultural majority in any given society, and so finding expression in literatures on multinationalism (Kymlicka, 1995). These authors are useful in providing a present-focused account, some of which will be picked up on below, but there is also a prior historical literature which speaks to this question. This literature provides an understanding of the ways in which 'the history of whiteness is one of transitions and changes' (Bonnett, 2008: 18), as well as the ways in which this history also serves as 'a geography' of the West (ibid.).

While 'white' and 'Western' are often conflated in contemporary discussion, according to Bonnet the idea that the 'West' has a coherent unity, something resembling an 'ethno-cultural repertoire' of whiteness, is a relatively novel conception that owes much (though not necessarily in a straightforward manner) to late nineteenth-century writers who anxiously debated the 'decline' of white dominance (ibid.: 23). Amongst others, Bonnett (2008) identifies Benjamin Kidd's *Social Evolution* (1894) and *Principles of Western Civilisation* (1902), each of which share something with the current theories of *Eurabia* and European decline discussed elsewhere (see **Euro-Islam**). Of course Kidd was writing at a time when the British Empire reigned over nearly a quarter of the planet's landmass (and nearly five hundred million people), and other European powers dominated the colonies they had taken. Nonetheless, pointing to the thesis of Charles Pearson (1984) in particular, Bonnett (2008: 18) describes some recurring features in this perception of decline:

> Pearson's principle explanation of why white expansion was at an end and white supremacy in retreat rests on demographics (notably Chinese and African fertility), geographical determinism (the unsuitability of the 'wet tropics' for white settlement) and the deleterious consequences of urbanisation on human 'character'. Moreover and crucially the economic ascendancy of those who Inge, following Pearson, was later to term 'the cheaper races' (Inge 1922, 27), meant the white 'will be driven from every neutral market and forced to confine himself within his own' (Pearson, 1894: 137).

There is much here which spans several presumed features of culture and civilisation (intertwined in biology and environment), but which is principally underwritten by the ways in which whiteness served as a form of *substantive rationality* that fashioned geopolitics in its own image. In this mode of thinking, empire and colonialism are understood as natural states of international relations and indicative of human progress – serving to illustrate how in such formulations the world was 'imaginatively seized, its parts compared and its centre and periphery established' (Bonnett, 2008: 17).

If we *verstehen* and place ourselves amongst the worldview(s) of the writers of the day, then unsettling challenges to this hegemony (and related geo-political formations) must have raised some profound existential concerns. Such concerns were certainly prompted by the Japanese naval annihilation of the Russian fleet in 1904, where 'for the first time since the Middle Ages, a non-European country had vanquished a European power in a major war' (Mishra, 2012: 1). What is especially interesting is that this violent disruption occurred just at the moment the transaction (a notion we will return to) between whiteness and the West had been taking place, but in a manner 'in which the mass of white people are treated with suspicion' (Bonnett, 2008: 20).

This seeming paradox is explained by an internal racial hierarchy that drew upon notions of both class and **race**, and informed what would later become familiar tropes of social Darwinism and eugenicist thinking. This tension, 'of asserting both white solidarity and class elitism was resolved, in part, by asserting that the "best stock" of the working class had long since climbed upwards' (ibid.: 21), and which continued to feed into parallel debates about culture and political economy (McDermott, 2006). The particularly relevant implications of the genealogy for our discussion in that '[w]hilst "Westerner" can and does sometimes operate as a substitute term for "white", it also operates within new landscapes of power and discrimination that have new and often fragile relationships with the increasingly widely repudiated language of race' (Bonnett, 2008: 18).

RACIAL SUPREMACY AND PRIVILEGE

Due in large part to these historical antecedents, two features of contemporary whiteness are those which turn on questions of supremacy and privilege. As Winant (1997: 76) describes:

> monolithic white supremacy is over, yet in a more concealed way, white power and privilege live on ... Whites are no longer the official 'ruling race' yet they still enjoy many of the privileges from the time when they were.

In thinking about these we need to focus on two slightly different frames. By supremacy what is meant is dominance, explicitly as coercion but also implicitly through kinds of prevailing consensus amongst white majority society. Illustrations of the latter include the ways in which once racially segregated societies continue to operate racial zones even while there is no formal policy to support it. Obvious examples are post-Apartheid South Africa and post-Segregation southern states in the US, where racial categories are keenly related to the exercise of power. Yet there are also less obvious examples found in every liberal-democratic European Union state, manifested in the reluctance of visible minorities to move or live outside of urban centres that are often considered much 'safer' than non-urban conurbations (Neal, 2009). This is a different kind of white dominance to that of explicitly 'white nationalist' movements such as the Ku Klux Klan in the US, though of course far right-wing parties in Europe often form part of the political mainstream and may also be in governing coalitions (see **Euro-Islam**).

Even though the historical practices and contemporary implications of white supremacy are therefore controversial, they are typically easier to debate than the ways in which whiteness serves as what Twine and Gallagher (2008: 8) describe as a 'public and psychological wage', and what others have termed a 'knapsack' (McIntosh, 1988) or 'possessive investment' (Lipsitz, 1998). Each of these refer to a kind of capital, and are illustrated in what Duster (2001: 114–15) elaborates as 'deeply embedded in the routine structures of economic and political life. From ordinary service at Denny's restaurants, to far greater access to bank loans to simple *police-event-free* driving – all these things have come unreflectively with the territory of being white.' Whiteness here is a type of habitus and the norm against which others are judged, in which 'culture and ideology constantly re-cloak whiteness as a normative identity' (ibid.: 12). Scholars and intellectuals have not stood outside these conventions, however, for:

> Throughout much of the twentieth-century mainstream, white social scientists did not focus on the institutions that created, reproduced and normalized white supremacy. The focus that guided whites in the academy primarily concerned itself with the pathology of racist individuals rather than the structural forces that produced racist social systems. (Twine and Gallagher, 2008: 10)

One of the sociological implications of this is that there is a documented tendency amongst 'ethnically ambiguous' minorities to seek the material and symbolic rewards of whiteness by positioning themselves as white in such things as applications for education employment, and other training (Warren and Twine, 1997; Lee, 2001) (see also **mixedness**). This is evidence, argue Twine and Gallagher (2008: 14), of how 'whiteness is continuing to expand in the United States, and that it continues to incorporate ethnicities of multiracial, Asian, Mexican and other Latinos of non-European heritage'.

CLASS AND NEGOTIATING IDENTITY

To a large extent, however, much of the discussion of whiteness has attributed a conscious or unwitting white dominance which under-recognises how '[t]he economic and psychological wages of whiteness may be more meagre (and thus more precious) the lower down the social hierarchy the white subject is located' (Garner, 2006: 262). In opening up these readings from a European perspective, Anoop Nayak's (2003a and 2003b) research has utilised ethnographic methods in post-industrial settings in order to explore how whiteness intersects with class and masculinities, and so is negotiated in ways that take on 'multiple and contingent' meanings (2003a: 319). This is especially evident in terms of how 'young people inhabit white ethnicities to different degrees and with varying consequences' (ibid.)

not least because 'whiteness is not simply constituted in relation to blackness as previous race studies expertly show, but is also fashioned *through and against other versions of whiteness*' (ibid.: 320, emphasis added). Nayak illustrates this by describing three different sub-cultures of working-class young boys:

> For the *Real Geordies*, global culture can be resisted and displaced through the re-staking of local identity in embodied football-related activities. For others such as the *Charver Kids*, restructuring has sharpened inequalities, allowing organised crime and street 'scams' to grow in the widening fissures of poverty and persistent unemployment. Finally, there is evidence to suggest that, for a cluster of *White Wannabes*, globalisation has opened up spaces in which a new transnationalism and multiculture now flourish. (Ibid., emphasis added)

What this emphasises is that whiteness needs to be read as more than supremacy, privilege and capital; it also needs to be understood as an identity that can be **intersectional** and negotiated, and so is much more than an outcome of racial dualism.

REFERENCES

Billig, M. (1995) *Banal Nationalism*. Sage.

Bonnett, A. (2008) 'Whiteness and the West', in C. Dwyer and C. Bressey (eds) *New Geographies of Race and Racism*. Aldershot: Ashgate.

Duster, T. (2001) 'The "morphing" of properties of whiteness', in B. B. Rasmussen, E. Klinenberg, I. Nexica and M. Wray (eds) *The Making and Unmaking of Whiteness*. Durham: Duke University Press.

Fenton, S. and Mann, R. (2010) 'Introducing the majority to ethnicity: do they like what they see?', in G. Calder, P. Cole and J. Seglow (eds) *Citizenship Acquisition and National Belonging*. Basingstoke: Palgrave.

Frankenberg, R. (2001) 'The mirage of an unmarked whiteness', in B. B. Rasmussen, E. Klinenberg, I. Nexica and M. Wray (eds) *The Making and Unmaking of Whiteness*. Durham: Duke University Press.

Garner, S. (2006) 'The uses of whiteness: what sociologists working on Europe can draw from US work on whiteness', *Sociology*, 40 (2): 257–75.

Hage, G. (1998) *White Nation: Fantasies of White Supremacy in a Multicultural Society*. Annandale: Pluto Press.

Hewitt, R. (2005) *White Backlash and the Politics of Multiculturalism*. Cambridge: Cambridge University Press.

Kidd, B. (1894) *Social Evolution*. London: Macmillan.

Kidd, B. (1902) *Principles of Western Civilization*. London: Macmillan.

Kymlicka, W. (1995) *Multicultural Nationalism*. Oxford: Oxford University Press.

Lee, S. (2001) *Using New Racial Categories in the 2000 Census*, Baltimore: Annie E. Casey Foundation.

Lipstiz, G. (1998) *The Possessive Investment in Whiteness: How White People Profit from Identity Politics*. Philadelphia: Temple University Press.

McDermott, M. (2006) *Working-Class White: The Making and Unmaking of Race Relations*. Berkeley: University of California Press.

McIntosh, P. (1988) 'White privilege and male privilege: a personal account of coming to see correspondences through work in women's studies', Working Paper #189, Wellesley College Center for Research on Women, Wellesley, MA.

Mishra, P. (2012) *From the Ruins of Empire*. London: Allen Lane.

Nayak, A. (2003a) '"Ivory lives": economic restructuring and the making of whiteness in a post-industrial youth community', *European Journal of Cultural Studies*, 6 (3): 305–25.

Nayak, A. (2003b) 'Last of the "real Geordies"? White masculinities and the subcultural response to deindustrialisation', *Environment and Planning D: Society and Space*, 21 (1): 7–25.

Neal, S. (2009) *Rural Identities: Ethnicity and Community in the English Countryside*. Farnham: Ashgate.

Pearson, C. (1894) *National Life and Character: A Forecast*. London: Macmillan.

Rhodes, J. (2013) 'Remaking whiteness in the "postracial" UK', in N. Kapoor, V. S. Kalra and J. Rhodes (eds) *The State of Race*. Basingstoke: Palgrave.

Twine, F. and Gallagher, C. (2008) 'The future of whiteness: a map of the "third wave"', *Ethnic and Racial Studies*, 31 (1): 4–24.

Warren, J. and Twine, F. W. (1997) 'White Americans, the new minority? Non-blacks and the ever-expanding boundaries of whiteness', *Journal of Black Studies*, 28 (2): 200–18.

Winant, O. (1997) 'Behind blue eyes: whiteness and contemporary US racial politics', *New Left Review*, 225 (September–October): 73–88.

index

Amis, M. 127
Anderson, B. 94–6
Anthias, F. 29–31, 65
antisemitism 1, 3, 8–13, 71, 73, 115, 126
  bigotry 8–10
  Judeophobia 9, 102
  new antisemtism 10–12
  object–subject 7–8
Arendt, H. 9, 1

Back, L. 9, 17, 40, 112, 123
Banton, M. 114, 121–3, 125
Barth, F. 38–40
Bauman, Z. 3
Bhabha, H. 52, 82, 83, 9, 94, 111
Billig, M. 96–7, 153
Black Power 16, 88, 128–9
blackness 1, 4, 13–19, 28, 35, 37, 40, 42,
    48, 50, 54, 64, 65, 66, 81–2, 84, 86,
    88, 105, 107–8, 114–5, 123, 128–9,
    132, 156
  The Black Atlantic 13, 17–8, 28
  political blackness 16
Bonnett, A. 153–4
Brah, A. 30
Brewer, J. 3
Brubaker, R. 4, 28–30

Cantle, T. 59, 146
Castles, S. 20–1, 23, 55, 57, 58, 76–9
capital 41, 78, 124, 148–50, 155, 156
citizenship 6, 8, 19–25, 32, 33, 34, 37,
    58, 61, 62, 63, 76, 77, 83–90, 92,
    93, 103–5, 123, 133, 141–2, 144, 149
  Athenian 21–2, 92
  Roman 2–22, 28,
  T. H. Marshall 22–3
  post-national 11, 19, 23–4
Crenshaw, K. 65–6

diaspora 4, 18, 27–30, 76, 87, 148–9
  co-ordinates 28
  diasporic space 30
discourse 8, 10, 28, 30, 37, 40, 41, 54, 57,
    61–3, 69, 83, 87–9, 93, 100, 103, 111,
    115, 129, 135, 142

diversity 28, 42, 54, 55–7, 58, 59–62, 64,
    75, 76, 83, 85, 86, 87, 114, 131, 133,
    144–7
DNA 30, 116
Dworkin, R. 32
Du Bois, W. E. B 14–16, 18, 125, 132–3

equality 1, 5, 13, 16, 21, 22, 23, 31–5
ethnicity 1–2, 4–6, 17, 2, 25, 28, 29, 31,
    33, 34, 35, 37–42, 46, 47, 48, 50, 55,
    59, 64, 65, 68, 80–2, 83, 84, 88, 94,
    106, 112. 114, 119, 122, 130, 139,
    145, 146, 147, 152
  assertiveness 38, 39, 88
  boundaries 24, 28, 29, 35, 38–9, 41, 46,
    52, 53, 66, 121, 145, 150, 151,
  new and old ethnicities 40–1
  primordial 38, 53
  subjective 4, 38, 39, 41, 54, 82, 97,
    134, 145
essentialism 29, 30, 35, 42, 53, 54, 62, 68,
    82, 36
Euro-Islam 1, 2, 43–6, 253, 155

Fanon, F. 14, 15, 112, 125, 132
feminisms 64–6, 86, 88

Geertz, C. 38
Gellner, E. 92–5, 98–9
gender 21, 34, 46, 63, 65, 67, 68, 72, 87,
    97, 146
Gilroy, P. 13, 16, 17, 18, 28, 53, 54, 114,
    149
Goldberg, D. T. 49–50, 117
groups 4, 5, 8, 11, 5, 16, 17, 20, 21, 23,
    24, 27, 29, 30, 32, 33–5, 37–9, 41–2,
    48–50, 55–7, 61–2, 66–7, 78, 84–5,
    87, 97, 99, 104, 106, 115, 117, 120–3,
    127–8, 133–4, 139, 145–6, 149

Habermas, J. 134, 135, 136
Hall, S. 4, 13, 28
Harding, S. 66
health 1, 16, 22, 35, 41, 47–51, 58, 147
Hegel, G. W. 85, 131–2
hooks, b. 65, 132

Honneth, A. 36, 130, 132, 133
hybridity 1, 2, 5, 17, 28, 29, 30, 35, 42, 46, 52–4, 62–3, 81, 149

identity 1, 3–6, 13, 32, 33–4, 65, 65–7, 115, 131, 134, 140
  autonomy 139–41
  blackness 13, 16
  citizenship 24–5
  diaspora 27–9
  ethnicity 38–41
  hybridity 53–4
  mixedness 81
  multiculturalism 83, 87–90
  nation 93–6
  superdiversity 145
  transnatonalism 148
  whiteness 152–3, 155–6
interculturalism 1, 3, 59–64, 90, 145, 147
integration 1, 43, 43, 55–9, 62, 64, 77, 87–90, 120, 122, 141
intersectionality 1, 35, 48, 64–9, 72, 102, 131, 145, 152, 156
Islamophobia 1, 11, 69–74, 126, 127

Kipling, R. 126
Klug, B. 8, 10, 11
Kushner, T. 11, 128
Kymlicka, W. 58, 84, 88, 89, 104, 133, 153

Lawrence, S. 129
liberalism 21–3, 36, 60, 61, 63–4, 86–8, 89, 131, 141–2

Marxism 36, 126,
migration 4, 28, 38, 45, 46, 55, 56, 62, 75–80, 81, 105–8, 120, 121, 123, 126, 139, 144, 145, 147–50
Miles, R. 72, 78, 117, 118, 125, 126
mixedness 1, 3, 35, 42, 52, 52, 71, 72, 80–2, 155
Meer, N. 20, 24, 25, 34, 46, 57, 58, 59, 65, 71, 83, 84, 85, 86, 87, 90, 97, 118, 126, 129, 133, 139, 140
Modood, T. 5, 6, 20, 24, 34, 35, 39, 40, 41, 46, 54, 57, 58, 59, 69, 71, 78, 83, 84, 85, 86, 87, 90, 106, 126, 133, 137, 139
multiculturalism 5, 6, 23, 34, 37, 56, 57–64, 83–92, 131–5, 140, 144–5, 147, 148, 149, 156
Murji, K. 128, 129

nationalism 3, 38, 40, 62, 92–7
  banal 96–7
  black 16, 17, 86
  British 62–3
  citizenship 23, 62
  diaspora 27, 29, 30
  English 10, 40
  identity 56, 57, 58, 62, 68, 72, 83, 84
  imagined 28, 94–5
  nation 18, 37, 61, 93–4, 95–6
  nation-state 8, 23–4, 75, 76, 92–3
  purity 11, 53, 71
  race 40, 53, 81
Nayak, A. 129, 155–6
Nazroo, J. 48, 50
new social movements 2–25

Parekh, B. 29, 35, 36, 56, 60, 63, 83, 84, 87, 89, 142
Plato 2
political participation 103–7
post-colonialism 81, 98, 109–13

race 113–19
  antisemitism 9
  Atlantic-centric 10
  blackness 14–5, 17
  class 17
  citizenship 21, 25
  critical theory 132
  discrimination 34
  equality 33
  ethnicity 37
  gender 65–8
  health 47, 48, 49, 50
  hybridity 53
  mixedness 80–2
  nation 40, 53, 81
  political participation 107
  post-colonialism 110–12
  whiteness 152–4
race relations 119–25
racism
  anti- 66, 121
  biological 15, 49, 116
  cultural 9–10, 48, 50, 71–2, 102
  institutional racism 17, 128–9
racialisation 125–30
Ramadan, T. 43–7
Rawls, J. 36, 56, 83, 131, 141
redistribution 35–6

reflexvity 3, 5
recognition 1, 3, 6, 13, 16, 17, 24, 25,
28, 35–6, 37, 39, 44, 56, 60, 62,
66, 81, 82, 83, 85, 112, 117, 118,
130–5, 138, 144, 147, 151

Said, E. 99–102, 111
Saussure, F. 2
Sayyid, B. 28–9, 138
Scott, J. 33–5, 84
secularism 136–42
Shakespeare 9–10, 126
Solomos, J. 9, 17, 40, 112, 123–4
space 27, 29, 30, 45, 61, 86, 87, 88, 89,
90, 137, 138, 146, 147, 149, 150, 156
super-diversity 29, 34. 35, 61, 62,
144–7, 148

Taylor, C. 5, 23, 60, 83, 88, 130, 132, 137
transnationalism 1, 27–8, 29, 30, 79,
144, 147–52

Young, I. M 5, 27, 67, 84, 86, 88, 101,
112, 133–4
Yuval-Davis, A. 65, 67–8, 97

Vertovec, S. 79, 144–52
Virdee, S. 118

Walby, S. 65–9
Weber, M. 38, 58, 123, 137
Werbner, P. 10, 30, 68
whiteness 152–55
Winant, O. 81, 118
Wittgenstein, L. 2